## RATS Handbook to Accompany
### *Introductory Econometrics for Finance*

Written to complement the second edition of best-selling textbook *Introductory Econometrics for Finance*, this book provides a comprehensive introduction to the use of the Regression Analysis of Time-Series (RATS) software for modelling in finance and beyond. It provides numerous worked examples with carefully annotated code and detailed explanations of the outputs, giving readers the knowledge and confidence to use the software for their own research and to interpret their own results. A wide variety of important modelling approaches is covered, including such topics as time-series analysis and forecasting, volatility modelling, limited dependent variable and panel methods, switching models and simulations methods. The book is supported by an accompanying website containing freely downloadable data and RATS instructions.

CHRIS BROOKS is Professor of Finance at the ICMA Centre, University of Reading, UK, where he also obtained his PhD. He has published over 60 articles in leading academic and practitioner journals including the *Journal of Business*, the *Journal of Banking and Finance*, the *Journal of Empirical Finance*, the *Review of Economics and Statistics* and the *Economic Journal*. He is associate editor of a number of journals including the *International Journal of Forecasting*. He has also acted as consultant for various banks and professional bodies in the fields of finance, econometrics and real estate.

# RATS Handbook to Accompany
## *Introductory Econometrics for Finance*

## Chris Brooks
ICMA Centre

CAMBRIDGE
UNIVERSITY PRESS

CAMBRIDGE UNIVERSITY PRESS
Cambridge, New York, Melbourne, Madrid, Cape Town, Singapore, São Paulo, Delhi

Cambridge University Press
The Edinburgh Building, Cambridge CB2 8RU, UK

Published in the United States of America by Cambridge University Press, New York

www.cambridge.org
Information on this title: www.cambridge.org/9780521721684

First published 2009

Printed in the United Kingdom at the University Press, Cambridge

*A catalogue record for this publication is available from the British Library*

*Library of Congress Cataloguing in Publication data*
Brooks, Chris
RATS handbook to accompany Introductory econometrics for finance / Chris Brooks.
    p.  cm.
Includes bibliographical references and index.
ISBN 978-0-521-89695-5 (hbk.) – ISBN 978-0-521-72168-4 (pbk.)   1. Finance–Econometric models.
2. Finance–Mathematical models.    3. Regression analysis–Data processing.    4. Econometrics.
I. Brooks, Chris, 1971. Introductory econometrics for finance.   II. Title.   III. Series.
HG173.B763 2009
332.01'519536 – dc22      2008033463

ISBN  978-0-521-89695-5 hardback
ISBN  978-0-521-72168-4 paperback

# Contents

# Figures

# Screenshots

# Preface

This RATS handbook accompanies the second edition of *Introductory Econometrics for Finance* (Cambridge University Press, ISBN: 9780521694681). The first edition of *Introductory Econometrics for Finance* incorporated a discussion of the use of the RATS software into the text, but the inclusion of additional material in the second edition has necessitated the switch to a separate RATS handbook to ensure that the text remains at a manageable length. It is not intended as a stand-alone textbook and it will not repeat all of the theory, background and case studies from *Introductory Econometrics for Finance*. Rather, it is intended to illustrate, using numerous examples with real data taken from that book, how RATS can be used to solve many problems of interest in empirical finance. The focus is on replicating the examples and not on demonstrating the full functionality of the software. Thus this handbook should be of benefit to anyone who wishes to learn how to use RATS, and it assumes no prior exposure to the software. While the illustrations here focus on topics in finance, most of the methodology is generic and hence it may be usefully employed in other areas of application such as economics, business or real estate.

As for the first edition of the main textbook, output from the RATS package is included in Courier 9-point font in a box, while instructions for readers to type, or actions that they must follow, are written in **bold type**. All of the sets of instructions developed in this book together with the data are available on the Cambridge University Press web site at www.cup.cam.ac.uk/brooks

I am grateful to Tom Doan and Tom Maycock at Estima for their support and for their assistance with my programs, and to Tom Doan for many useful comments on an earlier draft manuscript. Naturally, I alone bear responsibility for any remaining errors.

### About *Introductory Econometrics for Finance*

Now thoroughly revised and updated including two new chapters in its second edition, this best-seller was the first textbook to teach introductory econometrics to finance students. The text is based primarily on intuition rather than formulae, giving students the skills and confidence to estimate and interpret models, while having an intuitive grasp of the underlying theoretical concepts.

The approach, based on the successful courses I have taught at the ICMA Centre, one of the UK's leading finance schools, and the Cass Business School, London, ensures that the text focuses squarely on the needs of finance students. The book assumes no prior knowledge of econometrics, and covers important modern topics such as time-series forecasting, volatility modelling, switching models, limited dependent variable and panel approaches, and simulations methods. It includes detailed examples and case studies from the finance literature. Sample instructions and output from EViews are presented as an integral part of the text. Advice on planning and executing a project in empirical finance is also given.

### About the author

Chris Brooks is Professor of Finance at the ICMA Centre, University of Reading, UK, where he also obtained his PhD. He has published over 60 articles in leading academic and practitioner journals including the *Journal of Business*, *Journal of Banking and Finance*, *Journal of Empirical Finance*, *Review of Economics and Statistics*, and the *Economic Journal*. He is author of three Cambridge books in addition to this one and is an associate editor of a number of journals including the *International Journal of Forecasting* and the *Journal of Business Finance and Accounting*. He has also acted as consultant for various banks and professional bodies in the fields of finance, econometrics and real estate.

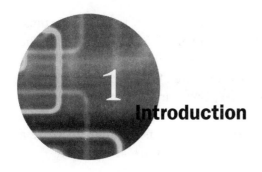

# 1 Introduction

## 1.1 Description

'RATS' stands for *Regression Analysis of Time-Series*. Although, as the title suggests, the program was initially developed for the estimation of time-series econometric models, recent versions of the software have a wide range of features which would be of use in the analysis of cross-sectional or panel data.

RATS is an econometric modelling package that enables the researcher to transform, analyse and estimate models for actual data, and also to conduct simulations using artificial data created in almost any way he chooses. The advantage of RATS over more traditional programming languages is that you do not have to 're-invent the wheel' since most of the tasks that are of interest will be available by issuing just a couple of commands. Thus, RATS provides a useful bridge between simple but inflexible packages which are entirely menu driven, and full programming languages (such as FORTRAN or C/C++), which would require you to code up even OLS regressions yourself. The advantage of instruction-based programs such as this is that they make it quick and easy to replicate a set of results or to repeat the same analysis using a large number of different series; both would be more troublesome and time-consuming with pure menu-driven packages.

Recent versions of RATS have made the software even more powerful and yet simpler for novices to get to grips with via the use of 'Wizards', which will be described in detail below. Over the past 12 years, I have used RATS for much of my empirical research, and have co-authored two software reviews that feature RATS and focus on the estimation of models for volatility – Brooks *et al.* (2001, 2003).[1]

---

[1] See Chapter 8 of this handbook for a discussion of how to estimate such models.

While this book has made use of version 7 of RATS throughout, most of the procedures are also available in older versions of the software. The discussion below assumes that the reader has obtained a licensed version of the package and has loaded it onto a computer. While there are broadly four platforms for RATS (Windows, Mac, UNIX and a command prompt from a PC), this guide assumes throughout that WinRATS, the Windows version, is used. In all three cases, the researcher is required to write a set of instructions and to run them. The interfaces are also similar.

## 1.2  RATSDATA

RATSDATA is a simple-to-use, menu-based program for handling data. It can be used to import data into files which have a special RATS format with a '.RAT' suffix, and also to export data from RATS to another format or to print or plot variables in the dataset. A principal advantage that previously existed in converting data files to RATS format was the increase in speed of reading and writing the data; now that computers are faster, this hardly matters and many of the features of RATSDATA are incorporated into RATS itself. Hence this book will not use RATSDATA or discuss it further.

## 1.3  Accomplishing simple tasks in RATS

There are essentially two ways to run programs in RATS: *interactively* or in *batch mode*. To use interactive mode, you write the instructions in the RATS Editor and RATS will execute each line after you have typed it and hit <ENTER>. Using batch mode involves writing all of the commands together and then running them in a single go. Any text editor could be used to write the instructions, including the RATS Editor, and there are also various ways to run them. These will be discussed in detail below.

## 1.4  Further reading

Readers who wish to learn more about the functionality of the software should consult the RATS *User Guide*, which is a highly detailed but surprisingly readable description of the features and working of RATS, including numerous examples and technical details. Enders' (2003) *RATS Programming Manual* is also useful for those already familiar with the software and who want to enhance their knowledge of how to write RATS programs. Finally, the RATS *Reference Manual* provides an alphabetical listing of all of the instructions and functions available in RATS. All three of these are distributed electronically with the software and hence should be freely available to all readers.

## 1.5 Other sources of information and programs

The Estima web site (www.estima.com) provides links to a long list of RATS procedures, which make the implementation of many complex tasks very easy. Some of these procedures will be described in subsequent chapters of this book.

Estima's site also includes a link to the RATS web-based discussion forum (www.estima.com/forum), where users can post or respond to questions about aspects of the software or programs, and there is also an e-mail-based discussion group, to which users can subscribe and make postings.

## 1.6 Opening the software

To load RATS from Windows, choose **Start**, **All Programs**, **WinRATS 7.0** and again **WinRATS 7.0**. An empty window called 'NONAME00.TXT{io}' will be opened. {io} denotes 'input-output', i.e. this file is both an input file (for writing instructions and telling RATS what to do) and an output file (for RATS to write the results in). The screen will appear like the one below.

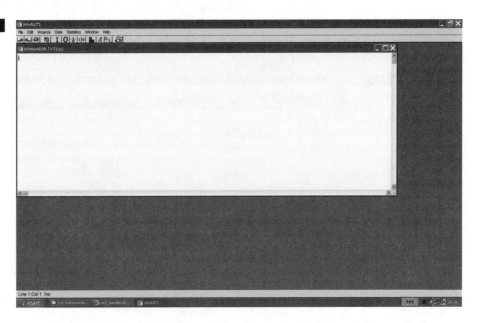

However, it is often desirable to have two separate files open on the screen at the same time – an input file where the program will be written and an output file where the results will be displayed. To achieve this, click on the **File menu** and choose **New**. A second file will be displayed on the screen called 'NONAME01.TXT'. Go into the **Window menu** and choose **'Use for Output'** – you will notice that the name has changed to 'NONAME01.TXT{o}' as shown on the left-hand side of the file tab. This will be the output file that the results will be placed in. If you look at the first file, the name has now changed to 'NONAME01.TXT{i}' – this is the program file where the commands will be written.

It is a good idea to save the files frequently. With RATS, you must save the input and output files separately (unless of course you do not want to save the output). The way to do this is to go into the **File menu** and choose **'Save As'**. Note that RATS will then be saving in a file the display window that is on the top, which is the output window. Assuming that you want to save the input file instead, click **Cancel** and select **the tab of the input window** underneath. Click '**File**' and '**Save As**' again and **save the open file 'NONAME00.PRG{io}'** as *XX.prg*. Replace 'XX' with any file name you consider appropriate. It is usually best to keep file names to a maximum of eight characters.

Finally, to have a nice window display so that you can see both the input and output files at the same time, click on the $\vdash\frac{I}{o}$ button. This is equivalent to going to the **Window menu** and choosing 'Tile Horizontal' rather than 'Tile Vertical'. The former will put the input window above the output window, while the latter will put the input window on the left and the output window on the right. The screen should now appear as shown below.

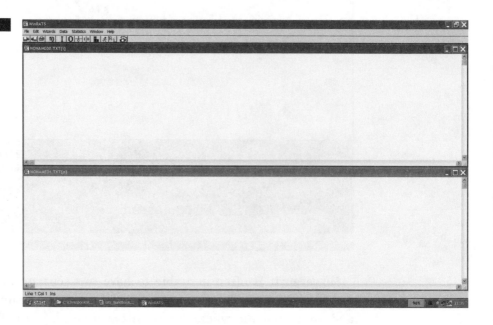

**Screenshot 1.2**

The 12 icons (buttons) that appear near the top of the window by default have the following functions (which are also available by clicking on the appropriate menu item):

Open file

Save file

Print the contents of the active window (the window on top)

Function look-up, which opens up the functions wizard

Use this window for input

Use this window for output

Tile windows horizontally (one below another)

Tile windows vertically (side by side)

Edit – select all

(RUNNING PERSON) Runs the selected instructions, or the instruction on the cursor line, if any (equivalent to hitting <ENTER>). Disabled if the active window is not the input window.

Ready/Local (R/L) – this is a toggle switch. Clicking on this icon switches RATS from Ready to Local (L/R) mode and clicking again would switch RATS back to (R/L). Instructions are keyed in when RATS is in local mode, and clicking on the L/R button will then enable the program to be run by clicking on the RUNNING PERSON. The RUNNING PERSON button is unavailable when RATS is in local mode. The R/L button is disabled if the active window is not the input window.

Clear program – this clears the memory.

## 1.7  Types of RATS files

The convention is to name program files (that is, files containing RATS instructions) with the extension '.PRG' or, less commonly, '.RTS' and the output files with the extension '.OUT'. It is usually best to follow this convention so that the file type is obvious from the extension. In the RATS directory, there are also files with the extension '.SRC'. These are special pre-programmed sets of instructions, known as *RATS procedures*, which can be called from within a program file to do certain tasks (e.g. testing for a unit root), rather like sub-routines in a programming language. Note that both input and output files are always saved as raw text (i.e. *ASCII format*), whatever they are called.

## 1.8  Reading (loading) data in RATS

Before performing any formal analysis, the data must be loaded into the software. Suppose that the data consist of monthly observations on Vodafone's Share Price (Vodafone) and the FTSE All Share Price Index (FTALL) from November 1984 to February 2007. Suppose also that the data file is in ASCII (i.e. raw text) format, has two columns of length 268 observations and is called THEDATA.DAT (initially saved in the WinRATS Directory).

The CALENDAR instruction will be the one that will read in the data. In previous versions of RATS, it was necessary to type these instructions manually in an editor, but now the Data Entry Wizard can be employed to do the job. The following example will show how to achieve that but first, various usages of CALENDAR are highlighted. The basic structure is CALENDAR(frequency) start date e.g.

    CALENDAR(M) 1998:4

would be used for monthly data starting in April 1998;

    CALENDAR(Q) 1980:1

would be used for quarterly data starting in quarter 1, 1980;

    CALENDAR(7) 2002:8:16

would be used for daily data with 7 days per week starting on 16 August 2002;

    CALENDAR(A) 1985:1

would be used for annual data starting in 1985. With annual data, the number after the colon must always be 1.

Note that this command, like most others in RATS, can be abbreviated to its first three letters, CAL, or the whole command can be used.

The ALLOCATE command works with CALENDAR and tells RATS when the sample period finishes. For example,

ALLOCATE 1999:10

would be used for data finishing in October 1999;

ALLOCATE 2007:10:30

would be used for data finishing on 30 October 2007.

Note that it is also possible to use numbers rather than dates with the ALLOCATE command. For example, if the series in the data file each contained 180 observations, it would be possible to use

ALLOCATE 180

Now that the arrays to store the data have been established with the CALENDAR and ALLOCATE instructions, the OPEN command can be used to open a new or existing file. For example

OPEN DATA C:\WINRATS\THEDATA.DAT
DATA(FORMAT=FREE,ORG=OBS) / VODAFONE FTALL

In this case, RATS opens the data file THEDATA.DAT that has been saved in the WINRATS directory on the C drive. Note that if the data file is saved elsewhere, you would have to specify the correct path, e.g. for data on a pen drive attached to a USB port that was named E:\

OPEN DATA E:\THEDATA.DAT

DATA reads data series from an external file into the working memory. The general 'syntax' (form of the command) is

DATA(options) *start end list of series*

where '*start end*' is the range of entries to read and '*list of series*' is the list of series names for RATS to read from the file. The following options are available on how the data are arranged in the file:

ORG=[VAR]/OBS: this tells whether the data are blocked horizontally by series – i.e. in rows (ORG=VAR) – or by observations – i.e. in columns (ORG=OBS). Note that the term appearing in square brackets is always the default.

Organised by Observation implies that the series appear in separate columns:

| X1 | X2 |
|------|-------|
| 100.0 | 405.0 |
| 105.3 | 905.2 |
| 103.9 | 630.1 |
| 206.7 | 890.2 |
| 200.1 | 332.2 |

Organised by Variable implies that the series occur one at a time in blocks:

| X1 | 100.0 | 105.3 | 103.9 | 206.7 | 200.1 |
|------|-------|-------|-------|-------|-------|
| X2 | 405.0 | 905.2 | 630.1 | 890.2 | 332.2 |

FORMAT=[FREE]/PRN/WKS/DBF/RATS/XLS '(FORTRAN Format)'
This tells RATS which format to use for your data set. For instance, if your data are in an ASCII (text) file, then you would use FREE and if your data are in a Lotus worksheet, use WKS, Microsoft Excel (XLS), etc. For text-based files, RATS assumes that there are no series labels (e.g. X1 or X2), so that the data file contains only data and no strings of row or column headers.

Putting this all together, the four lines of code below will load the data and assign the name VODAFONE to the first column of observations and FTALL to the second for monthly data starting in November 1984 and finishing in February 2007.

```
CALENDAR(M) 1984:11
ALLOCATE 2007:02
OPEN DATA C:\WINRATS\THEDATA.DAT
DATA(FORMAT=FREE,ORG=OBS) / VODAFONE FTALL
```

## 1.9 Reading in data on UK house prices

Open RATS version 7 and click File, New. Then click on the 'I' icon (▮) to use this as the input window, so that the other window will become that to receive the output. Next, tile the windows horizontally by clicking the 'I|O' icon. It is probably easier to be able to write several lines of code and then to run them in a batch rather than allowing RATS to run each line after we hit <ENTER>. Your screen should probably look like the one in Screenshot 1.3.

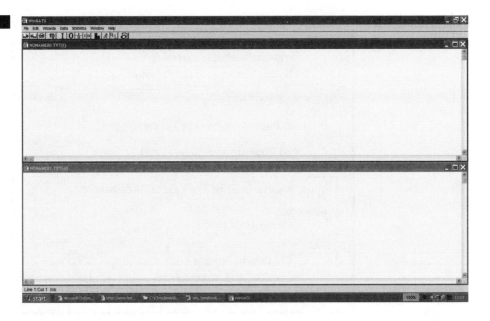

Note in particular that the 'R/L' button has R first and the running man icon is in darkened blue typeface on the screen. This means that RATS is in 'ready' or 'run' mode and will run instructions line by line. To switch this off, click the 'R/L' button. This will switch RATS to 'local' mode, where R/L will become L/R and the running man will be in grey, denoting that this button is now not operational. The top left part of the screen will now appear as

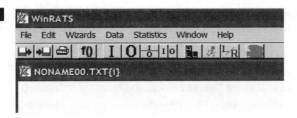

RATS is now in a position to be able to write a set of instructions together and then they will be run in a batch.

The first task is to read in (import) a series of UK average house prices from a Microsoft Excel spreadsheet called 'UKHPR.XLS'. There are 197 monthly observations running from January 1991 to May 2007. From inside RATS, click on **Data** and then **Data (Other Formats)**. You will then be asked to find the directory that the file has been placed in and the name of the file. Make sure you **change the file type** from 'Text Files (*.*)' to '**Excel Files(*.XLS)**'. Once you have done this, click **Open** and the 'Import Format' Screenshot 1.5 will be observed.

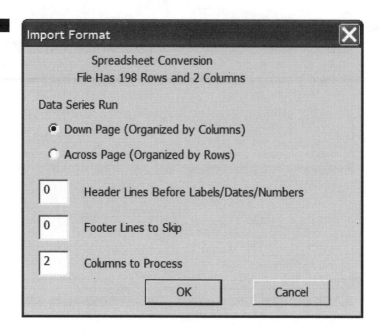

RATS has peeked inside the file and determined how the data are organised. Usually, it will do this correctly, but just to check: the data are
indeed organised in columns and there are two columns of data to process (including the dates column). There are no header lines before the
series labels and no footer lines, so click **OK**. Then the 'New Series Date'
window will appear.

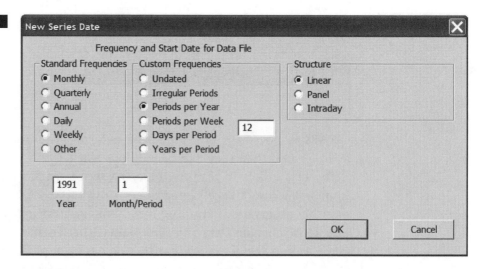

RATS has again peeked inside the file and correctly identified that
we have monthly time-series data, so verify again that the window is

completed correctly and click **OK**. RATS will then write and run the following lines of code:

```
OPEN DATA 'C:\Chris\book\RATS handbook\UKHPR.xls'
CALENDAR(M) 1991
ALL 2007:05
DATA(FORMAT=XLS,ORG=COLUMNS) 1991:01 2007:05 price
```

Note that RATS has listed only one variable, 'price', since it is not necessary to import the dates column because RATS can date the observations itself. There are no missing data points in this series, but if there were, RATS would code them as %NA. Note also that the column headers (variable names) in the spreadsheet must not contain any spaces, so 'HOUSEPRICE' is acceptable but 'HOUSE PRICE' is not.

## 1.10 Mixing and matching frequencies and printing

RATS permits the integration of various types of data (daily, weekly, monthly, quarterly, annual, etc.). It is also possible to convert the frequency of the data, for example, monthly to quarterly, quarterly to weekly and so on. This is achieved using the COMPACT (for switching to lower frequency) or DISTRIB and INTERPOL (for switching to higher frequency) procedures – see the RATS 7 *User Guide*, p. 77.

To look at the data within RATS, it would be possible to use the PRINT command. Type the following command after the four lines loading the data above:

**PRINT / PRICE**

This will display all the data entries of the house price series together with their dates. It is important when using any software package in an application that involves reading in data, to print at least a sub-sample of the observations to ensure that they have been read correctly by the program. Obviously, if they have not, any results obtained thereafter will be utterly meaningless. Another easy way to see whether the data as a whole look plausible is to use the TABLE instruction (simply type **TABLE** on its own). The name, number of observations, mean, standard error, minimum and maximum will be displayed for all series in RATS' memory.

## 1.11 Transformations

Variables of interest can be created in RATS by typing in the formulae using the 'SET' command. Suppose, for example, that a time-series called

Z has been read into the software. It can be used in the following ways so as to create new variables A, B, C, etc.:

SET A = Z/2              Dividing
SET B = Z*2             Multiplication
SET C = Z**2            Squaring
SET D = LOG(Z)          Taking the logarithms
SET E = EXP(Z)          Taking the exponential
SET F = Z{1}            Lagging the data
SET G = LOG(Z/Z{1})     Creating the log-returns

Note that it is also possible to create a series D, which is the log of Z, as

LOG Z / D

Other functions that can be used in the formulae include: *abs, sin, cos, sum,* etc. Some of these additional functions will be described subsequently.

Note the spaces that must be placed on either side of the equals signs in the SET command. These are necessary for the program to work. The SET command modifies or transforms the whole series at the same time. Modifying a single observation on a variable is accomplished using the COMPUTE command (or COM for short). For example, the line

COMPUTE lxx = LOG(x)

would take the log of a single number x and call it lxx.

For the house price series above, we might be interested in obtaining the simple percentage returns. To get these, type the following line into the input window after the print command:

**SET DHP = 100\*(price-price{1})/price{1}**

If, in the transformation, the new series is given the same name as the old series, then the old series will be overwritten.

## 1.12 Computing summary statistics

To get the summary statistics of a series, just type in a command such as

**STATISTICS PRICE**
**STATISTICS DHP**

This will give the number of observations, the sample mean, variance, skewness, kurtosis and their respective significances for the raw house price series and the percentage changes. We can also use the option 'FRACTILES' by typing

STATISTICS(FRACTILES) PRICE

which will show the main fractiles of the distribution of a series (the 1st, 5th, 10th, 90th, 95th, etc. percentiles and the median).

We should now have a set of instructions to read in the data, print the price series, construct a percentage returns series, and compute summary statistics for both the raw prices and the returns. To run this program and get the output, ensure that the input window is active, then click the L/R button to toggle switch RATS back to run mode. The running man icon will now be blue again. Then click the 'select ALL' icon to highlight the entire set of instructions and click on the running man icon.

Now in the output window (Box 1.1) we would first see the printed series followed by the summary statistics for the house price series and their simple returns as described above (with vertical dots added by me to denote that not all entries are shown to save some space).

### Box 1.1

```
ENTRY          PRICE
1991:01   53051.7211063
1991:02   53496.7987463
   ⋮           ⋮
2007:04   180314.1673158
2007:05   181584.4999830

Statistics on Series PRICE
Monthly Data From 1991:01 To 2007:05
Observations                    197
Sample Mean           88614.841417   Variance              1787641787.70088
Standard Error        42280.513096   of Sample Mean        3012.361830
t-Statistic (Mean = 0)   29.417064   Signif Level          0.000000
Skewness                  0.837734   Signif Level (Sk=0)   0.000002
Kurtosis (excess)        -0.833278   Signif Level (Ku = 0) 0.019021
Jarque-Bera              28.741849   Signif Level (JB = 0) 0.000001


Statistics on Series DHP
Monthly Data From 1991:02 To 2007:05
Observations                    196
Sample Mean               0.636252   Variance              1.313976
Standard Error            1.146288   of Sample Mean        0.081878
t-Statistic (Mean = 0)    7.770755   Signif Level          0.000000
Skewness                  0.036939   Signif Level (Sk = 0) 0.834052
Kurtosis (excess)         0.173202   Signif Level (Ku = 0) 0.626851
Jarque-Bera               0.289564   Signif Level (JB = 0) 0.865211
```

We can verify that indeed RATS has correctly read the raw price series. The interpretation of each of the terms in the summary statistics output is discussed in *Introductory Econometrics for Finance*, Chapter 4. It makes little sense to try to interpret the descriptive statistics for the raw price series because it is trending (non-stationary). Note that the number of observations for the returns series is one fewer because the first observation (January 1991) has been lost when constructing the lagged value. The mean monthly return is 0.636%, with a variance of 1.31%. The series is positively skewed and leptokurtic, but in neither case significantly so. Therefore, the Jarque–Bera test statistic for normality does not exceed the critical value.

## 1.13 Plots

RATS has two instructions for graphics:

- GRAPH produces time-series plots
- SCATTER produces scatter (x versus y) plots.

The syntax for producing the plots is

GRAPH(*options*) *number hfield vfield*
# *series start end symbol choice*

|  |  |
|---:|---|
| *number* : | number of series to graph (maximum being 20). |
| *hfield vfield* : | in conjunction with the HFIELDS and VFIELDS options of SPGRAPH), these parameters allow you to put multiple graphs on a single page. |
| *series* : | the series to be graphed. |
| *start end* : | the range to graph. |
| *symbol choice* : | selects the line type, pattern or colour that RATS uses for series. |
| *options* : | include, for example, Dates (label entries with dates), Style (style of graph, Grid (grid series), Height (graph height), Key (location of key), Max = (value of upper boundary), Header (header string for graph), etc. |

SCATTER(*options*) *number of pairs hfield vfield*
# *x-series y-series start end symbol choice*

|  |  |
|---:|---|
| *pairs* : | number of pairs of series to plot against each other (RATS can graph up to 20 pairs with a single instruction). |
| *x-series* : | the series on the horizontal axis. |
| *y-series* : | the series on the vertical axis. |

Customised graphs can easily be incorporated into other Windows applications using copy-and-paste, or by exporting as Windows metafiles.

There now follow some sample instructions for producing plots using RATS.

1 To produce a graph (time-series plot)
GRAPH(header='Plot of VODAFONE and FTALL SHARE Prices',hlabel='Sample Period',vlabel='Share Price',key=upleft) 2
# VODAFONE
# FT
Note that while the GRAPH command spills over onto a second line here, it must appear on a single line in the RATS program, as will be discussed in the following paragraph.
2 To produce a scatter diagram
SCATTER(Style=symbol,Header='BTvs.FT',Hlabel='FT',Vlabel='BT') 1
# VODAFONE FT

There is also a Wizard for constructing graphs. Click **Data**, **Graph** and the following window will appear.

Screenshot 1.7

The variable(s) to be plotted is(are) selected from the series list by clicking '<< Add <<'. Note that it is also possible to construct a two-scale graph, where one line is overlaid with another. In the 'Style' box, we can choose the type of graph we would like, and by choosing the appropriate options we can set the x- and y-axis labels, and whether a key and/or title are used. Suppose that we wished to generate a plot of the UK house price series from before. Clicking **OK** with the boxes completed as above would generate the following code:

```
GRAPH(STYLE=LINE, $
HEADER='Time-series Line Graph of Average House Prices', $
VLABEL='Price, GBP',HLABEL='Month', KEY=UPLEFT) 1
# PRICE
```

I have added the dollar signs ($) at the end of the first and second lines. A dollar sign is used by RATS to denote an instruction that spills over onto the following line, and hence the first three lines in the code sample above are all part of a single instruction. If we did not use the dollar sign, RATS would think that the word 'VLABEL' is a command like 'STATISTICS' or 'GRAPH' and so it would cause an error message.

To do the converse in RATS, i.e. to include more than one instruction on a single line, requires the separation of the commands with semicolons, e.g.

```
STATISTICS ABC; SET X = Y
```

Suppose that we also wished to construct a scatter plot of the price series against the returns.[2] There is no Wizard for this in RATS version 7.0, although there will be one in version 7.10. Type the following lines into the input window with the other instructions to produce the scatter plot:

```
scatter(Style=symbol,Header='House prices against house price returns', $
Hlabel='Price',Vlabel='DHP') 1
# PRICE DHP
```

Executing these two sets of instructions by running the program would generate Figures 1.1 and 1.2. By making the window containing the graph active (i.e. by clicking on it), there are a number of options. First, the graphs can be saved as encapsulated postscript files or as Windows metafiles by clicking on the disk icon. Second, the graphs can also be printed by clicking the print icon, or by selecting Edit and Copy, the

---

[2] This probably makes little sense to do but we have only two series as examples so far and hence nothing else to plot!

**Figure 1.1**

Time-series line graph of average house prices

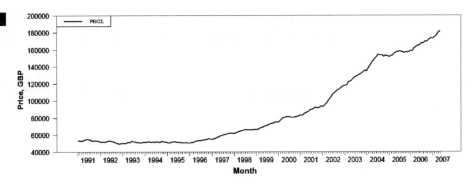

**Figure 1.2**

House prices against house price returns

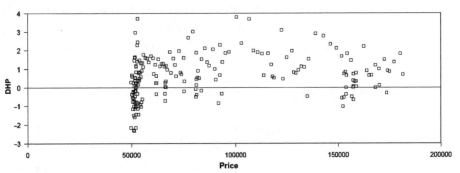

graphs can (separately) be copied to the Windows clipboard for pasting into another package such as Microsoft Word.

There is also an instruction, SPGRAPH, for constructing a panel containing several graphs together. For example, for plotting six graphs with three on the left and three on the right, the syntax would be

```
SPGRAPH(HFI=2,VFI=3)
```

[insert usual instructions to generate each of the six individual component graphs]

```
SPGRAPH(DONE)
```

## 1.14 Comment lines

When writing a complex set of instructions, it is often useful to be able to add comments to explain which sections do what in the code. This is useful not only for anyone else who might want to examine and possibly modify code that you have written but also if you want to come back to your own code after some time has elapsed! In RATS, comment lines (that will be skipped over and not executed) start with an asterisk, *, e.g.

```
* This line will not be executed
```

It is also possible to include a number of lines within a single comment statement using /* to open the comment block and */ to close it, e.g.

```
/*
This is
a comment
block */
```

## 1.15  Printing results

Both the Input and Output files (stored as text) can be printed by going into the 'File' menu and choosing 'Print'. These files can also be opened in a word processor and printed from the latter.

## 1.16  Saving the instructions and results

When exiting the program, you will be prompted with 'Save Changes Before Close?', in which case you choose 'Yes'. This will save changes to both the instructions file and the results. It is a good idea to periodically re-save the input window file to ensure that any changes or additions that you have made are retained in the event of a crash.

## 1.17  Econometric tools available in RATS

There now follows a list of some of the most important and useful features of RATS, taken from Estima's web site, and with techniques covered in this text highlighted in *italics* – see the *User Guide* version 7.0 for further details.

- *Graphics*
- *High-quality time-series graphics*
- *High-resolution X–Y scatter plots*
- Dual-scale graphs
- Contour graphs
- *Copy-and-paste graphs into other applications*
- Export graphs to many formats, including PostScript and WMF
- Data Entry and Output
- *Menu-driven 'Data Wizard' for reading in data*
- *Reads and writes Excel XLS, WKS, ASCII, DIF, PRN, DBF, and other data files*
- On-screen data editor
- *Can handle virtually any data frequency, including daily, weekly, intra-day and panel data*

- RATS data file format is fast and easy, supports all frequencies and allows you to store series of different frequencies on the same file
- Easy to convert data to different frequencies
- *Data transformations*
- Flexible transformations with algebraic formulas
- *Easy to create trend series, seasonal and time-period dummies*
- Specialised differencing and filtering operations
- *Multiple regressions including stepwise*
- Regression with autoregressive errors
- *Heteroscedasticity/serial-correlation correction, including Newey-West*
- *Non-linear least squares*
- *Two-stage least squares for linear, non-linear and autocorrelated models*
- *ARCH and GARCH estimation (univariate and multivariate)*
- Seemingly unrelated regressions and three-stage least squares
- Non-linear systems estimation
- Generalised Method of Moments
- *Maximum likelihood estimation*
- Constrained optimisation
- *Built-in hypothesis testing*
- *Logit and probit models*
- Censored/truncated data
- *Fixed/random effects estimators*
- Non-parametric regressions
- Kernel density estimation
- *Robust estimation*
- *Recursive least squares*
- State-space models
- Neural network models
- Linear and quadratic programming
- *ARIMA models*
- Transfer function/intervention models
- *Vector autoregressions, including structural VARs*
- *Impulse responses, variance decompositions*
- *Error-correction models*
- Kalman filter
- Spectral analysis
- *Forecasting*
- *Exponential smoothing*
- *Simultaneous equation models (unlimited number of equations)*
- *Simulations with random or user-supplied shocks*
- *Forecast performance statistics*

## 1.18  Outline of the remainder of this book

The outline of this book tracks the same format as the chapters with empirical material in the second edition of *Introductory Econometrics for Finance* (specifically Chapters 2–12). Each chapter contains detailed examples of implementation in RATS.

- Chapter 2 introduces the classical linear regression model (CLRM) and develops a hypothesis-testing framework.
- Chapter 3 continues and develops the material of Chapter 2 by generalising the bivariate model to multiple regression – i.e. models with many variables. The framework for testing multiple hypotheses is outlined, and measures of how well the model fits the data are described.
- Chapter 4 examines the important but often neglected topic of diagnostic testing. Testing for violations of the CLRM assumptions is described along with plausible remedial steps.
- Chapter 5 presents an introduction to time-series models, commencing by showing how the appropriate model can be chosen for a set of actual data, how the model is estimated and how model adequacy checks are performed. The generation of forecasts from such models is discussed, as are the criteria by which these forecasts can be evaluated.
- Chapter 6 extends the analysis from univariate to multivariate models. Estimation techniques for simultaneous equations models are outlined. Vector autoregressive (VAR) models, which have become extremely popular in the empirical finance literature, are also covered. The interpretation of VARs is explained by way of joint tests of restrictions, causality tests, impulse responses and variance decompositions.
- The first section of Chapter 7 discusses unit root processes and presents tests for non-stationarity in time-series. The concept of and tests for cointegration, and the formulation of error-correction models, are then discussed in the context of both the single equation framework of Engle–Granger, and the multivariate framework of Johansen.
- Chapter 8 covers the important topic of volatility and correlation modelling and forecasting. The class of ARCH (autoregressive conditionally heteroscedastic) models is then discussed. Other models are also presented, including extensions of the basic model such as GARCH, GARCH-M, EGARCH and GJR formulations. Multivariate GARCH models are described.
- Chapter 9 discusses testing for and modelling regime shifts or switches of behaviour in financial series. This chapter introduces the Markov switching approach to dealing with regime shifts. Threshold

autoregression is also discussed, along with issues relating to the estimation of such models.

- Chapter 10 focuses on how to deal appropriately with longitudinal data – that is, data having both time-series and cross-sectional dimensions. Fixed and random effects models are elucidated and distinguished.
- Chapter 11 describes logit and probit models that are appropriate for situations where the dependent variable is not continuous. Readers will learn how to construct, estimate and interpret such models.
- Finally, Chapter 12 presents an introduction to the use of simulations and bootstrapping in econometrics and finance. The reader is shown how to set up a simulation, and examples are given in options pricing and financial risk management to demonstrate the usefulness of these techniques.

# 2

# The classical linear regression model

In very general terms, regression is concerned with describing and evaluating the relationship between a given variable and one or more other variables. More specifically, regression is an attempt to explain movements in a variable by reference to movements in one or more other variables. To make this more concrete, denote the variable whose movements the regression seeks to explain by $y$ and the variables which are used to explain those variations by $x_1, x_2, \ldots, x_k$. Hence, in this relatively simple set-up, it would be said that variations in $k$ variables (the $x$s) cause changes in some other variable, $y$. The case where a single explanatory variable $x$ seeks to explain changes in a variable $y$ is known as the *bivariate regression model* and would be written:

$$y_t = \alpha + \beta x_t + u_t \tag{2.1}$$

where $u_t$ denotes a random disturbance term and the subscript $t(= 1, 2, 3, \ldots)$ denotes the observation number. This chapter demonstrates how to conduct bivariate regressions and simple hypotheses in RATS.

## 2.1 Hedge ratio estimation using OLS

This section shows how to run a bivariate regression using RATS. The example considers the situation where an investor wishes to hedge a long position in the S&P500 (or its constituent stocks) using a short position in futures contracts. Many academic studies assume that the objective of hedging is to minimise the variance of the hedged portfolio returns. If this is the case, then the appropriate hedge ratio (the number of units of the futures asset to sell per unit of the spot asset held) will be the slope estimate (i.e. $\hat{\beta}$) in a regression where the dependent variable is a time-series of spot returns and the independent variable is a time-series of futures returns.

This regression will be run using the file 'SandPhedge.xls', which contains monthly returns for the S&P500 index (in column 2) and S&P500 futures (in column 3). As described in Chapter 1, the first step is to import the data into RATS. To do this using the data Wizard, **open RATS** and **create an additional window**, so that there is one for each of the input and the output, then click the button to **tile these windows horizontally**.

Next, click **Data** and **Data (Other Formats)**, then **find the directory** where the Excel file is stored (also, don't forget to **change the 'Files of type' box** to 'Excel Files(*.XLS)') and click **Open**. RATS will correctly identify that there are 67 monthly data points and 3 columns, so there is no need to change anything in the 'Import Format' dialog box – just click **OK**. When the 'New Series Date' dialog box appears, as before, RATS will have correctly completed the required information so click **OK** again to choose monthly data with 12 periods per year starting in February 2002. The instructions to import the data will then be created automatically as

```
OPEN DATA 'C:\Chris\book\RATS handbook\SandPhedger.xls'
CALENDAR(M) 2002:2
ALL 2007:07
DATA(FORMAT=XLS,ORG=COLUMNS) 2002:02 2007:07 Spot Futures
```

Verify that the data have been imported correctly by printing the two series and checking a couple of entries at random against the original Excel file. The next step is to transform the levels of the two series into percentage returns. It is common in academic research to use continuously compounded returns rather than simple returns. To achieve this (i.e. to produce continuously compounded returns), type the lines

```
SET DSPOT = 100*LOG(SPOT/SPOT{1})
SET DFUTURES = 100*LOG(FUTURES/FUTURES{1})
```

**Save the input file as 'sandphedge.prg'** and don't forget to continue to save it at regular intervals to ensure that no work is lost! Before proceeding to estimate the regression, now that we have imported more than one series we can examine a number of descriptive statistics together and measures of association between them. We could obtain the summary statistics as described in Chapter 1, but in addition we can compute the cross-correlations between the spot and futures returns series. To do this using a Wizard, click **Statistics** and then **Cross Correlations**. Note that for this Wizard to work properly, we need to have already run the initial lines that read in the data, so that the series are in RATS memory and appear in the list to choose from. Then **complete the dialog box** as in screenshot 2.1.

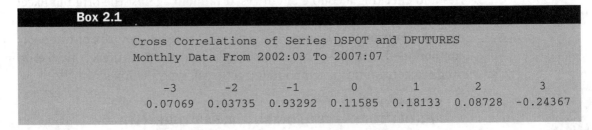

This will not only compute the correlation between the spot and futures returns measured at the same time but also the correlation between $rspot_t$ with $rfutures_{t-3}$ through to $rfutures_{t+3}$ (the choice of $\pm 3$ lags is entirely arbitrary). The instruction line that this Wizard would create is

CROSS(FROM=-3,TO=3) DSPOT DFUTURES

and running this yields the output in Box 2.1.

**Box 2.1**

```
Cross Correlations of Series DSPOT and DFUTURES
Monthly Data From 2002:03 To 2007:07

    -3       -2       -1        0        1        2        3
 0.07069  0.03735  0.93292  0.11585  0.18133  0.08728 -0.24367
```

Interestingly, the correlation is highest when the futures returns lead the spot returns by one period (i.e. between $dspot_t$ and $dfutures_{t-1}$). This was a useful exercise for it illustrates either that information is incorporated into the futures market a whole month more quickly than it is in the spot market or, perhaps more likely, that the data have not been measured correctly. This issue is not pursued further here since the example is used only to illustrate how to run the regression in RATS.

Now proceeding to actually estimate the regression equation, this can be achieved either by writing the lines of code manually or by using a Wizard. The core command for running a linear regression is of the form

```
LINREG(OPTIONS) DEPVAR / RESIDS
# INDEPVARS
```

This will estimate a linear regression with dependent variable 'depvar' and a list of independent variables 'indepvars' (including a constant in the list if appropriate) following the hash (#) symbol. There is a variety of options that can be placed in parentheses after the linreg command, some of which are discussed below. '/ resids' will save the residuals in a series called resids.

We want to run a regression of the spot returns on an intercept and the futures returns, saving the residuals as a series called resids. To do this using the Wizard, having run the program already to read in the data etc., click **Statistics** and then **Regressions**. The 'Univariate Regressions' Wizard will then appear.

**Screenshot 2.2**

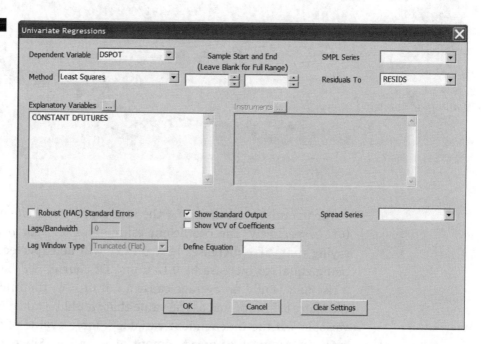

**Complete the boxes** as in the screen capture here for the dependent variable and the explanatory variables by selecting them from the appropriate lists and then typing '**RESIDS**' in the 'Residuals To' box. Finally, click **OK**. It is possible to set a sample range so that only a sub-set of the available observations is used (for example, starting the estimation in January 2003), or we can use robust standard errors – these will be discussed in Chapter 4. RATS will create the additional lines of code

```
LINREG DSPOT / RESIDS
# Constant DFUTURES
```

And the standard linear regression output will be as in Box 2.2.

### Box 2.2

```
Linear Regression — Estimation by Least Squares
Dependent Variable DSPOT
Monthly Data From 2002:03 To 2007:07
Usable Observations             65   Degrees of Freedom        63
Centered R**2            0.013422      R Bar **2    -0.002238
Uncentered R**2          0.027383      T X R**2      1.780
Mean of Dependent Variable       0.4212026598
Std Error of Dependent Variable  3.5429920081
Standard Error of Estimate       3.5469548972
Sum of Squared Residuals       792.59600968
Regression F(1,63)                 0.8571
Significance Level of F            0.35809281
Log Likelihood                  -173.51111
Durbin-Watson Statistic            2.116689


      Variable        Coeff         Std Error      T-Stat       Signif
************************************************************************
1.    Constant     0.3633022795   0.4443688425   0.81757    0.41668454
2.    DFUTURES     0.1238600322   0.1337898152   0.92578    0.35809281
```

The parameter estimates for the intercept ($\hat{\alpha}$) and slope ($\hat{\beta}$) are 0.36 and 0.12 respectively. The coefficient estimate of 0.12 for $\beta$ is interpreted as saying that, 'if $x$ increases by 1 unit, $y$ will be expected, everything else being equal, to increase by 0.12 units'. Of course, if $\hat{\beta}$ had been negative, a rise in $x$ would on average cause a fall in $y$. $\hat{\alpha}$, the intercept coefficient estimate, is interpreted as the value that would be taken by the dependent variable $y$ if the independent variable $x$ took a value of zero. 'Units' here refer to the units of measurement of $x_t$ and $y_t$. Since $x$ and $y$ are both measured as percentage returns, the slope would imply that a change in the futures return of one percentage point would lead to a 0.12 percentage point increase in the spot return.

A large number of other statistics are also presented in the regression output – the purpose and interpretation of these will be discussed later in this and subsequent chapters.

If we assume that the objective is to minimise the variance of the hedged portfolio returns, we can now work out how effective the hedge has been by comparing the variance of the spot returns with the variance of the residuals from the OLS regression that estimates the optimal hedge ratio. To do this, type the following additional lines of code:

```
STATS(NOPRINT) DSPOT
COM DSPOTVAR = %VARIANCE
STATS(NOPRINT) RESIDS
COM RESIDSVAR = %VARIANCE
COM FALL = 100*(DSPOTVAR-RESIDSVAR)/DSPOTVAR
DIS 'SPOT RETURN VARIANCE=' DSPOTVAR $
', HEDGED PORTFOLIO VARIANCE=' RESIDSVAR $
'% FALL IN VARIANCE=' FALL
```

The STATS (the short form and equivalent to the instruction STATISTICS) commands will construct summary statistics (for the spot returns and residual series respectively). The NOPRINT option that is used in parentheses will mean that these statistics are calculated but not printed to the output file. When a command is run, such as STATS or LINREG, RATS will automatically calculate a number of quantities and these will be stored as scalars with names starting in '%'. So %MEAN will store the mean of a series, %VARIANCE will store the variance, %NOBS will store the number of observations, %NDF will be the number of degrees of freedom, %NREG is the number of regressors, %RSQUARED is the $R^2$, and so on.

COM DSPOTVAR = %VARIANCE will construct a new scalar, DSPOTVAR, that takes the variance of the DSPOT series that was created using the STATS command preceding it. COM is short for COMPUTE and is used for the calculation of scalar quantities and not for series (where the SET command would be used). The next line, 'COM FALL = ...' calculates the percentage change in the variance when we move from the unhedged spot position to the hedged portfolio. Finally, the DIS command (short for DISPLAY) will print the listed quantities to the output file, with all of the text enclosed inside '' being displayed in the output window exactly as it is written. The output from this set of instructions is as shown in Box 2.3.

The variance of the hedged portfolio returns is 12.38, compared with 12.55 for the unhedged spot position, a fall of only 1.34%. Thus, at least on this measure, the hedge has performed poorly.

Now **estimate a regression for the levels of the series** rather than the returns (i.e. run a regression of spot on a constant and futures) and examine the parameter estimates. The return regression slope parameter estimated above measures the optimal hedge ratio and also measures the short-run relationship between the two series. By contrast, the slope

**Box 2.3**

```
SPOT RETURN VARIANCE= 12.55279 , HEDGED PORTFOLIO VARIANCE= 12.38431
% FALL IN VARIANCE=   1.34217
```

parameter in a regression using the raw spot and futures indices (or the log of the spot series and the log of the futures series) can be interpreted as measuring the long-run relationship between them. Type the two lines (or use the Wizard again) to estimate a new equation that regresses the spot prices on a constant and the futures prices, not saving the residuals this time.

The intercept estimate ($\hat{\alpha}$) in this regression is 21.11 and the slope estimate ($\hat{\beta}$) is 0.98. The intercept can be considered to approximate the cost of carry, while as expected the long-term relationship between spot and futures prices is almost 1:1 – see Chapter 7 for further discussion of the estimation and interpretation of this long-term relationship. Finally, Click **File** and **Save as** to save the input file as 'Sandphedge.prg'.

## 2.2 Standard errors and hypothesis testing

Any set of regression estimates $\hat{\alpha}$ and $\hat{\beta}$ are specific to the sample used in their estimation. In other words, if a different sample of data was selected from within the population, the data points (the $x_t$ and $y_t$) would be different, leading to different values of the OLS estimates. The standard errors give us an idea of how 'good' these estimates of $\alpha$ and $\beta$ are in the sense of having some measure of the reliability or precision of the estimators ($\hat{\alpha}$ and $\hat{\beta}$). They give an indication of whether the estimates are likely to vary much from one sample to another sample within the given population. In other words, they show the likely sampling variability and hence the precision of the estimates.

Often, financial theory will suggest that certain coefficients should take on particular values, or values within a given range. It is thus of interest to determine whether the relationships expected from financial theory are upheld by the data or not. Estimates of $\alpha$ and $\beta$ have been obtained from the sample, and inferences are made concerning the likely population values from the regression parameters that have been estimated from the sample data. In doing this, the aim is to determine whether the differences between the coefficient estimates that are actually obtained and expectations arising from financial theory are a long way from one another in a statistical sense. This chapter now continues to examine some hypothesis tests using the test of significance approach.

First, re-examine the regression output above for the spot and futures returns regression. The third column (taking the variable numbers as the first column) presents the coefficient standard errors, and the fourth presents the $t$-ratios, which are the statistics for testing the null hypothesis that the true values of these parameters are zero against a two-sided alternative – i.e. these statistics test $H_0: \alpha = 0$ versus $H_1: \alpha \neq 0$ in the first row of numbers and $H_0: \beta = 0$ versus $H_1: \beta \neq 0$ in the second. The fact that these test statistics are both very small is indicative that neither of these null hypotheses is likely to be rejected. This conclusion is confirmed by the *p*-values given in the final column. Both *p*-values are considerably larger than 0.1, indicating that the corresponding test statistics are not even significant at the 10% level.

Suppose now that we wanted to test the null hypothesis $H_0: \beta = 1$ rather than $H_0: \beta = 0$. We could test this, or any other hypothesis about the coefficients, by hand using the information we already have. But it is easier to let RATS do the work by using the TEST or RESTRICT or EXCLUDE commands.

For example, to test the restriction that parameters 1 and 2 (the intercept and slope) are both zero, use the command

```
TEST(ZEROS)
# 1 2
```

or to test the restriction that parameters 1 and 2 are both one, use the command

```
TEST
# 1 2
# 1 1
```

The TEST instruction is less cumbersome than RESTRICT but it does an identical job and could be used in any situation where we want to test linear hypotheses about the parameters. However, RESTRICT is more flexible and so it will be used throughout this book. Thus the relevant line of code to be inserted would be

```
RESTRICT 1
# 2
# 1 1
```

This command is interpreted as stating that there is one restriction (RESTRICT 1) on the second coefficient (# 2), which is that one times the value of that coefficient equals one (# 1 1). The output would be as in Box 2.4.

**Box 2.4**

```
t(63)= 6.548630 or F(1,63)= 42.884552 with Significance Level 0.00000001
```

Note that by using this command, it is possible to test multiple hypotheses, which will be discussed in Chapter 3. The test is performed in two different ways with identical conclusions by construction because the $t$-distribution is a special case of the $F$-distribution. Therefore, this nicely illustrates that if we take a $t$-distributed random variable with 63 degrees of freedom, the square of this random variable will follow an $F$-distribution with (1,63) degrees of freedom. Hence $6.548630^2 = 42.884552$. The results suggest that the null hypothesis should clearly be rejected as the $p$-value for the test is zero to four decimal places.

There is also a Wizard available for testing restrictions that will write the commands for you. This Wizard can be found by clicking 'Statistics' and then 'Regression Tests' after you have run a regression.

As an exercise, now go back to the regression in levels (i.e. with the raw prices rather than the returns) and test the null hypothesis that $\beta = 1$ in this regression. You should find in this case that the null hypothesis is not rejected since the parameter estimate ($\hat{\beta}$) is very close to the value under the null hypothesis ($\beta^*$). The results for the test in this case would be as in Box 2.5.

---

**Box 2.5**

```
t(64)= 0.751863 or F(1,64)= 0.565298 with Significance Level 0.45488966
```

---

## 2.3 Estimation and hypothesis testing with the CAPM

This exercise will estimate and test some hypotheses about the capital asset pricing model (CAPM) beta for several US stocks. First, **use the Data Wizard** to set up a program to accommodate monthly data commencing in January 2002 and ending in April 2007 to import the Excel file 'capm.xls'. The file is organised by observation and contains six columns of numbers plus the dates in the first column. The data comprise the monthly stock prices of four companies (Ford, General Motors, Microsoft and Sun), along with index values for the S&P500 ('sandp') and three-month US-Treasury bills ('ustb3m'). **Save the file** of instructions as capm.prg. **Verify a few observations for each series** by printing them and comparing them with the corresponding observations in the Excel file.

In order to estimate a CAPM equation for the Ford stock as an example, we need to first transform the price series into returns and then calculate the excess returns over the risk-free rate. To transform the series, we need to use the SET command and to type the following into the input window:

**SET RSANDP = 100*LOG(SANDP/SANDP{1})**

This will create a new series named RSANDP that will contain the percentage returns of the S&P500. Recall that the operator {1} is used to instruct RATS to use the one-period lagged observation of the series. To estimate the continuously compounded percentage returns on the Ford stock, type

**SET RFORD = 100*LOG(FORD/FORD{1})**

This will yield a new series named RFORD which will contain the returns of the Ford stock.

When we transform the returns into excess returns, we need to be slightly careful because the stock returns are monthly but the Treasury bill yields are annualised. We could run the whole analysis using monthly data or using annualised data and it should not matter which we use, but the two series must be measured consistently. So, to turn the T-bill yields into monthly figures and to write over the original series, type

**SET USTB3M = USTB3M/12**

Now, to compute the excess returns, type

**SET ERSANDP = RSANDP-USTB3M**

where ERSANDP will be used to denote the excess returns on the S&P500, so that the original (not excess) returns series will remain as RSANDP. Similarly **transform the Ford returns** into a set of excess returns.

Now that the excess returns have been obtained for the two series, before running the regression, plot the data in a scatter diagram and in a time-series graph to examine visually whether the series appear to move together. To do this, the Wizard can be used for the time-series plot but not the scatter, as before. For the time-series plot, because the Ford stock returns are considerably more volatile, it is perhaps more informative to use a two-scale plot. The required code is

```
SCATTER(STYLE=SYMBOL,HEADER='Scatter Plot of S&P versus Ford Excess Returns', $
VLABEL='Ford', HLABEL='S&P',KEY=NONE) 1
# ERSANDP ERFORD
GRAPH(STYLE=LINE, HEADER='Monthly Time-series Plot of S&P and Ford Excess Returns', $
VLABEL='Return (%) ', OVERLAY=LINE, HLABEL='Month',KEY=UPLEFT) 2
# ERSANDP
# ERFORD
```

The plots would be those shown in Figures 2.1 and 2.2.

**Figure 2.1**

Scatter plot S&P versus Ford excess returns

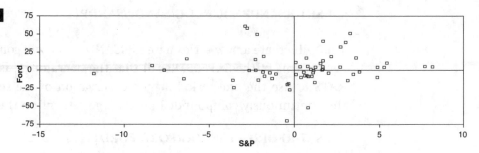

**Figure 2.2**

Monthly time-series plot of S&P and Ford excess returns

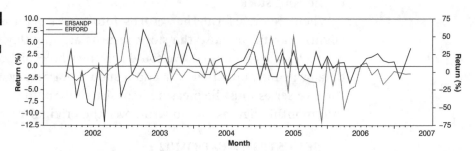

It seems fairly evident that there is a positive relationship between the S&P500 and Ford returns, although the latter are considerably more volatile. The time-series plot suggests that the S&P (left-scale) and Ford (right-scale) do indeed move together. Since the data have already been transformed to obtain the excess returns, to estimate the CAPM regression equation using OLS, just type the following in the equation window:

**LINREG ERFORD**
**# CONSTANT ERSANDP**

Make sure that you save the input file again to include the transformation commands and regression equation. The estimation output is shown in Box 2.6.

Take a couple of minutes to examine the results of the regression. What is the slope coefficient estimate and what does it signify? Is this coefficient statistically significant? The beta coefficient (the slope coefficient) estimate is 0.3597. The $p$-value of the $t$-ratio is 0.6523, signifying that the excess return on the market proxy has no significant explanatory power for the variability of the excess returns of Ford stock. What is the interpretation of the intercept estimate? Is it statistically significant?

How could the hypothesis that the value of the population beta is equal to one be tested? The answer is to use the RESTRICT command and type

```
  Box 2.6

Linear Regression - Estimation by Least Squares
Dependent Variable ERFORD
Monthly Data From 2002:02 To 2007:04
Usable Observations            63      Degrees of Freedom      61
Centered R**2               0.003350      R Bar **2   -0.012989
Uncentered R**2             0.012429       T X R**2      0.783
Mean of Dependent Variable          2.097444893
Std Error of Dependent Variable    22.051291229
Standard Error of Estimate         22.194037228
Sum of Squared Residuals        30047.092598
Regression F(1,61)                     0.2050
Significance Level of F             0.65229704
Log Likelihood                    -283.66580
Durbin-Watson Statistic             1.785699


        Variable        Coeff         Std Error       T-Stat        Signif
************************************************************************************
1.    Constant     2.0202193712    2.8013822756     0.72115      0.47357163
2.    ERSANDP      0.3597261387    0.7944429336     0.45280      0.65229704
```

```
  Box 2.7

t(61)= 0.805941 or F(1,61)= 0.649540 with Significance Level 0.42340784
```

**RESTRICT 1**
**# 2**
**# 1 1**

and the results are shown in Box 2.7.

The conclusion here is that the null hypothesis that the CAPM beta of Ford stock is 1 cannot be rejected and hence the estimated beta of 0.359 is not significantly different from 1.[3]

---

[3] Although the value 0.359 may seem a long way from 1, considered purely from an econometric perspective, the sample size is quite small and this has led to a large parameter standard error, which explains the failure to reject both $H_0: \beta = 0$ and $H_0: \beta = 1$.

# 3

## Further development and analysis of the classical linear regression model

### 3.1 Conducting multiple hypothesis tests

It is very easy to generalise the simple model to one with multiple regressors (independent variables). Equation (2.1) becomes

$$y_t = \beta_1 + \beta_2 x_{2t} + \beta_3 x_{3t} + \cdots + \beta_k x_{kt} + u_t, \quad t = 1, 2, \ldots, T \tag{3.1}$$

So the variables $x_{2t}, x_{3t}, \ldots, x_{kt}$ are a set of $k-1$ explanatory variables which are thought to influence $y$, and $\beta_1, \beta_2, \ldots, \beta_k$ are the parameters which quantify the effect of each of these explanatory variables on $y$. The coefficient interpretations are slightly altered in the multiple regression context. Each coefficient is now known as a partial regression coefficient, interpreted as representing the partial effect of the given explanatory variable on the explained variable, after holding constant, or eliminating the effect of, all other explanatory variables. For example, $\hat{\beta}_2$ measures the effect of $x_2$ on $y$ after eliminating the effects of $x_3, x_4, \ldots, x_k$. Stating this in other words, each coefficient measures the average change in the dependent variable per unit change in a given independent variable, holding all other independent variables constant at their average values.

Hypothesis tests involving more than one parameter can be conducted using an $F$-test. The residual sums of squares from each regression are determined, and the two residual sums of squares are 'compared' in the test statistic. The $F$-test statistic for testing multiple hypotheses about the coefficient estimates is given by

$$test\ statistic = \frac{RRSS - URSS}{URSS} \times \frac{T - k}{m} \tag{3.2}$$

where the following notation applies:

$URSS$ = residual sum of squares from unrestricted regression
$RRSS$ = residual sum of squares from restricted regression
$m$ = number of restrictions

```
  Box 3.1
```

```
Linear Regression - Estimation by Least Squares
Dependent Variable ERFORD
Monthly Data From 2002:02 To 2007:04
Usable Observations              63   Degrees of Freedom         61
Centered R**2            0.003350       R Bar **2   -0.012989
Uncentered R**2          0.012429        T X R**2     0.783
Mean of Dependent Variable          2.097444893
Std Error of Dependent Variable   22.051291229
Standard Error of Estimate        22.194037228
Sum of Squared Residuals          30047.092598
Regression F(1,61)                    0.2050
Significance Level of F             0.65229704
Log Likelihood                     -283.66580
Durbin-Watson Statistic              1.785699


        Variable        Coeff        Std Error        T-Stat        Signif
*************************************************************************************
1.    Constant      2.0202193712    2.8013822756     0.72115      0.47357163
2.    ERSANDP       0.3597261387    0.7944429336     0.45280      0.65229704
```

$T$ = number of observations

$k$ = number of regressors in unrestricted regression

We will now reconsider the CAPM example constructed in the previous chapter. As a reminder, the results are included again in Box 3.1.

If we examine the regression $F$-test, this also shows that the regression slope coefficient is not significantly different from zero, which in this case is exactly the same result as the $t$-test for the beta coefficient (since there is only one slope coefficient). Thus, in this instance, the $F$-test statistic is equal to the square of the slope $t$-ratio.

Now suppose that we wish to conduct a joint test that both the intercept and slope parameters are one. We would perform this test exactly as for a test involving only one coefficient. Type the code

**RESTRICT 2**
**# 1**
**# 1 1**
**# 2**
**# 1 1**

The command RESTRICT 2 is used here since we wish to test two restrictions! Then the two sets of 'supplementary cards' (the items that follow the # symbol) state first that we wish to test a hypothesis concerning

---

**Box 3.2**

```
F(2,61) = 0.37460 with Significance Level 0.68913177
```

---

parameter 1 (the intercept) that $1 \times$ parameter $1 = 1$ and second that we wish to test a hypothesis concerning parameter 2 (the slope) that $1 \times$ parameter $2 = 1$. RATS uses a Wald form of the test (an $F$-test). The output is shown in Box 3.2.

The test statistic follows an $F$-distribution with $(m, T-k)$ degrees of freedom, where $m = 2$, $k = 2$ and $T = 63$ in this case. The conclusion is that the joint null hypothesis, $H_0$: $\beta_1 = 1$ and $\beta_2 = 1$, is not rejected since the test statistic is lower than the critical value and the $p$-value is considerably larger than 0.05.

## 3.2 Multiple regression using an APT-style model

In the spirit of arbitrage pricing theory (APT), the following example will examine regressions that seek to determine whether the monthly returns on Microsoft stock can be explained by reference to unexpected changes in a set of macroeconomic and financial variables. First, **set up a new RATS program that reads in the data**. There are 254 monthly observations in the file 'macror.xls' starting in March 1986 and ending in April 2007. There are 13 series plus a column of dates. The series in the Excel file are the Microsoft stock price, the S&P500 index value, the consumer price index, an industrial production index, Treasury bill yields for the following maturities: three months, six months, one year, three years, five years and ten years, a measure of 'narrow' money supply, a consumer credit series and a 'credit spread' series. The latter is defined as the difference in annualised average yields between a portfolio of bonds rated AAA and a portfolio of bonds rated BAA. Save the resulting input file as 'MACRO.PRG'.

The first stage is to generate a set of changes or *differences* for each of the variables, since the APT posits that the stock returns can be explained by reference to the *unexpected changes* in the macroeconomic variables rather than their levels. The unexpected value of a variable can be defined as the difference between the actual (realised) value of the variable and its expected value. The question then arises about how we believe that investors might have formed their expectations, and while there are many ways to construct measures of expectations, the easiest is to assume that investors have naive expectations that the next period value of the variable is equal to the current value. This being the case, the entire change in the variable from one period to the next is the unexpected change (because investors are assumed to expect no change).[4]

Transforming the variables can be done as described in Chapter 2 by typing the following lines of code into the input window:

```
SET DSPREAD = SPREAD - SPREAD{1}
SET DCREDIT = CONSUMERCREDIT - CONSUMERCREDIT{1}
SET DPROD = INDPROD - INDPROD{1}
SET RMSOFT = 100*LOG(MICROSOFT/MICROSOFT{1})
SET RSANDP = 100*LOG(SANDP/SANDP{1})
SET DMONEY = M1MONEY - M1MONEY{1}
SET INFLATION = 100*LOG(CPI/CPI{1})
SET TERM = USTB10Y - USTB3M
```

We also need to apply further transformations to some of the transformed series, so add the following commands:

```
SET DINFLATION = INFLATION - INFLATION{1}
SET MUSTB3M = USTB3M/12
SET RTERM = TERM - TERM{1}
SET ERMSOFT = RMSOFT - MUSTB3M
SET ERSANDP = RSANDP - MUSTB3M
```

The final two of these calculate excess returns for the stock and for the index respectively.

We can now run the regression. Type the following:

```
LINREG ERMSOFT
# CONSTANT ERSANDP DPROD DCREDIT DINFLATION $
DMONEY DSPREAD RTERM
```

to use Least Squares over the whole sample period. Run this input file and the table of results will appear as in Box 3.3.

Take a few minutes to examine the main regression results. Which of the variables has a statistically significant impact on the Microsoft excess returns? Using your knowledge of the effects of the financial and macro-economic environment on stock returns, examine whether the coefficients have their expected signs and whether the sizes of the parameters are plausible.

The regression $F$-statistic takes a value 8.908. Remember that this is a special $F$-test that examines the null hypothesis that all of the slope

---

[4] It is an interesting question as to whether the differences should be taken on the levels of the variables or their logarithms. If the former, we have absolute changes in the variables, whereas the latter would lead to proportionate changes. The choice between the two is essentially an empirical one, and this example assumes that the former is chosen, apart from for the stock price series themselves and the consumer price series. In these latter cases, convention is followed in using percentage changes.

**Box 3.3**

```
Linear Regression — Estimation by Least Squares
Dependent Variable ERMSOFT
Monthly Data From 1986:05 To 2007:04
Usable Observations            252     Degrees of Freedom      244
Centered R**2              0.203545      R Bar **2   0.180696
Uncentered R**2            0.204141       T X R**2      51.443
Mean of Dependent Variable     -0.42080264
Std Error of Dependent Variable  15.41135106
Standard Error of Estimate       13.94964949
Sum of Squared Residuals      47480.623879
Regression F(7,244)                 8.9082
Significance Level of F        0.00000000
Log Likelihood                 -1017.64215
Durbin-Watson Statistic           2.156221
```

| | Variable | Coeff | Std Error | T-Stat | Signif |
|---|---|---|---|---|---|
| 1. | Constant | -0.58760337 | 1.45789822 | -0.40305 | 0.68726564 |
| 2. | ERSANDP | 1.48943369 | 0.20327634 | 7.32714 | 0.00000000 |
| 3. | DPROD | 0.28932249 | 0.50091896 | 0.57758 | 0.56407798 |
| 4. | DCREDIT | -0.00005584 | 0.00016049 | -0.34792 | 0.72819661 |
| 5. | DINFLATION | 4.24780859 | 2.97734151 | 1.42671 | 0.15494127 |
| 6. | DMONEY | -1.16152636 | 0.71397392 | -1.62685 | 0.10506027 |
| 7. | DSPREAD | 12.15775447 | 13.55096915 | 0.89719 | 0.37050347 |
| 8. | RTERM | 6.06760945 | 3.32136337 | 1.82684 | 0.06894503 |

parameters are jointly zero. The *p*-value of zero attached to the test statistic shows that this null hypothesis should be rejected. However, there are a number of parameter estimates that are not significantly different from zero – specifically those on the DPROD, DCREDIT and DSPREAD variables. Let us test the null hypothesis that the parameters on these three variables are jointly zero using an *F*-test. To test this, we use the RESTRICT command with three restrictions. Given the order that the variables are listed, these are numbers 3, 4 and 7. We could conduct this test with either the TEST command or with RESTRICT; the latter is used here.

```
RESTRICT 3
# 3
# 1 0
# 4
# 1 0
# 7
# 1 0
```

**Box 3.4**

```
F(3,244) = 0.40163 with Significance Level 0.75195457
```

The resulting $F$-test statistic follows an $F(3, 244)$ distribution as there are 3 restrictions, 252 usable observations and 8 parameters to estimate in the unrestricted regression. The output is shown in Box 3.4.

The $F$-statistic value is 0.402 with $p$-value 0.752, suggesting that the null hypothesis cannot be rejected. The parameters on DINFLATION and DMONEY are almost significant at the 10% level and so the associated parameters are not included in this $F$-test and the variables are retained.

## 3.3 Stepwise regression

There is a procedure known as a stepwise regression that is available in RATS. Stepwise regression is an automatic variable selection procedure which chooses the jointly most 'important' (variously defined) explanatory variables from a set of candidate variables. There are a number of different stepwise regression approaches, but the simplest is the forwards method. This starts with no variables in the regression (or only those variables that are always required by the researcher to be in the regression) and then it selects first from the list of candidate variables the one with the lowest $p$-value (largest $t$-ratio) if it were included, then the variable with the second lowest $p$-value conditional upon the first variable already being included, and so on. The procedure continues until the next lowest $p$-value relative to those of the variables already included is larger than some specified threshold value, at which point the selection stops, with no more variables being incorporated into the model.

To conduct a stepwise regression which will automatically select from among these variables the most important ones for explaining the variations in Microsoft stock returns, we would use the STWISE command

    **STWISE ERMSOFT**
    **# CONSTANT ERSANDP DPROD DCREDIT DINFLATION \$**
      **DMONEY DSPREAD RTERM**

An alternative stepwise procedure is to start with all the variables included and then to sequentially delete the least significant variable until only those variables with $p$-values lower than the threshold remain – this is known as *backwards stepwise*. Finally, it is possible to conduct a *full stepwise* procedure that combines the forwards and backwards approaches so that the procedure starts with no variables but at each stage after variables have been added, the backwards approach is then used to delete variables that now have higher *p*-values than the threshold.

There are various options that can be used with the STWISE instruction, including 'FORCE=x', where x is a number. This will force the first x listed variables to be in the regression irrespective of their significance; method=[stepwise]/forwards/backwards will use the full stepwise (the default), the forwards or the backwards version of the procedure respectively. The default criterion is to include variables in the forwards procedure if the *p*-value is less than 0.2 and to delete variables in the backwards procedure if their *p*-value is greater than 0.2. These can be changed using the options slenter=y and slstay=z where y and z are numbers between 0 and 1 with z required to be no smaller than y. It is a good idea to ensure that the constant is always in the regression, even if the parameter attached to it is not statistically significant, so use the FORCE=1 option and ensure that CONSTANT is the first listed explanatory variable. The output we see on running this command is shown in Box 3.5.

---

### Box 3.5

```
Stepping In with P = 0.000000 Variable ERSANDP
Stepping In with P = 0.115338 Variable RTERM
Stepping In with P = 0.099449 Variable DMONEY
Stepping In with P = 0.164257 Variable DINFLATION

Stepwise Regression
Dependent Variable ERMSOFT
Monthly Data From 1986:05 To 2007:04
Usable Observations              252   Degrees of Freedom        247
Centered R**2              0.199612     R Bar **2   0.186650
Uncentered R**2            0.200211       T X R**2     50.453
Mean of Dependent Variable          -0.42080264
Std Error of Dependent Variable     15.41135106
Standard Error of Estimate          13.89886631
Sum of Squared Residuals         47715.085734
Regression F(4,247)                   15.4001
Significance Level of F              0.00000000
Log Likelihood                     -1018.26281
Durbin-Watson Statistic                2.150604
```

| | Variable | Coeff | Std Error | T-Stat | Signif |
|---|---|---|---|---|---|
| 1. | Constant | -0.947197550 | 0.878699808 | -1.07795 | 0.28210611 |
| 2. | ERSANDP | 1.471399746 | 0.201458819 | 7.30372 | 0.00000000 |
| 3. | DINFLATION | 4.013511671 | 2.876986089 | 1.39504 | 0.16425681 |
| 4. | DMONEY | -1.171272592 | 0.702522559 | -1.66724 | 0.09673438 |
| 5. | RTERM | 6.121657473 | 3.292863158 | 1.85907 | 0.06420669 |

As can be seen, the excess market return, the term structure, money supply and unexpected inflation variables have all been included while the default spread and credit variables have been omitted.

Stepwise procedures have been strongly criticised by statistical purists. At the most basic level, they are sometimes argued to be no better than automated procedures for data mining, especially if the list of potential candidate variables is long and results from a 'fishing trip' rather than a strong prior financial theory. More subtly, the iterative nature of the variable selection process implies that the size of the tests on parameters attached to variables in the final model will not be the nominal values (e.g. 5%) that would have applied had this model been the only one estimated. Thus the *p*-values for tests involving parameters in the final regression should really be modified to take into account that the model results from a sequential procedure, although they are usually not in statistical packages such as RATS.

## 3.4 Constructing reports

It is often the case that the final output from a piece of empirical research will be a written report of some sort that includes the regression results. It is poor form to copy the entire output from a standard computer package, but re-typing the results is also to be avoided as it wastes time and is likely to introduce errors. Fortunately, RATS has a REPORT instruction that can be used to prepare regression parameter estimates and their standard errors in a useful format for pasting directly into a report in, for example, Microsoft Word. If we want to put the output from the Microsoft regression containing all of the variables and of the stepwise procedure in two columns in a table, we could use the following instructions:

```
REPORT(ACTION=DEFINE)
LINREG ERMSOFT / RESIDS
# CONSTANT ERSANDP DPROD DCREDIT DINFLATION $
   DMONEY DSPREAD RTERM
REPORT(REGRESSION)
STWISE(FORCE=1) ERMSOFT
# CONSTANT ERSANDP DPROD DCREDIT DINFLATION $
   DMONEY DSPREAD RTERM
REPORT(REGRESSION)
REPORT(ACTION=SHOW)
```

The basic engine for producing formatted output is the REPORT instruction. 'REPORT(ACTION=DEFINE)' will set up a report. We then run any desired regression and add the command 'REPORT(REGRESSION)' after-wards – and this will append the parameter and standard error output from the most recent regression to the report. We can run as many regressions as we want, adding 'REPORT(REGRESSION)' after each one. Finally, when we are done, we add the line 'REPORT(ACTION=SHOW)', which will print the report to the output window. A number of options are also available, for example, to restrict the number of decimal places displayed, or to add column headers – see the RATS 7 *User Guide*, pp. 169–73 for more details.

The results from these instructions will appear in two columns (Box 3.6), with the blank spaces indicating variables that were not selected in the final model by the stepwise procedure.

**Box 3.6**

| | | |
|---|---|---|
| Constant | -0.587603 | -0.947198 |
| | (1.457898) | (0.878700) |
| ERSANDP | 1.489434 | 1.471400 |
| | (0.203276) | (0.201459) |
| DPROD | 0.289322 | |
| | (0.500919) | |
| DCREDIT | -0.000056 | |
| | (0.000160) | |
| DINFLATION | 4.247809 | 4.013512 |
| | (2.977342) | (2.876986) |
| DMONEY | -1.161526 | -1.171273 |
| | (0.713974) | (0.702523) |
| DSPREAD | 12.157754 | |
| | (13.550969) | |
| RTERM | 6.067609 | 6.121657 |
| | (3.321363) | (3.292863) |

# 4

# Diagnostic testing

Recall that five assumptions are made relating to the classical linear regression model. These are required to show that the estimation technique, ordinary least squares, has a number of desirable properties, and also so that hypothesis tests regarding the coefficient estimates can validly be conducted. Specifically, it is assumed that

1. $E(u_t) = 0$
2. $Var(u_t) = \sigma^2 < \infty$
3. $Cov(u_i, u_j) = 0$
4. $Cov(u_t, x_t) = 0$
5. $u_t \sim N(0, \sigma^2)$

This chapter will now examine the main diagnostic procedures that are used to test these assumptions in the context of the classical linear regression model. A pragmatic approach to 'solving' problems associated with the use of models where one or more of the assumptions is not supported by the data will then be adopted.

The text below discusses various regression diagnostic (mis-specification) tests that are based on the calculation of a test statistic. These tests can be constructed in several ways and the precise approach to constructing the test statistic will determine the distribution that the test statistic is assumed to follow. Two particular approaches are in common usage and their results are given by the statistical packages: the Lagrange Multiplier (LM) test and the Wald test. Further details concerning these procedures are given in Chapter 8 of *Introductory Econometrics for Finance*. For now, all that readers need to know is that LM test statistics in the context of the diagnostic tests presented here follow a $\chi^2$ distribution with degrees of freedom equal to the number of restrictions placed on the model, denoted $m$. The Wald version of the test follows an $F$ distribution with $(m, T - k)$ degrees of freedom. Asymptotically, these two tests are equivalent, although their results will differ somewhat in small samples. They are equivalent as the sample size increases towards infinity since there is a direct relationship between the $\chi^2$ and $F$ distributions. Taking a $\chi^2$-variate and dividing by its degrees of freedom asymptotically gives an $F$-variate:

$$F(m, T - k) \to \frac{\chi^2(m)}{m} \text{ as } T \to \infty.$$

Computer packages typically present results using both approaches, although only one of the two will be illustrated for each test below. They will usually give the same conclusion, although if they do not, the $F$ version is usually considered preferable for finite samples, since it is sensitive to sample size (one of its degrees of freedom parameters depends on sample size) in a way that the $\chi^2$ version is not.

## 4.1  Testing for heteroscedasticity

Re-open the Microsoft regression instructions file that was examined in the previous chapter and that included all the macroeconomic explanatory variables. First, **plot the residuals** by re-running the regression and using the option to create a residual series. If the residuals of the regression have systematically changing variability over the sample, that is a sign of heteroscedasticity. The resulting plot is shown in Figure 4.1.

In this case, it is hard to see any clear pattern, so we need to run a formal statistical test. We can calculate the statistics for a large number of heteroscedasticity tests using RATS, including the Breusch-Pagan, Goldfeld-Quandt, ARCH and White tests. We will consider the Goldfeld-Quandt (hereafter GQ) and White tests here and the ARCH test in Chapter 8.

One of the simplest methods for testing for heteroscedasticity is the Goldfeld-Quandt (1965) formulation. Their approach is based on splitting

**Figure 4.1**

Plot of residuals over time

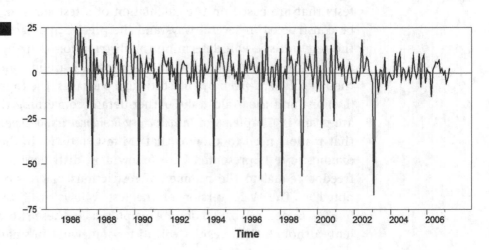

the total sample of length $T$ into two sub-samples of length $T_1$ and $T_2$. The regression model is estimated on each sub-sample and the two residual variances are calculated as $s_1^2 = \hat{u}_1'\hat{u}_1/(T_1 - k)$ and $s_2^2 = \hat{u}_2'\hat{u}_2/(T_2 - k)$ respectively. The null hypothesis is that the variances of the disturbances are equal, which can be written $H_0: \sigma_1^2 = \sigma_2^2$, against a two-sided alternative. The test statistic, denoted $GQ$, is simply the ratio of the two residual variances where the larger of the two variances must be placed in the numerator (i.e. $s_1^2$ is the higher sample variance for the sample with length $T_1$, even if it comes from the second sub-sample)

$$GQ = \frac{s_1^2}{s_2^2} \tag{4.1}$$

The test statistic is distributed as an $F(T_1 - k, T_2 - k)$ under the null hypothesis, and the null of a constant variance is rejected if the test statistic exceeds the critical value.

To use the $GQ$ test requires us to make a particular assumption concerning the method to order the series and also where to split them into sub-parts. I assume here that the time ordering is retained and that the sample is split at January 1997, roughly half way through the period. Type the following lines in the input file:

```
SMPL 1986:3 1996:12
   LINREG(NOPRINT) ERMSOFT
# CONSTANT ERSANDP DPROD DCREDIT DINFLATION DMONEY $
   DSPREAD RTERM
COMPUTE RSS1=%RSS, NDF1 = %NDF
SMPL 1997:1 2007:04
LINREG(NOPRINT) ERMSOFT
# CONSTANT ERSANDP DPROD DCREDIT DINFLATION DMONEY $
   DSPREAD RTERM
COMPUTE RSS2=%RSS, NDF2 = %NDF
CDF(TITLE='Goldfeld-Quandt Test') FTEST $
(RSS2/NDF2)/(RSS1/NDF1) NDF2 NDF1
SMPL 1986:3 2007:04
```

The SMPL instructions set the samples for the two regressions so that the first runs from the start of the whole sample until December 1996 and the second runs from January 1997 until the end of the whole sample. After setting the sample, we run the two sub-sample regressions, taking the residual sums of squares and calling them RSS1 and RSS2 respectively. Then we take the numbers of degrees of freedom and call them NDF1 and NDF2. The CDF command computes the *p*-value for a given test statistic,

**Box 4.1**

```
Goldfeld-Quandt Test
F(120,116)=   1.19700 with Significance Level 0.16545607
```

a given distribution and given degrees of freedom. The form for the command is

CDF DISTRIBUTION STATISTIC DOF1 DOF2

where distribution is either FTEST, TTEST, CHISQUARED or NORMAL; STATISTIC is the test statistic, which can be calculated within the instruction as it is here; DOF1 and DOF2 are the degrees of freedom for the numerator and denominator in the FTEST but only the first would be used for the $t$ and $\chi^2$ while neither are used for the normal. Note that in this case, because RSS2 is bigger, we have to place this in the numerator rather than RSS1. The final SMPL instruction resets the sample back to the entire available period so that all subsequent instructions in this input file will use all the observations. The results are given in Box 4.1.

It is apparent that according to the Goldfeld-Quandt test with this ordering and this break date, there is no evidence of heteroscedasticity. Put another way, there is no evidence of a difference in the regression standard errors before and after January 1997.

Now, turning to White's (1980) test, it is particularly useful because it makes few assumptions about the likely form of the heteroscedasticity and is carried out as follows.

1. Assume that the regression model estimated is of the standard linear form, e.g.

$$y_t = \beta_1 + \beta_2 x_{2t} + \beta_3 x_{3t} + u_t \tag{4.2}$$

To test $\mathrm{Var}(u_t) = \sigma^2$, estimate the model above, obtaining the residuals, $\hat{u}_t$.

2. Then run the auxiliary regression

$$\hat{u}_t^2 = \alpha_1 + \alpha_2 x_{2t} + \alpha_3 x_{3t} + \alpha_4 x_{2t}^2 + \alpha_5 x_{3t}^2 + \alpha_6 x_{2t} x_{3t} + v_t \tag{4.3}$$

where $v_t$ is a normally distributed disturbance term independent of $u_t$. This regression is of the squared residuals on a constant, the original explanatory variables, the squares of the explanatory variables and their cross-products.

The reason that the auxiliary regression takes this form is that it is desirable to investigate whether the variance of the residuals (embodied in $\hat{u}_t^2$) changes systematically with any known variables relevant to the model. Relevant variables will include the original explanatory variables, their squared values and their cross-products. Note also that this regression should include a constant term, even if the original regression did not. This is as a result of the fact that $\hat{u}_t^2$ will always have a non-zero mean, even if $\hat{u}_t$ has a zero mean.

3. Given the auxiliary regression, the test can be conducted using two different approaches. First, it is possible to use the $F$-test framework described in Chapter 3. This would involve estimating (4.3) as the unrestricted regression and then running a restricted regression of $\hat{u}_t^2$ on a constant only. The RSS from each specification would then be used as inputs to the standard $F$-test formula.

   With many diagnostic tests, an alternative approach can be adopted that does not require the estimation of a second (restricted) regression. This approach is known as a Lagrange Multiplier (LM) test, which centres on the value of $R^2$ for the auxiliary regression. If one or more coefficients in (4.3) is statistically significant, the value of $R^2$ for that equation will be relatively high, while if none of the variables is significant, $R^2$ will be relatively low. The LM test would thus operate by obtaining $R^2$ from the auxiliary regression and multiplying it by the number of observations, $T$. It can be shown that

$$TR^2 \sim \chi^2 (m)$$

   where $m$ is the number of regressors in the auxiliary regression (excluding the constant term), equivalent to the number of restrictions that would have to be placed under the $F$-test approach.

4. The test is one of the joint null hypothesis that $\alpha_2 = 0$, $\alpha_3 = 0$, $\alpha_4 = 0$, $\alpha_5 = 0$, and $\alpha_6 = 0$. For the LM test, if the $\chi^2$ test statistic from step 3 is greater than the corresponding value from the statistical table then reject the null hypothesis that the errors are homoscedastic.

In order to estimate White's test in RATS, we could either use the procedure REGWHITETEST or compute the test statistic manually by re-running the entire period regression and then adding several lines of code to calculate the required elements for the auxiliary regression.

RATS procedures are the equivalents of sub-routines in a programming language and they have the suffix '.SRC'. There are many of these procedure files, which are pre-written sets of instructions that are distributed with the RATS software and are used for conducting a particular task. The command to call the White's test procedure would be

SOURCE REGWHITETEST.SRC

The 'SOURCE' command does not actually do the estimation; rather, it just puts the relevant commands into memory. As a word of caution, when you first run this command after opening RATS, you may see the following window, entitled 'File for SOURCE(1)'.

Screenshot 4.1

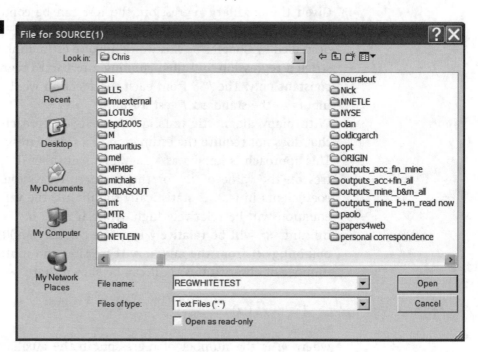

What has happened in this case is that RATS cannot find automatically where the REGWHITETEST.SRC file is located. So you have three choices:

1. Press cancel and copy the REGWHITETEST.SRC file to your working directory (the one where the .PRG files are being run from).
2. Show RATS where the SOURCE file is. The file will be located where the RATS executable file is located; on my computer, the directory is 'C:\Program Files\Estima\WinRATS 7', but yours may have a different name depending on what was specified when RATS was installed.[5]

---

[5] If you choose option two of the three above, you will need to show RATS where it is every time you shut down and re-open the software.

3. The best solution is to click on File and Preferences ... and then click on the Directories tab. You will see the following screen.

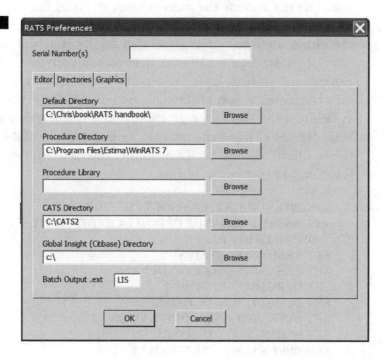

The 'Default Directory' will be the one that you save your work in, whereas the other fields are likely to be blank initially. If you find out where your source (.SRC) files are located, then type this into the 'Procedure Directory' box; similarly, in Chapter 7, a particular sub-routine for analysing cointegrated systems called CATS2 (CATS version 2) will be used, and so it is also worth finding where this is located[6] and specifying this directory as well. Then click OK and respond 'Yes' to the question 'Make Permanent?'.

To run the automated procedure for White's test after the SOURCE line, write

**@REGWHITETEST(TYPE=NOCROSSTERMS)**

The TYPE=NOCROSSTERMS option means that the cross-product terms are not used in the auxiliary regression (the default is that they are included).

---

[6] (if you have purchased CATS, which must be bought in addition to RATS).

To see what the test is doing and how it works, we could code it up manually. Given the relatively large number of variables in this regression, I do not include the cross-product terms in the auxiliary regression, only the squares of the original explanatory variables. It is possible to use either an $F$-test or a $\chi^2$ version of the test, and we produce both here. The $F$-statistic for White's heteroscedasticity test will simply be the regression $F$-statistic from the auxiliary regression, and this is automatically calculated as part of the standard output; the $\chi^2$ version is calculated as $TR^2$ from the auxiliary regression, and this will follow a $\chi^2$ distribution with degrees of freedom equal to the number of variables being used in the auxiliary regression, not including the constant (14 in this case). The resulting instructions would be

```
LINREG(NOPRINT) ERMSOFT / RESIDS
# CONSTANT ERSANDP DPROD DCREDIT DINFLATION DMONEY $
   DSPREAD RTERM
SET RESIDSSQ = RESIDS**2
SET ERSANDPSQ = ERSANDP**2
SET DPRODSQ = DPROD**2
SET DCREDITSQ = DCREDIT**2
SET DINFLATIONSQ = DINFLATION**2
SET DMONEYSQ = DMONEY**2
SET DSPREADSQ = DSPREAD**2
SET RTERMSQ = RTERM**2
LINREG RESIDSSQ
# CONSTANT ERSANDP DPROD DCREDIT DINFLATION DMONEY $
   DSPREAD RTERM ERSANDPSQ DPRODSQ DCREDITSQ $
DINFLATIONSQ DMONEYSQ DSPREADSQ RTERMSQ
CDF CHISQR %NOBS*%RSQUARED 14
```

The output is shown in Box 4.2.

Both the $F$- and $\chi^2$ ('LM') versions of the test statistic give the same conclusion that there is no evidence for the presence of heteroscedasticity, since the $p$-values are considerably in excess of 0.05. In fact, examining the individual explanatory variables in the auxiliary regression, there is no evidence that any of them are significantly related to the variance of the residuals.[7] The value of the test statistic is identical to that obtained from the REGWHITETEST procedure.

---

[7] It is also worth noting that RATS presents two versions of $R^2$ – a centred and an uncentred one. The former contains the total sum of squares about its mean value and constitutes the normal measure that is in common use. $TR^2$ as reported automatically by RATS is based on the uncentred $R^2$ and so it should be interpreted carefully.

```
   Box 4.2

Linear Regression - Estimation by Least Squares
Dependent Variable RESIDSSQ
Monthly Data From 1986:03 To 2007:04
Usable Observations         252    Degrees of Freedom        237
Total Observations          254    Skipped/Missing             2
Centered R**2          0.029426      R Bar **2   -0.027908
Uncentered R**2        0.113545      T X R**2     28.613
Mean of Dependent Variable         188.41517412
Std Error of Dependent Variable    612.85584641
Standard Error of Estimate         621.34876334
Sum of Squared Residuals           91499605.712
Regression F(14,237)                    0.5132
Significance Level of F             0.92437922
Log Likelihood                     -1970.67694
Durbin-Watson Statistic               2.069685


       Variable           Coeff      Std Error      T-Stat      Signif
   ********************************************************************************
   1.   Constant        250.477230    87.974784     2.84715    0.00479825
   2.   ERSANDP          -2.319256    10.055780    -0.23064    0.81779414
   3.   DPROD            16.167627    22.650950     0.71377    0.47607013
   4.   DCREDIT          -0.002092     0.018245    -0.11468    0.90879336
   5.   DINFLATION      -20.650617   133.390241    -0.15481    0.87710007
   6.   DMONEY           32.760569    34.486665     0.94995    0.34310591
   7.   DSPREAD        -541.681162   646.832591    -0.83744    0.40319099
   8.   RTERM            42.099763   161.287560     0.26102    0.79430144
   9.   ERSANDPSQ        -0.259966     0.912839    -0.28479    0.77605470
   10.  DPRODSQ          -7.283578     7.764219    -0.93810    0.34915040
   11.  DCREDITSQ        -0.000000     0.000001    -0.02924    0.97669388
   12.  DINFLATIONSQ   -103.711814   230.896763    -0.44917    0.65371975
   13.  DMONEYSQ         16.985813    14.693347     1.15602    0.24883671
   14.  DSPREADSQ       382.275437  3381.902184     0.11304    0.91009800
   15.  RTERMSQ        -508.016054   433.852586    -1.17094    0.24279820

 Chi-Squared(14)= 7.415250 with Significance Level 0.91751743
```

## 4.2 A digression on SMPL

The SMPL instruction provides an extremely useful method for dropping observations from a sample or for selecting a sub-sample. The simplest use of this instruction, for picking a sub-sample through time, was presented above, but there are also many others. For example, if you precede a LINREG instruction with SMPL(SERIES=FEMALE), RATS will conduct all subsequent commands (until told otherwise) on only observations for which the variable FEMALE is non-zero. So if FEMALE had been constructed as a dummy for which observations on male subjects were denoted by a zero, the regression would be conducted for women only. We could also use SMPL(SERIES=.NOT.FEMALE) to run the instructions only on the male sub-sample.

An alternative to using SMPL as a separate instruction is to use it as an option with the LINREG instruction in a single step. For example

```
LINREG(SMPL=FEMALE) Y
# CONSTANT X2 X3
```

Finally, we can also use the SMPL option to remove outliers from a regression sample. For example, suppose that in the context of the CAPM regression for Microsoft, we were worried about the possible undue influence of outliers on the parameters and we decided to remove any outlying observations where the corresponding residual from the estimated model was more than three standard errors from its mean. We would use the code

```
LINREG(NOPRINT) ERMSOFT / RESIDS
# CONSTANT ERSANDP
COM CUTOFF = 3*SQRT(%SEESQ)
LINREG(SMPL=(ABS(RESIDS)<CUTOFF) ERMSOFT
# CONSTANT ERSANDP
```

The first LINREG instruction is estimated purely to get the residuals. The COM instruction specifies the cut-off or threshold as three times the square root of the residual standard error squared, then the second LINREG command estimates the CAPM but using only the sample of observations where the residuals from the first stage fell within ±3 standard errors of their mean.

## 4.3   Using White's modified standard error estimates

If the form (i.e. the cause) of the heteroscedasticity is known, then an alternative estimation method which takes this into account can be used, such as generalised least squares (GLS). However, in reality, researchers are typically unsure of the exact cause of the heteroscedasticity and hence this technique is usually infeasible in practice. Other possible 'solutions' for heteroscedasticity include the following.

1. Transforming the variables into logs or reducing by some other measure of 'size'. This has the effect of re-scaling the data to 'pull in'

extreme observations. The regression would then be conducted upon the natural logarithms or the transformed data. Taking logarithms also has the effect of making a previously multiplicative model, such as the exponential regression model (with a multiplicative error term), into an additive one. However, logarithms of a variable cannot be taken in situations where the variable can take on zero or negative values, for the log will not be defined in such cases.

2. Using heteroscedasticity-consistent standard error estimates. Most standard econometrics software packages have an option (usually called something like 'robust') that allows the user to employ standard error estimates that have been modified to account for the heteroscedasticity following White (1980). In RATS, heteroscedasticity-robust standard error estimates can be obtained easily by using the robust option with the LINREG statement

> **LINREG(ROBUST) ERMSOFT / RESIDS**
> **# CONSTANT ERSANDP DPROD DCREDIT DINFLATION DMONEY $**
> **DSPREAD RTERM**

While White's correction does not require any user input, the Newey–West (1987) procedure requires the specification of a truncation lag length to determine the number of lagged residuals used to evaluate the autocorrelation. In RATS, the Newey–West standard errors can be invoked automatically when the user specifies the number of lags to use with the 'LAGS=' option of the LINREG command

> **LINREG(ROBUST, LAGS=5) ERMSOFT / RESIDS**

etc.

The Newey–West procedure in fact produces 'HAC' (Heteroscedasticity and Autocorrelation Consistent) standard errors that correct for both autocorrelation and heteroscedasticity that may be present in the residuals.

## 4.4 Autocorrelation and dynamic models

The third assumption that is made of the classical linear regression model's disturbance terms is that the covariance between the error terms over time (or cross-sectionally, for that type of data) is zero. In other words, it is assumed that the errors are uncorrelated with one another. If the errors are not uncorrelated with one another, it would be stated that they are 'autocorrelated' or 'serially correlated'.

The simplest test for autocorrelation is due to Durbin and Watson (1951). Durbin–Watson ($DW$) is a test for first-order autocorrelation – i.e. it tests only for a relationship between an error and its immediately previous value. One way to motivate the test and to interpret the test statistic would be in the context of a regression of the time $t$ error on its previous value

$$u_t = \rho u_{t-1} + v_t \tag{4.4}$$

where $v_t \sim N(0, \sigma_v^2)$. The $DW$ test statistic has as its null and alternative hypotheses

$$H_0 : \rho = 0 \text{ and } H_1 : \rho \neq 0.$$

Thus, under the null hypothesis, the errors at time $t - 1$ and $t$ are independent of one another, and if this null were rejected it would be concluded that there was evidence of a relationship between successive residuals. In fact, it is not necessary to run the regression given by (4.4) since the test statistic can be calculated using quantities that are already available after the first regression has been run

$$DW = \frac{\sum_{t=2}^{T} (\hat{u}_t - \hat{u}_{t-1})^2}{\sum_{t=1}^{T} \hat{u}_t^2} \tag{4.5}$$

The Durbin–Watson test statistic is approximately equal to $2(1 - \hat{\rho})$. Since $\hat{\rho}$ is a correlation, it implies that $-1 \leq \hat{\rho} \leq 1$, i.e. $\hat{\rho}$ is bounded to lie between $-1$ and $+1$. Substituting in these limits for $\hat{\rho}$ to calculate $DW$ would give the corresponding limits for Durbin–Watson as $0 \leq DW \leq 4$. A $DW$ statistic close to 0 corresponds to strong positive first-order autocorrelation, a statistic close to 4 corresponds to strong negative first-order autocorrelation, while a value close to 2 corresponds to there being very little first-order autocorrelation.

The Durbin–Watson test does not follow a standard statistical distribution such as a $t$, $F$, or $\chi^2$. $DW$ has two critical values – an upper critical value ($d_u$) and a lower critical value ($d_L$) – and there is also an intermediate region where the null hypothesis of no autocorrelation can be neither rejected nor not rejected! The null hypothesis is rejected and the existence of positive autocorrelation presumed if $DW$ is less than the lower critical value; the null hypothesis is rejected and the existence of negative autocorrelation presumed if $DW$ is greater than 4 minus the lower critical value; the null hypothesis is not rejected and no significant

**Box 4.3**

| Durbin–Watson Statistic | 2.156221 |
|---|---|

residual autocorrelation is presumed if *DW* is between the upper and 4-upper limits.

The Durbin–Watson statistic is calculated automatically and is presented in the standard regression output. For the model above containing the macroeconomic variables (that is, the original regression rather than the auxiliary regression of the test for heteroscedasticity!), recall that the value was as shown in Box 4.3.

For that example, $T = 252$, $k' = 7$ so $T - k' = 245$. The 1% critical values are not available in Durbin and Watson's original study since the number of degrees of freedom we have here is too large, but this figure of 2.16 would be safely within the non-rejection region, indicating that there is no evidence for the presence of first-order serial correlation in the residuals from this regression.

*DW* is a test only of whether consecutive errors are related to one another so there will also be many forms of residual autocorrelation that *DW* cannot detect. For example, if $\text{Corr}(\hat{u}_t, \hat{u}_{t-1}) = 0$, but $\text{Corr}(\hat{u}_t, \hat{u}_{t-2}) \neq 0$, *DW* as defined above will not find any autocorrelation. The Breusch–Godfrey test is a more general test for autocorrelation up to *r*th order. The model for the errors under this test is

$$u_t = \rho_1 u_{t-1} + \rho_2 u_{t-2} + \rho_3 u_{t-3} + \cdots + \rho_r u_{t-r} + v_t, v_t \sim N\left(0, \sigma_v^2\right) \quad (4.6)$$

The null and alternative hypotheses are:

$H_0 : \rho_1 = 0$ and $\rho_2 = 0$ and ... and $\rho_r = 0$
$H_1 : \rho_1 \neq 0$ or $\rho_2 \neq 0$ or ... or $\rho_r \neq 0$

So, under the null hypothesis, the current error is not related to any of its *r* previous values. The test is carried out in the following steps.

1. Estimate the linear regression using OLS and obtain the residuals, $\hat{u}_t$.
2. Regress $\hat{u}_t$ on all of the regressors from stage 1 (the *x*s) plus $\hat{u}_{t-1}, \hat{u}_{t-2}, \ldots, \hat{u}_{t-r}$. The regression will thus be

$$\hat{u}_t = \gamma_1 + \gamma_2 x_{2t} + \gamma_3 x_{3t} + \gamma_4 x_{4t} + \rho_1 \hat{u}_{t-1} + \rho_2 \hat{u}_{t-2} + \rho_3 \hat{u}_{t-3}$$
$$+ \cdots + \rho_r \hat{u}_{t-r} + v_t, v_t \sim N\left(0, \sigma_v^2\right) \quad (4.7)$$

Obtain $R^2$ from this auxiliary regression.

3. Letting $T$ denote the number of observations, the test statistic is given by

$$(T - r)R^2 \sim \chi_r^2$$

Note that $(T - r)$ pre-multiplies $R^2$ in the test for autocorrelation rather than $T$ (as was the case for the heteroscedasticity test). This arises because the first $r$ observations will effectively have been lost from the sample in order to obtain the $r$ lags used in the test regression, leaving $(T - r)$ observations from which to estimate the auxiliary regression. If the test statistic exceeds the critical value from the $\chi^2$ statistical tables, reject the null hypothesis of no autocorrelation.

The Breusch–Godfrey test for higher-order autocorrelation would be conducted in RATS by running the regression of the residuals on a constant and a number of lags of the residuals. The RESTRICT (or TEST) commands would then be used to test the restriction that the coefficients on all of the lagged residuals are jointly zero. Suppose, for example, that we wanted to test for autocorrelation of order up to 4. Recall that the auxiliary regression must also include the original explanatory variables (but which do not form part of the restriction):

```
LINREG RESIDS
# CONSTANT RESIDS{1 to 4} ERSANDP $
DPROD DCREDIT DINFLATION DMONEY DSPREAD RTERM
RESTRICT 4
# 2
# 1 0
# 3
# 1 0
# 4
# 1 0
# 5
# 1 0
CDF CHISQR %NOBS* %RSQUARED 4
```

The RESTRICT instruction tells RATS that there will be four elements in the restriction, involving coefficients 2 through 5, and that one times each of them should be set to zero. Note that the expression '{1 to 4}' can be used as shorthand in RATS to denote that all of lags 1 to 4 are included instead of writing 'RESIDS{1} RESIDS{2} ...' Running this code segment will give the $F$ and $\chi^2$ versions of the test statistic respectively as those in Box 4.4.

---

**Box 4.4**

```
F(4,236)=      0.81340 with Significance Level 0.51769028
Chi-Squared(4)=      3.535014 with Significance Level 0.47257447
```

Clearly there is no evidence of autocorrelation of any order up to 4 in the residuals of this regression according to either version of the test.

## 4.5 Testing for non-normality

One of the most commonly applied tests for normality is the Bera–Jarque (1981, hereafter BJ) test. BJ uses the property of a normally distributed random variable that the entire distribution is characterised by the first two moments – the mean and the variance. The (standardised) third and fourth moments of a distribution are known as its skewness and kurtosis. Skewness measures the extent to which a distribution is not symmetric about its mean value and kurtosis measures how fat the tails of the distribution are. A normal distribution is not skewed and is defined to have a coefficient of kurtosis of 3. It is possible to define a coefficient of excess kurtosis, equal to the coefficient of kurtosis minus three; a normal distribution will thus have a coefficient of excess kurtosis of zero. A normal distribution is symmetric and said to be mesokurtic.

Bera and Jarque formalise these ideas by testing whether the coefficient of skewness and the coefficient of excess kurtosis are jointly zero. Denoting the errors by $u$ and their variance by $\sigma^2$, it can be shown that the coefficients of skewness and kurtosis can be expressed respectively as

$$b_1 = \frac{E[u^3]}{\left(\sigma^2\right)^{3/2}} \quad \text{and} \quad b_2 = \frac{E[u^4]}{\left(\sigma^2\right)^2} \tag{4.8}$$

The kurtosis of the normal distribution is 3 so its excess kurtosis ($b_2 - 3$) is zero. The Bera–Jarque test statistic is given by

$$W = T\left[\frac{b_1^2}{6} + \frac{(b_2 - 3)^2}{24}\right] \tag{4.9}$$

where $T$ is the sample size. The test statistic asymptotically follows a $\chi^2(2)$ under the null hypothesis that the distribution of the series is symmetric and mesokurtic. $b_1$ and $b_2$ can be estimated using the residuals from the OLS regression, $\hat{u}$. The null hypothesis is of normality and this would be rejected if the residuals from the model were either significantly skewed or leptokurtic/platykurtic (or both).

```
     Box 4.5

Statistics on Series RESIDS
Monthly Data From 1986:03 To 2007:04
Observations                    252    Skipped/Missing        2
Sample Mean                0.000000    Variance          189.165832
Standard Error            13.753757    of Sample Mean      0.866405
t-Statistic (Mean=0)       0.000000    Signif Level        1.000000
Skewness                  -2.400256    Signif Level (Sk=0) 0.000000
Kurtosis (excess)          8.734048    Signif Level (Ku=0) 0.000000
Jarque-Bera             1042.949339    Signif Level (JB=0) 0.000000
```

The normality test statistic is computed automatically in RATS when the STATS command is run on the residuals

**LINREG ERMSOFT / RESIDS**
**# CONSTANT ERSANDP DPROD DCREDIT DINFLATION DMONEY $**
**DSPREAD RTERM**
**STATS RESIDS**

The first three lines of this code ensure that the test is conducted using the residuals from the Microsoft regression rather than on the residuals of one of the auxiliary regressions for the diagnostic tests that we ran most recently. The output in this case would be given by Box 4.5.

What is the appropriate conclusion? Note that, like Microsoft Excel, RATS reports excess kurtosis as 'kurtosis'. Are the residuals skewed? Are they mesokurtic, leptokurtic or platykurtic?

In this case, the null hypothesis of error normality is rejected, implying that the inferences we make about the coefficient estimates could be wrong, although the sample is probably sufficiently large for the non-normality to give little cause for concern.

## 4.6  Dummy variable construction and use

What should be done if evidence of non-normality is found? It is, of course, possible to employ an estimation method that does not assume normality, but such a method may be difficult to implement and one can be less sure of its properties. It is thus desirable to stick with OLS if possible, since its behaviour in a variety of circumstances has been well researched. For sample sizes that are sufficiently large, violation of the normality assumption is virtually inconsequential. Appealing to a central limit theorem, the test statistics will asymptotically follow the appropriate distributions even in the absence of error normality.

In economic or financial modelling, it is quite often the case that one or two very extreme residuals cause a rejection of the normality assumption. Such observations would appear in the tails of the distribution and would therefore lead $u^4$, which enters into the definition of kurtosis, to be very large. Such observations that do not fit in with the pattern of the remainder of the data are known as *outliers*. If this is the case, one way to improve the chances of error normality is to use dummy variables or some other method to effectively remove those observations. This type of dummy variable that takes the value one for only a single observation has an effect exactly equivalent to knocking out that observation from the sample altogether, by forcing the residual for that observation to zero. The estimated coefficient on the dummy variable will be equal to the residual that the dummied observation would have taken if the dummy variable had not been included in the model.

In RATS, the residuals can be plotted or printed using commands discussed previously to get an idea of whether there are specific outliers that may be usefully removed from the sample. To plot the actual and fitted values and the residuals, use the commands

```
SET FITTED = ERMSOFT – RESIDS
GRAPH(SCALE=BOTH) 3
# ERMSOFT
# FITTED
# RESIDS
```

From the graph (not shown), it can be seen that there are several large (negative) outliers, but the largest of all occur in early 1998 and early 2003. All of the large outliers correspond to months where the actual return was much smaller (i.e. more negative) than the model would have predicted. Interestingly, the residual in October 1987 is not quite so prominent because even though the stock price fell, the market index value fell as well, so that the stock price fall was at least in part predicted by the model (this can be seen by comparing the actual and fitted values during that month).

In order to specify the precise dates of the largest outliers, this would be best achieved by printing the RESIDS series and looking at the numbers by eye. Rather than printing the entire series if it were a very long one, we could use a command like

```
PRINT(SMPL=ABS(RESIDS)>20) / RESIDS
```

This would print the values of any residuals greater than 20 in absolute value.

If we did this, it would be evident that the two most extreme residuals (with values to the nearest integer) were in February 1998 ($-68$) and February 2003 ($-67$). One way to remove these big outliers from the data would be to delete them from the sample, but a much better way would be to use dummy variables. It would be tempting but incorrect to construct one dummy variable that takes the value one for both Feb 98 and Feb 03 (and zero elsewhere), but this would not have the desired effect of setting both residuals to zero. Instead, to remove two outliers requires us to construct two separate dummy variables. In order to create the Feb 98 dummy, we generate a series called FEB98DUM very simply in RATS using the SET command. The syntax is

```
SMPL 1986:03 2007:04
SET FEB98DUM = T == 98:2
```

RATS will always use the same observations as set previously. For example, if the sample has been set to consist only of the first 100 observations, RATS will continue to use this sample until told otherwise. Hence the SMPL instruction ensures that RATS returns to using the entire sample of observations, in case any sub-samples have been selected during a previous step. An alternative method of constructing the same dummy variable for February 98 would be to use the %IF command – for example

```
SET FEB98DUM = %IF(T<98:02.or.T>98:02,0,1)
```

The dummy is set up to say that if the time index is before February 1998 or after February 1998, the variable will take the value 0, otherwise 1. Hence only the observation for February 1998 will be given a value of 1. If we similarly construct a dummy for February 2003 and run the regression including the two dummy variables, we need to add the following code segment:

```
SET FEB03DUM = T == 2003:2
LINREG ERMSOFT / RESIDS
# CONSTANT ERSANDP DPROD DCREDIT DINFLATION DMONEY $
DSPREAD RTERM FEB98DUM FEB03DUM
```

We need to be careful when we use year identifiers for times after 1999 since these need to use the full four digits (e.g. '2003' and not '03'). The regression results would be those shown in Box 4.6.

```
         Box 4.6

Linear Regression - Estimation by Least Squares
Dependent Variable ERMSOFT
Monthly Data From 1986:03 To 2007:04
Usable Observations          252     Degrees of Freedom      242
Total Observations           254     Skipped/Missing           2
Centered R**2          0.358962      R Bar **2  0.335122
Uncentered R**2        0.359441      T X R**2     90.579
Mean of Dependent Variable        -0.42080264
Std Error of Dependent Variable   15.41135106
Standard Error of Estimate        12.56642604
Sum of Squared Residuals       38215.445332
Regression F(9,242)               15.0570
Significance Level of F            0.00000000
Log Likelihood                 -990.28982
Durbin-Watson Statistic            2.142031


       Variable         Coeff         Std Error        T-Stat         Signif
***********************************************************************************
1.     Constant        -0.08660581     1.31519419     -0.06585     0.94755145
2.     ERSANDP          1.54797081     0.18394457      8.41542     0.00000000
3.     DPROD            0.45501487     0.45187523      1.00695     0.31496551
4.     DCREDIT         -0.00005917     0.00014465     -0.40907     0.68285371
5.     DINFLATION       4.91329662     2.68565861      1.82946     0.06856156
6.     DMONEY          -1.43060800     0.64460124     -2.21937     0.02738942
7.     DSPREAD          8.62489524    12.22705150      0.70539     0.48124316
8.     RTERM            6.89375431     2.99398166      2.30254     0.02215420
9.     FEB98DUM       -69.14177418    12.68402016     -5.45109     0.00000012
10.    FEB03DUM       -68.24391252    12.65390053     -5.39311     0.00000016
```

Note that the dummy variable parameters are both highly significant and take approximately the values that the corresponding residuals would have taken if the dummy variables had not been included in the model.[8] By comparing the results with those of the regression above that excluded the dummy variables, it can be seen that the coefficient estimates on the remaining variables change quite a bit in this instance and the significance levels improve considerably. The term structure and money supply

---

[8] Note that the correspondence between the values of the residuals and the values of the dummy variable parameters is not perfect because two dummies are being used together; had we included only one dummy, the value of the dummy variable coefficient and that which the residual would have taken without the inclusion of the dummy in the model would be identical.

parameters are now both significant at the 5% level, and the unexpected inflation parameter is now significant at the 10% level. The $R^2$ value has risen from 0.20 to 0.36 because of the perfect fit of the dummy variables to those two extreme outlying observations.

Finally, if we re-examine the normality test results by re-running the appropriate code segment on the residuals from the equation that includes the dummies, we will see that while the skewness and kurtosis are both slightly closer to the values that they would take under normality, the Bera–Jarque test statistic still takes a value of 861 (compared with over 1,000 previously). We would thus conclude that the residuals are still a long way from following a normal distribution. While it would be possible to continue to generate dummy variables, there is a limit to the extent to which it would be desirable to do so. With this particular regression, we are unlikely to be able to achieve a residual distribution that is close to normality without using an excessive number of dummy variables. As a rule of thumb, in a monthly sample with 252 observations, it is reasonable to include, perhaps, two or three dummy variables but more would probably be excessive. In this instance, we would therefore probably not include further dummies and should resign ourselves to the inherent non-normality of these residuals.

## 4.7  Testing for multicollinearity

An implicit assumption when using the OLS estimation method is that the explanatory variables are not correlated with one another. If there was no relationship between the explanatory variables, they would be said to be orthogonal to one another. If the explanatory variables were orthogonal, adding or removing a variable from a regression equation would not cause the values of the coefficients on the other variables to change.

In any practical context, the correlation between explanatory variables will be non-zero, although this will generally be relatively benign in the sense that a small degree of association will not cause too much loss of precision. However, a problem occurs when the explanatory variables are very highly correlated with each other and this problem is known as multicollinearity. A simple way to test for 'near' multicollinearity would be to examine the pair-wise correlations between all combinations of two of the explanatory variables.

In RATS, a correlation matrix for the independent variables would be constructed using the CMOMENT instruction

| Box 4.7 | | | | | | |
|---|---|---|---|---|---|---|
| 1.0000 | | | | | | |
| -0.0962 | 1.0000 | | | | | |
| -0.0129 | -2.7414e-03 | 1.0000 | | | | |
| -0.0130 | 0.1680 | 0.0713 | 1.0000 | | | |
| -0.0336 | 0.1217 | 0.0353 | 6.7016e-03 | 1.0000 | | |
| -0.0380 | -0.0738 | 0.0253 | -0.1694 | -0.0751 | 1.0000 | |
| 0.0138 | -0.0425 | -0.0624 | -6.5182e-03 | 0.1704 | 0.0185 | 1.0000 |

**CMOMENT(CORR,PRINT)**
**# ERSANDP DPROD DCREDIT DINFLATION DMONEY DSPREAD $**
**RTERM**
**WRITE %CMOM**

The CMOMENT(CORR) instruction tells RATS to construct a variance/covariance matrix for the variables using the list of variables in the list of supplementary cards (after the # symbol) and then to transform it into a correlation matrix. The WRITE command simply displays the estimated correlation matrix. The output from this command would be as in Box 4.7.

Do the results indicate any significant correlations between the independent variables? (Note that the correlations between the variables will be listed in the same order as they were in the supplementary cards, i.e. starting with ERSANDP and finishing with RTERM.) In this particular case, the largest observed correlation is 0.17 between the money supply and term structure variables and this is sufficiently small that it can reasonably be ignored.

## 4.8 The RESET test for functional form

A further implicit assumption of the classical linear regression model is that the appropriate 'functional form' is linear. This means that the appropriate model is assumed to be linear in the parameters, so that in the bivariate case, the relationship between $y$ and $x$ could be represented by a straight line. However, this assumption may not always be upheld. Whether the model should be linear can be formally tested using Ramsey's (1969) RESET test, which is a general test for mis-specification of functional form. Essentially, the method works by using higher-order terms of the fitted values (e.g. $\hat{y}_t^2$, $\hat{y}_t^3$ etc.) in an auxiliary regression. The auxiliary regression is thus one where $y$, the dependent variable from the original regression, is regressed on powers of the fitted values

$$y_t = \beta_1 + \beta_2 \hat{y}_t^2 + \beta_3 \hat{y}_t^3 + \cdots + \beta_p \hat{y}_t^p + \text{original regressors} + v_t \tag{4.10}$$

Higher-order powers of the fitted values of $y$ can capture a variety of non-linear relationships, since they embody higher-order powers and cross-products of the original explanatory variables, e.g.

$$\hat{y}_t^2 = (\hat{\gamma}_1 + \hat{\gamma}_2 x_{2t} + \hat{\gamma}_3 x_{3t} + \cdots + \hat{\gamma}_k x_{kt})^2 \tag{4.11}$$

The value of $R^2$ is obtained from the regression (4.10) and the test statistic, given by $TR^2$, is distributed asymptotically as $\chi^2(p-1)$. Note that the degrees of freedom for this test will be $(p-1)$ and not $p$. This arises because $p$ is the highest-order term in the fitted values used in the auxiliary regression and thus the test will involve $p-1$ terms, one for the square of the fitted value, one for the cube, ..., one for the $p^{th}$ power. If the value of the test statistic is greater than the $\chi^2$ critical value, reject the null hypothesis that the functional form is correct.

The Ramsey RESET test would be constructed in RATS manually following the regression. The variable FITTED has already been specified in a previous instruction above, but we also need to construct a series that is the square of the fitted value:

```
SET FITTEDSQ = FITTED**2
LINREG(NOPRINT) ERMSOFT
# CONSTANT ERSANDP DPROD DCREDIT DINFLATION DMONEY $
DSPREAD RTERM FITTEDSQ
RESTRICT 1
# 9
# 1 0
```

The regression is conducted of the Microsoft excess returns on the original variables plus the square of the fitted values. The RESTRICT command computes the *F*-version of the test statistic. Think about how you would instruct RATS to compute the LM version. The RATS RESET output is given for the *F*-version (and an exactly equivalent *t*-test) by Box 4.8.

The Ramsey RESET test for this regression is in effect determining whether the relationship between the Microsoft stock excess returns and

**Box 4.8**

```
t(243) =   -0.958963 or F(1,243) =   0.919609 with Significance Level 0.33853070
```

the explanatory variables is linear or not. It can be seen that there is no apparent non-linearity in the regression equation and so overall it would be concluded that the linear model in the returns is appropriate.

RATS also has a built-in procedure for running the RESET test, which should be placed immediately after the main regression (not the auxiliary regression, which is now redundant anyway). The form of the command to call the sub-routine would be

**SOURCE REGRESET**

And then to run the RESET procedure, write

**@REGRESET(h=2)**

to include the squared fitted value term in the test regression only (use h = 3 to also include the cubic term and so on).

## 4.9 Parameter stability tests

So far, the regressions estimated have embodied the implicit assumption that the parameters ($\beta_1$, $\beta_2$ and $\beta_3$) are constant for the entire sample, both for the data period used to estimate the model and for any subsequent period used in the construction of forecasts. This implicit assumption can be tested using parameter stability tests. The idea is essentially to split the data into sub-periods and then to estimate up to three models for each of the sub-parts and for all the data and then to 'compare' the *RSS* of each of the models. There are two types of test that will be considered, namely the Chow (analysis of variance) test and predictive failure tests.

### 4.9.1 The Chow test

The steps involved in conducting a Chow test are as follows:

1. Split the data into two sub-periods. Estimate the regression over the whole period and then for the two sub-periods separately (three regressions). Obtain the *RSS* for each regression.
2. The restricted regression is now the regression for the whole period while the 'unrestricted regression' comes in two parts: one for each of the sub-samples. It is thus possible to form an *F*-test, which is based on the difference between the *RSS*s. The statistic is

$$\text{Test statistic} = \frac{RSS - (RSS_1 + RSS_2)}{RSS_1 + RSS_2} \times \frac{T - 2k}{k} \tag{4.12}$$

where:

> $RSS$ = residual sum of squares for whole sample
> $RSS_1$ = residual sum of squares for sub-sample 1
> $RSS_2$ = residual sum of squares for sub-sample 2
> $T$ = number of observations
> $2k$ = number of regressors in the 'unrestricted' regression (since it comes in two parts)
> $k$ = number of regressors in (each) 'unrestricted' regression.

The unrestricted regression is the one where the restriction has not been imposed on the model. Since the restriction is that the coefficients are equal across the sub-samples, the restricted regression will be the single regression for the whole sample. Thus, the test is one of how much the residual sum of squares for the whole sample ($RSS$) is bigger than the sum of the residual sums of squares for the two sub-samples ($RSS_1 + RSS_2$). If the coefficients do not change much between the samples, the residual sum of squares will not rise much upon imposing the restriction.

Thus the test statistic in (4.12) can be considered a straightforward application of the standard $F$-test formula discussed in Chapter 3. The restricted residual sum of squares in (4.12) is $RSS$, while the unrestricted residual sum of squares is ($RSS_1 + RSS_2$). The number of restrictions is equal to the number of coefficients that are estimated for each of the regressions, i.e. $k$. The number of regressors in the unrestricted regression (including the constants) is $2k$, since the unrestricted regression comes in two parts, each with $k$ regressors.

3. Perform the test. If the value of the test statistic is greater than the critical value from the $F$-distribution, which is an $F(k, T - 2k)$, then reject the null hypothesis that the parameters are stable over time.

Note that it is also possible to use a dummy variables approach to calculating both Chow and predictive failure tests. In the case of the Chow test, the unrestricted regression would contain dummy variables for the intercept and for all of the slope coefficients (see also Chapter 9). For example, suppose that the regression is of the form

$$y_t = \beta_1 + \beta_2 x_{2t} + \beta_3 x_{3t} + u_t \tag{4.13}$$

If the split of the total of $T$ observations is made so that the sub-samples contain $T_1$ and $T_2$ observations (where $T_1 + T_2 = T$), the unrestricted regression would be given by

$$y_t = \beta_1 + \beta_2 x_{2t} + \beta_3 x_{3t} + \beta_4 D_t + \beta_5 D_t x_{2t} + \beta_6 D_t x_{3t} + v_t \tag{4.14}$$

where $D_t = 1$ for $t \in T_1$ and zero otherwise. In other words, $D_t$ takes the value one for observations in the first sub-sample and zero for observations in the second sub-sample. The Chow test viewed in this way would then be a standard $F$-test of the joint restriction $H_0$: $\beta_4 = 0$ and $\beta_5 = 0$ and $\beta_6 = 0$, with (4.14) and (4.13) being the unrestricted and restricted regressions respectively.

### 4.9.2 The predictive failure test

The predictive failure test works by estimating the regression over a 'long' sub-period (i.e. most of the data) and then using those coefficient estimates for predicting values of $y$ for the other period. These predictions for $y$ are then implicitly compared with the actual values. Although it can be expressed in several different ways, the null hypothesis for this test is that the prediction errors for all of the forecasted observations are zero.
To calculate the test:

- Run the regression for the whole period (the restricted regression) and obtain the *RSS*.
- Run the regression for the 'large' sub-period and obtain the *RSS* (called $RSS_1$). Note that in this book, the number of observations for the long estimation sub-period will be denoted by $T_1$ (even though it may come second). The test statistic is given by

$$\text{Test statistic} = \frac{RSS - RSS_1}{RSS_1} \times \frac{T_1 - k}{T_2} \tag{4.15}$$

where $T_2$ = number of observations that the model is attempting to 'predict'. The test statistic will follow an $F(T_2, T_1 - k)$.

For an intuitive interpretation of the predictive failure test statistic formulation, consider an alternative way to test for predictive failure using a regression containing dummy variables. A separate dummy variable would be used for each observation that was in the prediction sample. The unrestricted regression would then be the one that includes the dummy variables, which will be estimated using all $T$ observations and will have $(k + T_2)$ regressors (the $k$ original explanatory variables and a dummy variable for each prediction observation, i.e. a total of $T_2$ dummy variables). Thus the numerator of the last part of (4.15) would be the total number of observations $(T)$ minus the number of regressors in the unrestricted regression $(k + T_2)$. Noting also that $T - (k + T_2) = (T_1 - k)$, since $T_1 + T_2 = T$, this gives the numerator of the last term in (4.15). The restricted regression would then be the original regression containing the explanatory variables but none of the dummy variables. Thus the number of restrictions would be the number of observations in the prediction period, which would be equivalent to the number of dummy variables included in the unrestricted regression, $T_2$.

The Chow test and the predictive failure test must be computed manually using RATS. For the break at 1996M10, the regressions for the whole sample and each of the sub-samples would be conducted and then the test statistics calculated for the $F$-version of the tests using the commands

```
* WHOLE SAMPLE
LINREG(NOPRINT) ERMSOFT
# CONSTANT ERSANDP DPROD DCREDIT DINFLATION DMONEY $
DSPREAD RTERM
COM RSST = %RSS
COM NOBST = %NOBS
COM DF1 = NOBST – 16
COM DF2 = 8
* FIRST SUB-SAMPLE
SMPL 1986:03 1996:01
LINREG(NOPRINT) ERMSOFT
# CONSTANT ERSANDP DPROD DCREDIT DINFLATION DMONEY $
DSPREAD RTERM
COM RSS1 = %RSS
* SECOND SUB-SAMPLE
SMPL 1996:02 2007:04
LINREG(NOPRINT) ERMSOFT
# CONSTANT ERSANDP DPROD DCREDIT DINFLATION DMONEY $
DSPREAD RTERM
COM RSS2 = %RSS
COM FCHOW = ((RSST – (RSS1+RSS2))/(RSS1+RSS2))*DF1/DF2
CDF FTEST FCHOW DF2 DF1
```

There are no new commands here, but perhaps a few comments are in order. 'COM RSST = %RSS' defines the residual sum of squares for the whole sample regression (the restricted regression) as RSST; 'COM NOBST = %NOBS' similarly sets up the number of observations for the whole sample as NOBST; 'COM DF1 = NOBST – 16' sets the number of degrees of freedom in the numerator ($T - 2k$ in the formula), while the denominator degrees of freedom is the number of restrictions, which is the number of parameters to be estimated, $k$, is 8 in this case. Similar definitions are then made for the second sub-sample, and then the 'COM FCHOW = ...' puts these ingredients together to calculate the test statistic. The final 'CDF...' command finds the critical value and $p$-value for this test statistic,

---

**Box 4.9**

```
F(8,236)=      0.53806 with Significance Level 0.82719294
```

**Box 4.10**

```
F(4,240)= 0.05658 with Significance Level 0.99401923
```

---

which has DF2 and DF1 degrees of freedom. The output is shown in Box 4.9.

It is clear here that there is no evidence for parameter instability across the two sub-sample periods according to the Chow test. To run the predictive failure test to determine whether the model can adequately forecast the last four observations (January–April 2007), we have already estimated the restricted regression (for the whole sample), which has residual sum of squares RSST and number of observations NOBST, so we need the following additional code:

```
* LONG SUB-SAMPLE (UNRESTRICTED REGRESSION)
SMPL 1986:03 2006:12
LINREG(NOPRINT) ERMSOFT
# CONSTANT ERSANDP DPROD DCREDIT DINFLATION DMONEY $
DSPREAD RTERM
COM RSS1 = %RSS
COM NOBS1 = %NOBS
COM NOBS2 = NOBST – NOBS1
COM FFORC = ((RSST – RSS1)/RSS1)*(NOBS1-8)/NOBS2
COM DF = NOBS1 - 8
CDF FTEST FFORC NOBS2 DF
```

The result is shown in Box 4.10.

This indicates that the model can indeed adequately predict the 2007 observations. Thus the conclusion from both forms of the test is that there is no evidence of parameter instability. However, the conclusion should really be that the parameters are stable *with respect to these particular break dates*. It is important to be aware that for the model to be deemed adequate, it needs to be stable with respect to any break dates that we may choose.

Note that it is not possible to conduct a Chow test or a parameter stability test when there are outlier dummy variables in the regression. This occurs because when the sample is split into two parts, the dummy variable for one of the parts will have values of zero for all observations, which would thus cause perfect multicollinearity with the column of ones that is used for the constant term. So ensure that the Chow test is performed using the regression containing all of the explanatory variables except the outlier dummies. It would also be possible, of course, to remove the outlying observations from the sample altogether before running the parameter stability test.

# Formulating and estimating ARMA models

Univariate time-series models are a class of specifications where one attempts to model and to predict financial variables using only information contained in their own past values and current and possibly past values of an error term. This practice can be contrasted with structural models, which are multivariate in nature and attempt to explain changes in a variable by reference to the movements in the current or past values of other (explanatory) variables. Time-series models are usually a-theoretical, implying that their construction and use is not based upon any underlying theoretical model of the behaviour of a variable. Instead, time-series models are an attempt to capture empirically relevant features of the observed data that may have arisen from a variety of different (but unspecified) structural models.

An important class of time-series models is the family of AutoRegressive Moving Average (ARMA) models, usually associated with Box and Jenkins (1976). Time-series models may be useful when a structural model is inappropriate. For example, suppose that there is some variable $y_t$ whose movements a researcher wishes to explain. It may be that the variables thought to drive movements of $y_t$ are not observable or not measurable, or that these forcing variables are measured at a lower frequency of observation than $y_t$. Additionally, as will be examined later in this chapter, structural models are often not useful for out-of-sample forecasting. These observations motivate the consideration of pure time-series models, which are the focus of this chapter.

ARMA($p, q$) models state that the current value of some series $y$ depends linearly on its own previous values plus a combination of the current and previous values of a white noise error term. The model could be written

$$\phi(L)y_t = \mu + \theta(L)u_t \qquad (5.1)$$

where $\phi(L) = 1 - \phi_1 L - \phi_2 L^2 - \cdots - \phi_p L^p$ and $\theta(L) = 1 + \theta_1 L + \theta_2 L^2 + \cdots \theta_q L^q$

or

$$y_t = \mu + \phi_1 y_{t-1} + \phi_2 y_{t-2} + \cdots + \phi_p y_{t-p} + \theta_1 u_{t-1}$$
$$+ \theta_2 u_{t-2} + \cdots + \theta_q u_{t-q} + u_t \qquad (5.2)$$

with $E(u_t) = 0$; $E(u_t^2) = \sigma_2$; $E(u_t u_s) = 0$, $t \neq s$.

The characteristics of an ARMA process will be a combination of those from the autoregressive and moving average parts. Note that the partial autocorrelation function (pacf) is particularly useful in this context. The autocorrelation function (acf) alone can distinguish between a pure autoregressive and a pure moving average process. However, an ARMA process will have a geometrically declining acf, as will a pure AR process. So, the pacf is useful for distinguishing between an AR($p$) process and an ARMA($p, q$) process – the former will have a geometrically declining autocorrelation function, but a partial autocorrelation function which cuts off to zero after $p$ lags, while the latter will have both autocorrelation and partial autocorrelation functions which decline geometrically.

## 5.1 Getting started

This example uses the monthly UK house price series which was already employed in the file HPR.PRG used in Chapter 1. There were a total of 196 monthly observations running from February 1991 (recall that the January observation was 'lost' in constructing the lagged value) to May 2007 for the percentage change in house price series.

The objective of this exercise is to build an ARMA model for the house price changes. There are three stages involved in constructing such a model according to Box and Jenkins (1976): identification, estimation and diagnostic checking.

- **Step 1**: involves determining the order of the model required to capture the dynamic features of the data. Graphical procedures are used (plotting the data over time and plotting the acf and pacf) to determine the most appropriate specification.
- **Step 2**: involves estimation of the parameters of the model specified in step 1. This can be done using least squares or another technique, known as maximum likelihood, depending on the model.

- **Step 3**: involves model checking – i.e. determining whether the model specified and estimated is adequate. Box and Jenkins suggest two methods: overfitting and residual diagnostics. Overfitting involves deliberately fitting a larger model than that required to capture the dynamics of the data as identified in step 1. If the model specified at step 1 is adequate, any extra terms added to the ARMA model would be insignificant. Residual diagnostics imply checking the residuals for evidence of linear dependence, which if present would suggest that the model originally specified was inadequate to capture the features of the data. The acf, pacf or Ljung–Box tests could be used.

It is worth noting that 'diagnostic testing' in the Box–Jenkins world essentially involves only autocorrelation tests rather than the whole barrage of tests outlined in the previous chapter. Also, such approaches to determining the adequacy of the model could only reveal a model that is under-parameterised ('too small') and would not reveal a model that is over-parameterised ('too big').

The first of these stages is carried out by looking at the autocorrelation and partial autocorrelation coefficients to identify any structure in the data. Estimating the autocorrelation coefficients in RATS would be achieved using the CORRELATE command, or by using the BJIDENT procedure. The following instructions will estimate the first 12 autocorrelation and partial autocorrelation coefficients, and will calculate the Ljung–Box test statistic for all 12 lags. The resulting autocorrelation coefficients for the raw house price series (PRICE) and the returns (DHP) are stored in arrays called CORRPRICE and CORRDHP respectively, while the corresponding partial autocorrelation coefficients will be stored in PCORRPRICE and PCORRDHP. The acf and the pacf are also plotted for each series using the GRAPH instruction:

```
CORRELATE(NUMBER=12,QSTATS,PARTIAL=PCORRPRICE) PRICE / CORRPRICE
GRAPH(STYLE=BARGRAPH,NUMBER=0,HEADER='ACF for House prices')
# CORRPRICE
GRAPH(STYLE=BARGRAPH,NUMBER=0,HEADER='PACF for House prices')
# PCORRPRICE
CORRELATE(NUMBER=12,QSTATS,PARTIAL=PCORRDHP) DHP / CORRDHP
GRAPH(STYLE=BARGRAPH,NUMBER=0,HEADER='ACF for Changes in house prices')
# CORRDHP
GRAPH(STYLE=BARGRAPH,NUMBER=0,HEADER='PACF for Changes in house prices')
# PCORRDHP
```

**Box 5.1**

```
Correlations of Series PRICE
Monthly Data From 1991:01 To 2007:05


Autocorrelations
    1          2          3          4          5          6          7
0.999549   0.998575   0.997056   0.995077   0.992695   0.989950   0.986885
    8          9         10         11         12
0.983499   0.979746   0.975547   0.970998   0.965950


Partial Autocorrelations
    1          2          3          4          5          6          7
 0.999549  -0.579044  -0.406717  -0.122825  -0.013181  -0.022742  -0.011484
    8          9         10         11         12
-0.083959  -0.191077  -0.291994   0.085478  -0.241597


Ljung-Box Q-Statistics
  Lags   Statistic   Signif Lvl
   12     2402.391     0.000000
```

**Box 5.2**

```
Correlations of Series DHP
Monthly Data From 1991:02 To 2007:05


Autocorrelations
    1          2          3          4          5          6          7
0.254161   0.373062   0.169310   0.121754   0.095566   0.088003   0.064804
    8          9         10         11         12
0.112205   0.217159   0.146580   0.300724   0.325522


Partial Autocorrelations
    1          2          3          4          5          6          7
0.254161   0.329767   0.026324  -0.040401   0.019797   0.045781   0.010557
    8          9         10         11         12
0.067493   0.192390   0.031511   0.164233   0.225022


Ljung-Box Q-Statistics
  Lags   Statistic   Signif Lvl
   12     111.945      0.000000
```

The RATS autocorrelation and partial autocorrelation output for the house prices will be that shown in Box 5.1 and for the changes in house prices see Box 5.2.

The plots for the autocorrelation and partial autocorrelations for the house price levels are shown in Figures 5.1 and 5.2 and for the house price percentage changes in Figures 5.3 and 5.4.

**Figure 5.1**
ACF for house prices

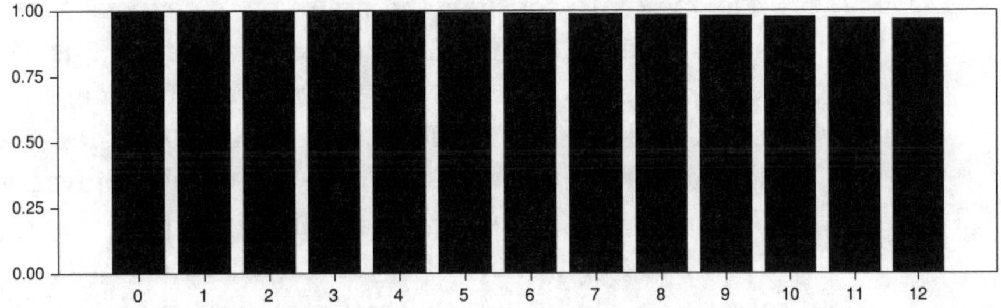

**Figure 5.2**
PACF for house prices

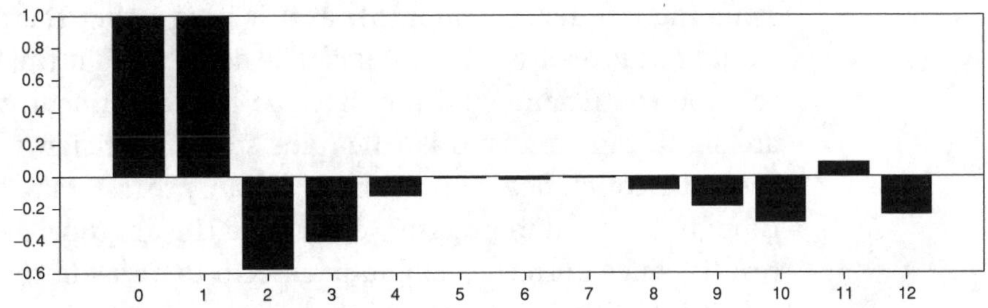

**Figure 5.3**
ACF for changes in house prices

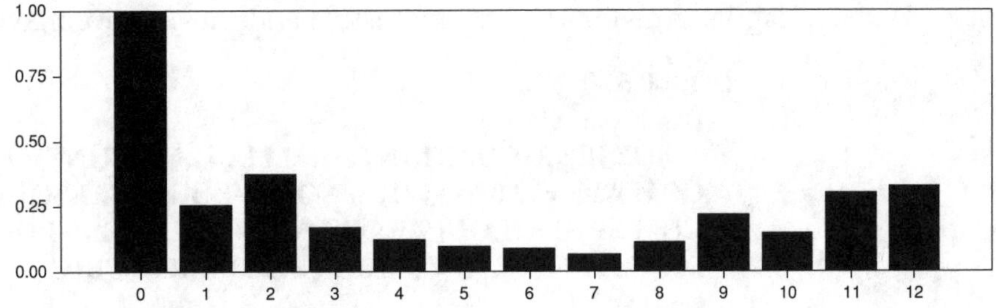

**Figure 5.4**
PACF for changes in house prices

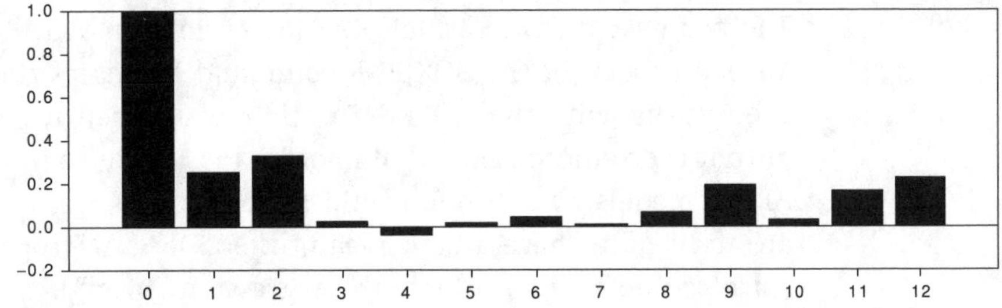

The extreme levels of persistence (slow decay) in the autocorrelations of the house price levels series are clearly evident from the autocorrelation function plot, and in fact this series is non-stationary (see Chapter 7) and so it is not appropriate to consider the time-series properties further.

Moving on to consider the house price changes, this is also a fairly persistent series. The Ljung-Box test statistic of 111.9 is significant at the 1% level ($p$-value = 0.0000). The autocorrelation coefficients decline slowly from a peak of 0.37 at the second lag to 0.06 at lag 7, before rising again slightly. Remember that as a rule of thumb, a given autocorrelation coefficient is classed as significant if it is outside a $\pm 1.96 \times (1/T^{1/2})$ band, where $T$ is the number of observations. In this case, it would imply that a correlation coefficient is classed as significant if it is bigger than approximately 0.14 or smaller than $-0.14$. The band is of course wider when the sampling frequency is monthly as it is here rather than daily where there would be more observations. It can be deduced that the first three autocorrelation coefficients and the first two partial autocorrelation coefficients are significant under this rule (plus some coefficients at lags 9 to 12). It could be concluded that a mixed ARMA process may be appropriate, although it is hard to precisely determine the appropriate order given these results, since both the acf and pacf seem to decay fairly slowly. In order to investigate this issue further, the information criteria are now employed. These can be constructed simply in RATS using a loop over the possible lag lengths for the autoregressive and moving average components[9]

```
DO I=0,5
  DO J=0,5
     BOXJENK(CONSTANT,AR=I,MA=J,NOPRINT) DHP
  COM AIC = (2.0*(I+J+1)/%NOBS)+LOG(%SEESQ)
  COM SBIC = (LOG(%NOBS)*(I+J+1)/%NOBS)+LOG(%SEESQ)
  DISPLAY 'P=' I 'Q=' J 'AIC=' AIC 'SBIC=' SBIC
  END DO J
END DO I
```

The two nested DO loops tell RATS to cycle over the AR lag length (I) and MA lag length (J). The BOXJENK command estimates the ARMA model for the returns (with the NOPRINT option again ensuring that no unwanted output is produced). Note that in order to include an intercept in the fitted ARMA models (which one would almost always want to do as the series are unlikely to have a zero mean), the CONSTANT option must be used since the default is to force the regression through the origin. The next two lines code the formulae for constructing the information criteria, and finally the DISPLAY command tells RATS what output to display. Computer program loops always operate so that the inner loop finishes first – so, in

---

[9] There is a procedure for determining the optimal ARMA model length, BJAUTOFIT, which is much easier to use than writing the nested loop instructions, but the latter demonstrate some structures that will be useful later in the book.

the example above, RATS will set I = 0 and then cycle around the loop for J, setting J = 1, then 2, 3, 4, 5, before changing I to 1, and running J = 1, 2, 3, 4, 5 etc. %NOBS and %SEESQ are the number of observations used in the Box–Jenkins model estimation and the residual variance respectively. These items are automatically created and defined in this way every time RATS runs any kind of regression.

The output from this set of commands would be as shown in Box 5.3.

**Box 5.3**

| | | |
|---|---|---|
| P= 0 Q= 0 AIC= | 0.28326 SBIC= | 0.29999 |
| P= 0 Q= 1 AIC= | 0.25878 SBIC= | 0.29223 |
| P= 0 Q= 2 AIC= | 0.15489 SBIC= | 0.20506 |
| P= 0 Q= 3 AIC= | 0.16070 SBIC= | 0.22760 |
| P= 0 Q= 4 AIC= | 0.16928 SBIC= | 0.25291 |
| P= 0 Q= 5 AIC= | 0.17390 SBIC= | 0.27425 |
| P= 1 Q= 0 AIC= | 0.23694 SBIC= | 0.27051 |
| P= 1 Q= 1 AIC= | 0.17613 SBIC= | 0.22648 |
| P= 1 Q= 2 AIC= | 0.15772 SBIC= | 0.22485 |
| P= 1 Q= 3 AIC= | 0.15059 SBIC= | 0.23451 |
| P= 1 Q= 4 AIC= | 0.16561 SBIC= | 0.26632 |
| P= 1 Q= 5 AIC= | 0.19432 SBIC= | 0.31181 |
| P= 2 Q= 0 AIC= | 0.12867 SBIC= | 0.17921 |
| P= 2 Q= 1 AIC= | 0.14423 SBIC= | 0.21161 |
| P= 2 Q= 2 AIC= | 0.15730 SBIC= | 0.24152 |
| P= 2 Q= 3 AIC= | 0.02866 SBIC= | 0.12973 |
| P= 2 Q= 4 AIC= | 0.00174 SBIC= | 0.11965 |
| P= 2 Q= 5 AIC= | 0.01325 SBIC= | 0.14801 |
| P= 3 Q= 0 AIC= | 0.14343 SBIC= | 0.21105 |
| P= 3 Q= 1 AIC= | 0.15703 SBIC= | 0.24156 |
| P= 3 Q= 2 AIC= | 0.16534 SBIC= | 0.26678 |
| P= 3 Q= 3 AIC= | 0.17927 SBIC= | 0.29761 |
| P= 3 Q= 4 AIC= | 0.17680 SBIC= | 0.31204 |
| P= 3 Q= 5 AIC= | 0.19298 SBIC= | 0.34512 |
| P= 4 Q= 0 AIC= | 0.15718 SBIC= | 0.24201 |
| P= 4 Q= 1 AIC= | 0.17293 SBIC= | 0.27472 |
| P= 4 Q= 2 AIC= | -0.05299 SBIC= | 0.06577 |
| P= 4 Q= 3 AIC= | 0.03058 SBIC= | 0.16631 |
| P= 4 Q= 4 AIC= | -0.02568 SBIC= | 0.12701 |
| P= 4 Q= 5 AIC= | 0.07854 SBIC= | 0.24820 |
| P= 5 Q= 0 AIC= | 0.17768 SBIC= | 0.27985 |
| P= 5 Q= 1 AIC= | 0.09912 SBIC= | 0.21832 |
| P= 5 Q= 2 AIC= | -0.03802 SBIC= | 0.09820 |
| P= 5 Q= 3 AIC= | 0.11018 SBIC= | 0.26343 |
| P= 5 Q= 4 AIC= | 0.13377 SBIC= | 0.30404 |
| P= 5 Q= 5 AIC= | 0.10933 SBIC= | 0.29664 |

In this application, Akaike's and Schwarz's criteria both select an ARMA(4,2). To run this model and examine the output, we re-use the command at the core of the previous loop, but without the NOPRINT option.

**BOXJENK(CONSTANT,AR=4,MA=2) DHP**

If we try to estimate the (4,2) model, we see that the optimisation routine does not converge on an optimum, and the parameter values proposed are rather implausible with coefficients larger than one in absolute value, indicating instability in the estimated model. Unfortunately, this occurs frequently in practice when a non-linear, iterative procedure is used to estimate the parameters rather than an analytical formula as would be the case with ordinary least squares. It would be possible to modify some of the options concerning the optimisation method used to conduct the estimation (e.g. by changing the starting values, changing the convergence criterion, or switching optimisation method entirely). This issue is investigated in detail in Chapter 8, but given the modest sample size used here, it is arguably preferable to leave the model chosen by the criteria on the shelf and to estimate a simpler one. So suppose that we choose to estimate an ARMA(1,1) using the same command as above but with AR=1, MA=1. We would obtain the output shown in Box 5.4.

---

### Box 5.4

```
Box-Jenkins - Estimation by LSGauss-Newton
Convergence in 24 Iterations. Final criterion was 0.0000080 <= 0.0000100
Dependent Variable DHP
Monthly Data From 1991:03 To 2007:05
Usable Observations            195   Degrees of Freedom        192
Centered R**2             0.133283        R Bar **2   0.124254
Uncentered R**2           0.336930        T x R**2      65.701
Mean of Dependent Variable          0.6352120917
Std Error of Dependent Variable     1.1491458064
Standard Error of Estimate          1.0753853943
Sum of Squared Residuals          222.03911929
Log Likelihood                     -289.35378
Durbin-Watson Statistic               2.064236
Q(36-2)                               87.815571
Significance Level of Q               0.00000120
```

| | Variable | Coeff | Std Error | T-Stat | Signif |
|---|---|---|---|---|---|
| 1. | CONSTANT | 0.651899748 | 0.198432681 | 3.28524 | 0.00121118 |
| 2. | AR{1} | 0.877168930 | 0.072768960 | 12.05416 | 0.00000000 |
| 3. | MA{1} | -0.686523384 | 0.109779962 | -6.25363 | 0.00000000 |

We can see that now convergence has been achieved, with the AR part of the model being stationary and the MA part invertible. The fact that the AR and MA coefficients are almost equal and opposite is again evidence of some instability in the estimated model, but both parameters are highly statistically significant.

It would be useful to check whether this model has been able to capture all of the dynamic structure in the house price changes or whether some remains in the residuals. So re-run the estimation, this time, adding '/ RESIDS' and then estimating the acf/pacf on those residuals

```
BOXJENK(NOPRINT,AR=1,MA=1) DHP / RESIDS
CORRELATE(NUMBER=12,QSTATS,PARTIAL=PACFR) RESIDS
```

The LB-Q(12) statistic takes a value 31.820, with $p$-value $= 0.001$, so the conclusion would be that this model is not sufficient and that a 'larger' model allowing for more structure should be specified.

## 5.2 Forecasting using ARMA models

Once a specific model order has been chosen and the model estimated for a particular set of data, it may be of interest to use the model to forecast future values of the series. Forecasting using ARMA models is a fairly simple exercise in calculating conditional expectations. Let $f_{t,s}$ denote a forecast made using an ARMA($p,q$) model at time $t$ for $s$ steps into the future for some series $y$. The forecasts are generated by what is known as a forecast function, typically of the form

$$f_{t,s} = \sum_{i=1}^{p} a_i f_{t,s-i} + \sum_{j=1}^{q} b_j u_{t+s-j} \tag{5.3}$$

where $f_{t,s} = y_{t+s}, k \leq 0; \quad u_{t+s} = 0, \quad s > 0$
$$= u_{t+s}, s \leq 0$$

and $a_i$ and $b_j$ are the autoregressive and moving average coefficients respectively.

Suppose that an ARMA(1,1) model for the house price percentage changes series were estimated using observations February 1991 – December 2004, leaving 29 observations remaining to construct forecasts and to test forecast accuracy (for the period January 2005 – May 2007). The model would be estimated and the multi-step ahead forecast production would be achieved using the following code segment:

```
SMPL 1991:03 2004:12
BOXJENK(CONSTANT,DEFINE=BJEQ,AR=1,MA=1) DHP / RESIDS
FORECAST 1 29 2005:01
# BJEQ DHPFOR
PRINT 2005:01 2007:05 DHP DHPFOR
SMPL 2005:01 2007:05
GRAPH(STYLE=LINE) 2
# DHP
# DHPFOR
SET MSE1 = (DHP-DHPFOR)**2
STATS(NOPRINT) MSE1
COM RMSEBJ = %MEAN**0.5
DIS 'RMSE-MULTI-STEP AHEAD =' RHSEBJ
```

The model is again estimated using the BOXJENK command, with the option DEFINE=BJEQ used to give the estimated equation a name that can be called when forecasting. Note that a vector of residuals must be saved at this stage (called RESIDS in this example) in order for RATS to be able to produce the forecasts. Prediction is achieved using the FORECAST command, with the numbers 1 29 2005:01 telling RATS to produce forecasts from one equation (the ARMA model is a single-equation set-up – see the following chapter for a multi-equation framework) up to 29 steps ahead, with the first forecast being produced for the January 2005 observation. The supplementary cards in the next line tell RATS to use the model BJEQ defined above and to put the forecasts in an array called DHPFOR. The PRINT line will then display the house price changes and the forecasts; they can then be plotted using the GRAPH command. Note that the SMPL 2005:01 2007:05 instruction is necessary in order to ensure that RATS plots only the forecast sample rather than the entire sample including the observations 1991:02 2004:12 used for model estimation.

There is also a single-equation forecasting Wizard on the Data menu, which is simpler to use than writing the code manually but which offers less flexibility.

The block of code beginning 'SET MSE1...' will open up a new array called MSE1, each element of which will be the square of the forecasted minus the actual value for each forecast observation. The mean squared error will just be the average of the observations in this series. Other forecast error measures can be constructed in a similar way. For example, the absolute forecast errors could be calculated using 'SET MAE1 = ABS(DHP-DHPFOR)', and so on.

The above code will produce a set of multi-step ahead forecasts with horizon from 1 to 29 observations. This means that the starting point in each case will be the same. Alternatively, we could produce a series of rolling one-step ahead forecasts, where the horizon is always one observation and so the starting point moves forward by one observation as we produce each forecast.

We could do this by estimating only one model and using the most recently available observations to construct the forecast, but this would imply that as we rolled through the sample, not all of the available information would be used to estimate the model parameters. This would make sense only if the time required to estimate the parameters were extremely large so that the computational time saved by estimating the model only once would be worth the potential loss of accuracy from using out-dated parameters in producing the forecasts. However, this is unlikely to be a relevant scenario, so the model should be re-estimated within the loop so that the parameters are updated when more data become available as the horizon increases. We can achieve this using the following loop:

```
DO J=1,29
SMPL 1991:03 2004:11+J
BOXJENK(CONSTANT,DEFINE=BJEQ,AR=1,MA=1,NOPRINT) $
DHP / RESIDS
FORECAST 1 1 2004:12+J
# BJEQ DHPFOR
END DO J
SMPL 2005:01 2007:05
GRAPH(STYLE=LINE, $
HEADER='DHP RECURSIVE 1-STEP AHEAD FORECASTS') 2
# DHP
# DHPFOR
SET MSE1 = (DHP-DHPFOR)**2
STATS(NOPRINT) MSE1
COM RMSEBJ = %MEAN**0.5
DIS 'RMSE - RECURSIVE 1-STEP AHEAD =' RMSEBJ
```

The loop over J from 1 to 29 is used to roll through the sample one observation at a time. The first cycle of the loop will start with $J = 1$ and therefore the sample starts by using observations from March 1991 to 'November 2004 + 1' (i.e. December 2004), then a forecast is made for one step ahead for observation 'December 2004 + 1' (i.e. January 2005), which is placed in the January 2005 element of the RTFOR series. The value of J is then increased by 1, the model re-estimated, another one-step ahead forecast produced and so on until 29 such predictions have been made. Finally, the 'SET MSE...' block will again calculate the mean of the squared forecast errors over the out-of-sample period, and 'COM MSEBJ...' will give the MSE.

**Figure 5.5**

DHP multi-step
ahead forecasts

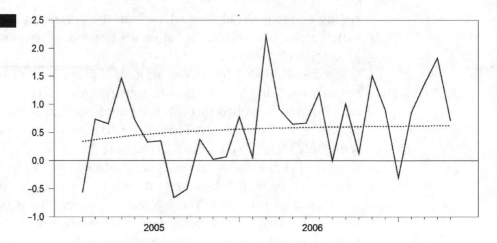

**Figure 5.6**

DHP recursive
one-step ahead
forecasts

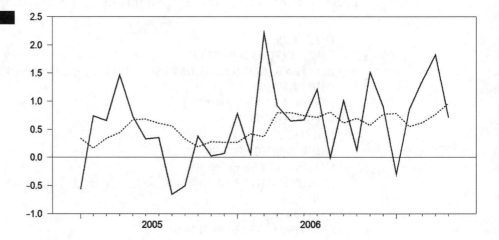

Note that the above code produces a set of one-step ahead forecasts *recursively* – i.e. with a fixed starting point and an increasing window length as we move through the sample. If, instead, we wanted to estimate the model with a *rolling window* of fixed length, how would we modify the above code? Try it and see whether the forecasts produced are more accurate.

The graphs will appear as in Figures 5.5 and 5.6 for the multi-step and rolling one-step horizons respectively, with the actual series as the solid line and the forecasts as the dotted line (not forgetting to click on the 'Use black & white (patterns)' button to switch from a two-colour figure to one that uses symbols instead).

As we would expect, the multi-step ahead predictions are smoother than the one-step ahead ones, and the former converge upon the long-term average change in house prices (since the AR part of the model is stationary)

---

**Box 5.5**

```
RMSE - MULTI-STEP AHEAD =          0.67402
RMSE - RECURSIVE 1-STEP AHEAD =   0.69328
```

---

over the in-sample period as the forecast horizon increases. But which set of forecasts is the more accurate, in terms of having the lowest root mean squared error (RMSE)? The results are shown in Box 5.5.

So in this particular exercise, the one-step ahead forecasts have a marginally lower RMSE and so would be classified as the more accurate. While the out-of-sample period was small at only 29 monthly observations, this is probably the result that we would have expected. In general, predictions usually become less accurate the longer the forecast horizon. A robust forecasting exercise would of course employ a longer out-of-sample period than the two years or so used here, and would perhaps employ several competing models in parallel. A good framework would also compare the accuracy of the predictions by examining several other error measures such as the mean absolute error (MAE) or Theil's U-statistic.

RATS provides a procedure for automatically analysing forecast errors. The syntax is

> SOURCE UFOREERRORS
> @UFOREERRORS *actual forecast start end*

where *actual* and *forecast* are the names of the series containing the actual and forecast series respectively and *start/end* are optional specifications for the sample range to be used in the calculation of the error measures. The mean forecast error (ME), MAE, RMSE, mean percentage error (MPE), mean absolute percentage error (MAPE) and RMSPE can all be calculated by the procedure (not all of these measures are presented by default).

There is also a THEIL instruction that computes a number of forecast error measures, although it is slightly more complicated to use – see the RATS *Reference Manual* entry for details.

## 5.3 Exponential smoothing models

Exponential smoothing is another modelling technique (not based on the ARMA approach) that uses only a linear combination of the previous values of a series for modelling it and for generating forecasts of its future values. Given that only previous values of the series of interest are used, the remaining question is how much weight should be attached to each of the previous observations. Recent observations would be expected to have the most power in helping to forecast future values of a series. If this is accepted, a model that places more weight on recent observations than those further in the past would be desirable. However, observations a long way in the past may still contain some information useful for forecasting future values of a series, which would not be the case under a centred moving average. An exponential smoothing model will achieve this by imposing a geometrically declining weighting scheme on the lagged values of a series. The equation for the model is

$$S_t = \alpha y_t + (1 - \alpha)S_{t-1} \tag{5.4}$$

where $\alpha$ is the smoothing constant with $0 \leq \alpha \leq 1$, $y_t$ is the current realised value, and $S_t$ is the current smoothed value.

Since $\alpha + (1 - \alpha) = 1$, $S_t$ is modelled as a weighted average of the current observation $y_t$ and the previous smoothed value. The forecasts from an exponential smoothing model are simply set to the current smoothed value, for any number of steps ahead, $s$

$$f_{t+s} = S_t, \quad s = 1, 2, 3, \ldots \tag{5.5}$$

In RATS, exponential smoothing is conducted using the ESMOOTH command. To produce a smoothed series called DHPS (the smoothed series) from a data series DHP, with observations 1991:03 to 2004:12 used for in-sample estimation and 29 (multi-step ahead) forecasts produced and placed in the series DHPFORS, the command would be

```
ESMOOTH(ESTIMATE,SMOOTHED=DHPS,FORECAST=DHPFORS, STEPS=29) $
DHP 1991:03 2004:12
```

with output as in Box 5.6.

There is also a Wizard that can conduct a number of filters and smoothers. The estimated smoothing coefficient of 0.106 is quite small. The forecasts or the in-sample smoothed values could then be printed or summary accuracy measures computed as desired. The RATS ESMOOTH instruction also has options to incorporate a trend or seasonal components – see the on-line help or user manual for details. If we wished to

**Box 5.6**

```
Exponential Smoothing for Series DHP
Model with TREND=None, SEASONAL=None
Alpha (level) 0.105888
```

**Box 5.7**

```
   ENTRY        DHPFORS              DHP
2005:01    0.854498397707    -0.567119992410
2005:02    0.648427330528     0.739184250621
2005:03    0.662800230007     0.652298726732

   ⋮             ⋮                 ⋮

2007:04    0.714032304948     1.824919006203
2007:05    0.845416249937     0.704510735997


Forecast Analysis for DHP
From 2005:01 to 2007:05
Mean Error                  0.00815655
Mean Absolute Error         0.54769622
Root Mean Square Error      0.72142363
Mean Square Error           0.520452
Theil's U                   0.813486
```

produce a series of recursive one-step ahead forecasts from the smoothed values, we would need to nest a slightly modified version of the ESMOOTH instruction in a loop:

```
DO J=1,29
SMPL 1991:03 2004:11+J
ESMOOTH(ESTIMATE,SMOOTHED=DHPS,NOPRINT,FORECAST=DHPFORS,STEPS=1) $
DHP 1991:03 2004:11+J
END DO J
PRINT 2005:01 2007:05 DHPFORS DHP
SOURCE UFOREERRORS
@UFOREERRORS DHP DHPFORS 2005:01 2007:05
```

We would then obtain the output in Box 5.7, with the dots indicating the omission of some rows.

Interpreting the forecast error analysis is difficult in the absence of a similar analysis of the forecasts from a benchmark model and so is not attempted here.

# 6  Multivariate models

One of the assumptions of the classical linear regression model is that the explanatory variables are non-stochastic, or fixed in repeated samples. There are various ways of stating this condition, some of which are slightly more or less strict, but all of which have the same broad implication. It could also be stated that all of the variables contained in the $X$ matrix are assumed to be exogenous or that the model is 'conditioned on' the variables in $X$. However, this assumption will be violated when there is feedback from the explained variable to the explanatory variable(s) – in other words, if there is a simultaneous relationship between them. This chapter first considers how to model simultaneous equations using an example on the relationship between inflation and stock returns.

## 6.1  Setting up a system

What is the relationship between inflation and stock returns? Holding stocks is often thought to provide a good hedge against inflation, since the payments to equity holders are not fixed in nominal terms and represent a claim on real assets (unlike the coupons on bonds, for example). However, the majority of empirical studies that have investigated the sign of this relationship have found it to be negative. Various explanations of this puzzling empirical phenomenon have been proposed, including a link through real activity, so that real activity is negatively related to inflation but positively related to stock returns so that stock returns and inflation vary negatively. Clearly, inflation and stock returns ought to be simultaneously related given that the rate of inflation will affect the discount rate applied to cashflows and therefore the value of equities, but the performance of the stock market may also affect consumer demand

and therefore inflation through its impact on householder wealth (perceived or actual).[10]

This simple example uses the same macroeconomic data as used previously to estimate this relationship simultaneously. Suppose (without justification) that we wish to estimate the following model, which does not allow for dynamic effects or partial adjustments and does not distinguish between expected and unexpected inflation:

$$inflation_t = \alpha_0 + \alpha_1 returns_t + \alpha_2 dcredit_t + \alpha_3 dprod_t + \alpha_4 dmoney_t + u_{1t}$$

(6.1)

$$returns_t = \beta_0 + \beta_1 dprod_t + \beta_2 dspread_t + \beta_3 inflation_t + \beta_4 rterm_t + u_{2t}$$

(6.2)

where 'returns' are stock returns and all of the other variables are defined as in a previous example in Chapter 3. It is evident that there is feedback between the two equations since the *inflation* variable appears in the *returns* equation and vice versa.

Are the equations (6.1) and (6.2) identified? Broadly, the answer to this question depends upon how many and which variables are present in each structural equation. Two conditions could be examined to determine whether a given equation from a system is identified – the order condition and the rank condition. There are a number of ways of stating the order condition; that employed here is an intuitive one (taken from Ramanathan, 1995, p. 666, and slightly modified):

> Let $G$ denote the number of structural equations. An equation is just identified if the number of variables excluded from an equation is $G-1$, where 'excluded' means the number of all endogenous and exogenous variables that are not present in this particular equation. If more than $G-1$ are absent, it is over-identified. If less than $G-1$ are absent, it is not identified.

Since there are two equations, each will be identified if one variable is missing from that equation. Equation (6.1), the inflation equation, omits two variables. It does not contain the default spread or the term spread and so is over-identified. Equation (6.2), the stock returns equation, omits two variables as well – the consumer credit and money supply variables –

---

[10] Crucially, good econometric models are based on solid financial theory. This model is clearly not, but represents a simple way to illustrate the estimation and interpretation of simultaneous equations models using RATS with freely available data!

and so it over-identified too. Two-stage least squares (2SLS) is therefore the appropriate technique to use.

In RATS, the 2SLS estimation can be done all in one go by specifying an instruments list of exogenous variables and then using the 'INST' option with the LINREG command.

**INSTRUMENTS CONSTANT DSPREAD DCREDIT DMONEY $**
**DPROD RTERM**
**LINREG(ROBUST,INST,FRML=INFLEQ) INFLATION**
**# CONSTANT RSANDP DCREDIT DPROD DMONEY**
**LINREG(ROBUST,INST,FRML=RETEQ) RSANDP**
**# CONSTANT DPROD DSPREAD INFLATION RTERM**

The output for the returns equation is shown in Box 6.1 and for the inflation equation in Box 6.2.

The results overall are not very enlightening. None of the parameters is even close to statistical significance in either equation, although interestingly, the fitted relationship between the stock returns and inflation series is positive (albeit not significantly so).

---

### Box 6.1

```
Linear Regression - Estimation by Instrumental Variables
With Heteroscedasticity/Misspecification Adjusted Standard Errors
Dependent Variable RSANDP
Monthly Data From 1986:03 To 2006:12
Usable Observations            249     Degrees of Freedom     244
Total Observations             250     Skipped/Missing          1
Mean of Dependent Variable         0.7153289944
Std Error of Dependent Variable    4.3803216103
Standard Error of Estimate         4.4110060716
Sum of Squared Residuals        4747.5017936
J-Specification(1)                 0.137710
Significance Level of J            0.71056805
Durbin-Watson Statistic            2.013944
```

| | Variable | Coeff | Std Error | T-Stat | Signif |
|---|---|---|---|---|---|
| 1. | Constant | 0.62953277 | 3.47174224 | 0.18133 | 0.85610816 |
| 2. | DPROD | -0.23342570 | 0.25568617 | -0.91294 | 0.36127499 |
| 3. | DSPREAD | -2.40710960 | 10.44817678 | -0.23039 | 0.81779214 |
| 4. | INFLATION | 0.51818652 | 14.15997915 | 0.03660 | 0.97080781 |
| 5. | RTERM | 0.11623999 | 1.40907152 | 0.08249 | 0.93425386 |

---

**Box 6.2**

```
Linear Regression - Estimation by Instrumental Variables
With Heteroscedasticity/Misspecification Adjusted Standard Errors
Dependent Variable INFLATION
Monthly Data From 1986:03 To 2006:12
Usable Observations           249      Degrees of Freedom     244
Total Observations            250      Skipped/Missing          1
Mean of Dependent Variable           0.2480987042
Std Error of Dependent Variable      0.2663603881
Standard Error of Estimate           1.1479452577
Sum of Squared Residuals           321.53790877
J-Specification(1)                     0.000011
Significance Level of J                0.99732485
Durbin-Watson Statistic                1.928535
```

| | Variable | Coeff | Std Error | T-Stat | Signif |
|---|---|---|---|---|---|
| 1. | Constant | 0.0573731323 | 0.3479002620 | 0.16491 | 0.86901278 |
| 2. | RSANDP | 0.2479339432 | 0.3755872977 | 0.66012 | 0.50917468 |
| 3. | DCREDIT | 0.0000001101 | 0.0000140221 | 0.00785 | 0.99373648 |
| 4. | DPROD | 0.0682047885 | 0.0902135151 | 0.75604 | 0.44962679 |
| 5. | DMONEY | 0.0280912552 | 0.0737764201 | 0.38076 | 0.70337988 |

## 6.2 A Hausman test

How can a researcher tell whether variables really need to be treated as endogenous or not? In other words, financial theory might suggest that there should be a two-way relationship between two or more variables, but how can it be tested whether a simultaneous equations model is necessary in practice? This would be done using a Hausman test and the steps involved are as follows:

1. Obtain the reduced form equations corresponding to each of the structural equations. Estimate these reduced form equations using OLS and obtain the fitted values.
2. Run the regression corresponding to the structural form equations, at this stage ignoring any possible simultaneity.
3. Run the structural form regressions again, but now also including the fitted values from the reduced form equations as additional regressors.
4. Use an $F$-test to examine the joint restriction that the parameters on the reduced form fitted values are zero. If the null hypothesis is

rejected, the variable(s) should be treated as endogenous because there is extra important information from the reduced form equations for modelling the dependent variable. However, if the null is not rejected, the variable(s) can be treated as exogenous for that dependent variable.

It is of interest to conduct a Hausman specification test for the endogeneity of the returns and inflation variables. There are two ways to do this in RATS – either using the REGWUTEST procedure or writing the instructions manually. The REGWUTEST approach involves only adding the lines

```
SOURCE REGWUTEST.SRC
@REGWUTEST
```

just after each of the supplementary cards of the LINREG instruction.

If we opted to conduct the test manually, sample RATS code to achieve this would be as follows:

```
* REDUCED FORM ESTIMATION
LINREG(ROBUST,NOPRINT) RSANDP / U
# CONSTANT DSPREAD DCREDIT DMONEY DPROD RTERM
SET SANDPF = RSANDP - U
LINREG(ROBUST,NOPRINT) INFLATION / V
# CONSTANT DSPREAD DCREDIT DMONEY DPROD RTERM
SET INFLATIONF = INFLATION - V
* HAUSMAN TEST FOR RSANDP
LINREG(ROBUST) RSANDP
# CONSTANT DSPREAD DPROD RTERM INFLATION INFLATIONF
* HAUSMAN TEST FOR INFLATION
LINREG(ROBUST) INFLATION
# CONSTANT DCREDIT DPROD DMONEY RSANDP RSANDPF
```

To do the Hausman test manually requires the reduced form equations to be estimated. U and V will be the residuals for the RSANDP and INFLATION reduced form regressions respectively, while RSANDPF and INFLATIONF will be the fitted values for the RSANDP and INFLATION reduced form regressions respectively. The Hausman regressions now involve adding the fitted values from the reduced form estimations to the relevant structural equation. The test then becomes one of the significance of the coefficients on the fitted values. The results from RATS estimation are shown in Box 6.3.

The conclusion is that the inflation fitted value term is not significant in the stock return equation and so inflation can be considered exogenous for stock returns. Thus it would be valid to simply estimate this equation (minus the fitted value term) on its own using OLS.

**Box 6.3**

```
Linear Regression - Estimation by Least Squares
With Heteroscedasticity-Consistent (Eicker-White) Standard Errors
Dependent Variable RSANDP
Monthly Data From 1986:03 To 2006:12
Usable Observations             249    Degrees of Freedom          243
Total Observations              250    Skipped/Missing               1
Centered R**2                0.022495  R Bar **2       0.002382
Uncentered R**2              0.047986  T x R**2        11.949
Mean of Dependent Variable             0.7153289944
Std Error of Dependent Variable        4.3803216103
Standard Error of Estimate             4.3751024489
Sum of Squared Residuals            4651.3897096
Log Likelihood                         -717.78551
Durbin-Watson Statistic                2.049035
```

| | Variable | Coeff | Std Error | T-Stat | Signif |
|---|---|---|---|---|---|
| 1. | Constant | 0.62953277 | 3.45795027 | 0.18205 | 0.85554055 |
| 2. | DSPREAD | -2.40710960 | 10.32283935 | -0.23318 | 0.81561939 |
| 3. | DPROD | -0.23342570 | 0.25713326 | -0.90780 | 0.36398364 |
| 4. | RTERM | 0.11623999 | 1.40195057 | 0.08291 | 0.93392068 |
| 5. | INFLATION | -1.88517898 | 0.97169753 | -1.94009 | 0.05236896 |
| 6. | INFLATIONF | 2.40336550 | 14.13950430 | 0.16998 | 0.86502962 |

```
Linear Regression - Estimation by Least Squares
With Heteroscedasticity-Consistent (Eicker-White) Standard Errors
Dependent Variable INFLATION
Monthly Data From 1986:03 To 2006:12
Usable Observations             249    Degrees of Freedom          243
Total Observations              250    Skipped/Missing               1
Centered R**2                0.066193  R Bar **2       0.046979
Uncentered R**2              0.500926  T x R**2        124.731
Mean of Dependent Variable             0.2480987042
Std Error of Dependent Variable        0.2663603881
Standard Error of Estimate             0.2600284599
Sum of Squared Residuals              16.430396390
Log Likelihood                         -14.88487
Durbin-Watson Statistic                1.389761
```

| | Variable | Coeff | Std Error | T-Stat | Signif |
|---|---|---|---|---|---|
| 1. | Constant | 0.0574 | 0.0769 | 0.74577 | 0.45580493 |
| 2. | DCREDIT | 1.1008e-07 | 3.0268e-06 | 0.03637 | 0.97098942 |
| 3. | DPROD | 0.0682 | 0.0193 | 3.52938 | 0.00041654 |
| 4. | DMONEY | 0.0281 | 0.0130 | 2.15955 | 0.03080748 |
| 5. | RSANDP | -6.6642e-03 | 3.8066e-03 | -1.75068 | 0.08000077 |
| 6. | RSANDPF | 0.2546 | 0.0813 | 3.12989 | 0.00174872 |

But the fitted stock return term is significant in the inflation equation, suggesting that stock returns are endogenous. We could thus estimate a triangular system, where inflation is a function of stock returns but not the other way around. The REGWUTEST procedure gives qualitatively identical conclusions.

## 6.3  VAR estimation

Vector autoregressive models (VARs) were popularised in econometrics by Sims (1980) as a natural generalisation of the univariate autoregressive models discussed in the previous chapter. A VAR is a systems regression model (i.e. there is more than one dependent variable) that can be considered a kind of hybrid between the univariate time-series models considered in Chapter 5 and the simultaneous equations models described previously in this chapter. VARs have often been advocated as an alternative to large-scale simultaneous equations structural models.

The simplest case that can be entertained is a bivariate VAR, where there are only two variables, $y_{1t}$ and $y_{2t}$, each of whose current values depends on different combinations of the previous $k$ values of both variables, and error terms

$$y_{1t} = \beta_{10} + \beta_{11}y_{1t-1} + \cdots + \beta_{1k}y_{1t-k} + \alpha_{11}y_{2t-1} + \cdots + \alpha_{1k}y_{2t-k} + u_{1t}$$

(6.3)

$$y_{2t} = \beta_{20} + \beta_{21}y_{2t-1} + \cdots + \beta_{2k}y_{2t-k} + \alpha_{21}y_{1t-1} + \cdots + \alpha_{2k}y_{1t-k} + u_{2t}$$

(6.4)

where $u_{it}$ is a white noise disturbance term with $E(u_{it}) = 0$, $(i = 1,2)$, $E(u_{1t}u_{2t}) = 0$. Provided that the VAR does not contain any contemporaneous terms on the right-hand side, it can be estimated using OLS.

By way of illustration, a VAR is estimated in order to examine whether there are lead-lag relationships for the returns to three exchange rates against the US dollar – the euro, the British pound and the Japanese yen. So we will be able to answer the question, do any of these three series react to news more quickly than the others? The data are daily and run from 7 July 2002 to 7 July 2007, giving a total of 1,827 observations. The data are contained in the Excel file 'currenciesr.xls' and in this case there is no column of dates. So we need to **construct a new RATS instruction file (call it FX.PRG)** that will read in the data; use the Wizard again to do this, noting that the data are observed seven days per week (rather than the usual five). The following instructions will be created:

```
OPEN DATA 'C:\Chris\book\RATS handbook\currenciesr.xls'
CALENDAR(7) 2002:7:7
ALL 2007:07:07
DATA(FORMAT=XLS,ORG=COLUMNS) 2002:07:07 2007:07:07 EUR GBP JPY
```

We then need to construct continuously compounded percentage returns, using the following lines:

**SET REUR = 100*LOG(EUR/EUR{1})**
**SET RGBP = 100*LOG(GBP/GBP{1})**
**SET RJPY = 100*LOG(JPY/JPY{1})**

Fortunately, there is also a Wizard for constructing VAR models. To use this, click on the **Statistics** menu and then select **VAR (set-up/Estimate)** and the following window will appear.

**Screenshot 6.1**

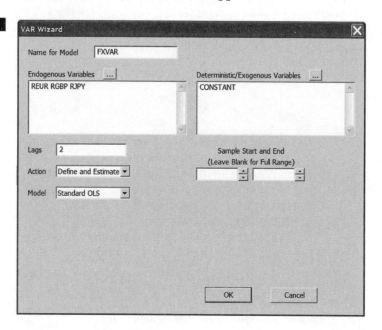

**Complete the window as above.** The endogenous variables in this case would be all three series of returns, and the only deterministic/exogenous variable would be the intercept. Suppose that we want to estimate a VAR(2) – that is, a VAR with two lags of each of the variables. We want to both define and estimate the VAR and to use OLS with the whole sample, so there is no need to change any of these default settings. (Hint: remember that to run a Wizard like this, you need to have already run the code to read in the data and construct the returns, so that RATS will recognise REUR and the other variables.) The code RATS creates would be

```
SYSTEM(MODEL=FXVAR)
VARIABLES REUR RGBP RJPY
LAGS 1 TO 2
DET CONSTANT
END(SYSTEM)
ESTIMATE
```

These instructions are fairly self-explanatory and so no comments are offered. The output in Box 6.4 will be seen when you click **OK**:

---

**Box 6.4**

```
VAR/System - Estimation by Least Squares
Dependent Variable REUR
Daily(7) Data From 2002:07:10 To 2007:07:07
Usable Observations        1824   Degrees of Freedom   1817
Mean of Dependent Variable       -0.017388537
Std Error of Dependent Variable   0.468678580
Standard Error of Estimate        0.468652261
Sum of Squared Residuals        399.07668973
Durbin-Watson Statistic            2.002212
```

| | Variable | Coeff | Std Error | T-Stat | Signif |
|---|---|---|---|---|---|
| 1. | REUR{1} | 0.031459843 | 0.036807837 | 0.85471 | 0.39282715 |
| 2. | REUR{2} | 0.011376649 | 0.036613231 | 0.31073 | 0.75604528 |
| 3. | RGBP{1} | -0.070258627 | 0.040505953 | -1.73453 | 0.08299439 |
| 4. | RGBP{2} | 0.026718893 | 0.040432484 | 0.66083 | 0.50880679 |
| 5. | RJPY{1} | -0.020697854 | 0.029999474 | -0.68994 | 0.49031967 |
| 6. | RJPY{2} | -0.014816511 | 0.029995174 | -0.49396 | 0.62139190 |
| 7. | Constant | -0.017229278 | 0.011001490 | -1.56609 | 0.11750264 |

```
F-Tests, Dependent Variable REUR
Variable    F-Statistic      Signif
REUR           0.4158      0.6598727
RGBP           1.6331      0.1956010
RJPY           0.3697      0.6910150


Dependent Variable RGBP
Daily(7) Data From 2002:07:10 To 2007:07:07
Usable Observations        1824   Degrees of Freedom   1817
Mean of Dependent Variable       -0.014450099
Std Error of Dependent Variable   0.411917771
Standard Error of Estimate        0.411763013
Sum of Squared Residuals        308.07013108
Durbin-Watson Statistic            2.003730
```

| | Variable | Coeff | Std Error | T-Stat | Signif |
|---|---|---|---|---|---|
| 1. | REUR{1} | 0.016776416 | 0.032339769 | 0.51875 | 0.60399480 |
| 2. | REUR{2} | 0.045542497 | 0.032168786 | 1.41574 | 0.15702430 |
| 3. | RGBP{1} | 0.040547409 | 0.035588975 | 1.13933 | 0.25471780 |
| 4. | RGBP{2} | -0.015074012 | 0.035524423 | -0.42433 | 0.67137676 |
| 5. | RJPY{1} | -0.029766428 | 0.026357867 | -1.12932 | 0.25891255 |
| 6. | RJPY{2} | -0.000392427 | 0.026354089 | -0.01489 | 0.98812113 |
| 7. | Constant | -0.012877997 | 0.009666029 | -1.33229 | 0.18293053 |

F-Tests, Dependent Variable RGBP

| Variable | F-Statistic | Signif |
|---|---|---|
| REUR | 1.1430 | 0.3190970 |
| RGBP | 0.7014 | 0.4960182 |
| RJPY | 0.6387 | 0.5280769 |

Dependent Variable RJPY
Daily(7) Data From 2002:07:10 To 2007:07:07

| | | | |
|---|---|---|---|
| Usable Observations | 1824 | Degrees of Freedom | 1817 |
| Mean of Dependent Variable | | 0.0021613882 | |
| Std Error of Dependent Variable | | 0.4386756314 | |
| Standard Error of Estimate | | 0.4385643628 | |
| Sum of Squared Residuals | | 349.47941851 | |
| Durbin-Watson Statistic | | 2.004680 | |

| | Variable | Coeff | Std Error | T-Stat | Signif |
|---|---|---|---|---|---|
| 1. | REUR{1} | 0.040970046 | 0.034444741 | 1.18944 | 0.23442090 |
| 2. | REUR{2} | 0.030551031 | 0.034262629 | 0.89167 | 0.37268676 |
| 3. | RGBP{1} | -0.060907457 | 0.037905435 | -1.60683 | 0.10826618 |
| 4. | RGBP{2} | -0.019407408 | 0.037836682 | -0.51293 | 0.60806562 |
| 5. | RJPY{1} | 0.011808562 | 0.028073481 | 0.42063 | 0.67407467 |
| 6. | RJPY{2} | 0.035523995 | 0.028069457 | 1.26557 | 0.20582764 |
| 7. | Constant | 0.002186587 | 0.010295184 | 0.21239 | 0.83182719 |

F-Tests, Dependent Variable RJPY

| Variable | F-Statistic | Signif |
|---|---|---|
| REUR | 1.1139 | 0.3284854 |
| RGBP | 1.5083 | 0.2215579 |
| RJPY | 0.9046 | 0.4048690 |

RATS presents the output for all three equations in the VAR model, and also a test of whether both lags of each variable are jointly significant in that equation. For example, the first equation is for the euro–dollar returns as the dependent variable, and under 'F-Tests, Dependent Variable REUR', the first entry, 'RGBP 1.6331 0.1956010', shows a test of whether both lags of the pound–dollar returns have a significant impact on the current value of the euro–dollar returns. Since the $F$-test statistic takes a value of only 1.6, with $p$-value 0.196, the conclusion would be that they do not have a significant impact. In fact, none of the joint tests on the lags of any of the variables shows significant results in any of the equations. So, rather boringly, none of the exchange rate returns is related to either of the others in a lead-lag sense!

Even if we look at the individual lags in each equation, only one of the total of 18 is significant at the 10% level, and none is significant at 5%. The one-period lag of the pound–dollar has a $p$-value of 0.08 in the euro–dollar equation. However, we need to remember that if we employ a 10% significance level, even if all three series were pure random variables, we would expect a couple of parameters that are significant by chance alone.

Note also that these results can be interpreted as Granger causality tests, since if variable $y_1$ causes $y_2$, lags of $y_1$ should be significant in the equation for $y_2$. If this were the case, we would say that $y_1$ 'Granger-causes' $y_2$, and so on. Since none of these tests shows statistically significant results, it could therefore be concluded that all of the variables are weakly exogenous with respect to the others and hence there is no Granger causality.

## 6.4  Selecting the optimal lag length for a VAR

The example above assumed that the lag length was known. But usually the first step in the specification of any VAR model, once the variables that will enter the VAR have been decided, would be to determine the appropriate lag length. This can be achieved in a variety of ways, but one of the easiest is to employ a multivariate information criterion.

Information criteria are not based on the construction of a test statistic that is compared with the critical value from a statistical distribution. Instead, the criteria trade off a fall in the *RSS* of each equation as more lags are added, against an increase in the value of the penalty term. The univariate criteria could be applied separately to each equation, but again, it is usually deemed preferable to require the number of lags to be the same for each equation. This requires the use of multivariate versions of the information criteria, which can be defined as

$$MAIC = T \log |\hat{\Sigma}| + 2k' \tag{6.5}$$

$$MSBIC = T \log |\hat{\Sigma}| + k' \log(T) \tag{6.6}$$

$$MHQIC = T \log |\hat{\Sigma}| + 2k' \log(\log(T)) \tag{6.7}$$

where $\hat{\Sigma}$ is the variance-covariance matrix of residuals, $T$ is the number of observations and $k'$ is the total number of regressors in all equations, which will be equal to $p^2 k + p$ for $p$ equations in the VAR system, each with $k$ lags of the $p$ variables, plus a constant term in each equation. As previously, the values of the information criteria are constructed for 0, 1, ..., $\bar{k}$ lags (up to some pre-specified maximum $\bar{k}$), and the chosen number of lags is that number minimising the value of the given information criterion.[11]

Returning to the example, suppose that lag orders from 1 to 10 are considered. We could take the code that the Wizard constructed for us above and we can nest it in a loop that estimates each candidate model over a fixed estimation range, calculating the values of AIC and SBIC in each case. However, a much easier way is to use the VARLAGSELECT procedure. The code would be

```
SOURCE VARLAGSELECT.SRC
@VARLAGSELECT(LAGS=10,CRIT=AIC)
# REUR RGBP RJPY
@VARLAGSELECT(LAGS=10,CRIT=SBC)
# REUR RGBP RJPY
```

CRIT=HQ can also be used to choose the lag length using the Hannan–Quinn criterion. The results would appear as in Box 6.5.

It is clear that both AIC and SBIC choose very small models, with AIC preferring a VAR(1) and SBIC being minimised when no lags of each variable are used, although this result is hardly surprising given that there was nothing that was significant in the VAR(2).

Often, it will be the case that we will want to choose between two different lag orders. For example, suppose that one researcher thought that a VAR(4) was optimal, while another deemed that a VAR(1) was preferable. Then, it might be of interest to test whether lags 2 through 4 for all three equations could be restricted to zero using a likelihood ratio test. This requires estimation of both the unrestricted model (i.e. the VAR(4)) and the restricted model (the VAR(1)). The logs of the determinants of the

---

[11] Note that there are several ways of writing the information criteria, as for their univariate counterparts.

---

**Box 6.5**

```
Lags    AICC
   0    4390.79516
   1    4375.89082*
   2    4383.94592
   3    4395.86353
   4    4395.29804
   5    4399.99767
   6    4405.49141
   7    4416.46819
   8    4415.50715
   9    4414.30798
  10    4428.75550


Lags    SBC/BIC
   0    4407.30393*
   1    4441.88611
   2    4499.36785
   3    4560.65191
   4    4609.39239
   5    4663.33719
   6    4718.01501
   7    4778.11447
   8    4826.21441
   9    4874.01418
  10    4937.39831
```

---

variance-covariance matrices of residuals for the two models are then 'compared'. Denote the variance-covariance matrix of residuals (given by $\hat{u}\hat{u}'$) as $\hat{\Sigma}$ and then the likelihood ratio test for this joint hypothesis is given by

$$LR = T \left\lfloor \log \left| \hat{\Sigma}_r \right| - \log \left| \hat{\Sigma}_u \right| \right\rfloor \tag{6.8}$$

where $\left| \hat{\Sigma}_r \right|$ is the determinant of the variance-covariance matrix of the residuals for the restricted model, $\left| \hat{\Sigma}_u \right|$ is the determinant of the variance-covariance matrix of residuals for the unrestricted VAR, and $T$ is the sample size. The test statistic is asymptotically distributed as a $\chi^2$ variate with degrees of freedom equal to the total number of restrictions. In the general case of a VAR with $g$ equations, to impose the restriction that the last $q$ lags have zero coefficients, there would be $g^2 q$ restrictions altogether. Intuitively, the test is a multivariate equivalent to examining the extent to which the $RSS$ rises when a restriction is imposed. If $\left| \hat{\Sigma}_r \right|$ and $\left| \hat{\Sigma}_u \right|$ are 'close together', the restriction is supported by the data.

The relevant block of RATS instructions is

```
SYSTEM 1 TO 3
VARIABLES REUR RGBP RJPY
LAGS 1 TO 4
DET CONSTANT
END(SYSTEM)
ESTIMATE(NOPRINT,OUTSIGMA=V)
COM SIGMAU = %LOGDET
COM NOBS = %NOBS
COM PARAMS = 39
SYSTEM 1 TO 3
VARIABLES REUR RGBP RJPY
LAGS 1 TO 1
DET CONSTANT
END(SYSTEM)
ESTIMATE(NOPRINT,OUTSIGMA=V)
COM SIGMAR = %LOGDET
COM LRSTAT = (NOBS-PARAMS)*(SIGMAR-SIGMAU)
CDF CHISQR LRSTAT 27
```

The equations are estimated as above with four lags and then one lag. The 'COM SIGMAU = %LOGDET', 'COM NOBS = %NOBS' and 'COM PARAMS = 39' commands define the log of the determinant of the residual variance-covariance matrix, the number of observations used for the regression, and the total number of parameters used in the unrestricted regression (three equations each with a constant and four lags of the three variables, so 13 parameters $\times$ 3 equations) respectively. Similarly, 'COM SIGMAR = %LOGDET' defines the log determinant of the residual variance-covariance matrix for the restricted model.

The final two lines define the likelihood ratio test. The penultimate line constructs the test statistic, while the last line states that the test statistic, 'LRSTAT', follows a Chi-squared distribution with 27 degrees of freedom (the number of restrictions placed on the model altogether, which will be the difference between the number of parameters in the unrestricted (39) and restricted (12) models). The result is shown in Box 6.6.

Surprisingly (given that the profligate criterion AIC chose a modest VAR(1)), the restriction is rejected by the likelihood ratio test, at least at the 5% level, suggesting that a VAR(4) should be employed in preference to a VAR(1).

**Box 6.6**

```
Chi-Squared(27)= 45.483985 with Significance Level 0.01444889
```

An alternative to computing the likelihood ratio test statistic by hand would be to use the RATIO instruction. To run this, we would have to save the residuals for each equation from the restricted and unrestricted models. For further details, see the RATS 7 *Reference Manual* entry.

## 6.5 Impulse responses and variance decompositions

Block $F$-tests and an examination of causality in a VAR will suggest which of the variables in the model have statistically significant impacts on the future values of each of the variables in the system. But $F$-test results will not, by construction, be able to explain the sign of the relationship or how long these effects require to take place. That is, $F$-test results will not reveal whether changes in the value of a given variable have positive or negative effects on other variables in the system, or how long it would take for the effect of that variable to work through the system. Such information will, however, be available from an examination of the VAR's impulse responses and variance decompositions.

Impulse responses trace out the responsiveness of the dependent variables in the VAR to shocks to each of the variables. So a unit shock is applied to the error from each equation separately, and the effects upon the VAR system over time are noted. Thus, if there are $g$ variables in a system, a total of $g^2$ impulse responses could be generated. The way that this is achieved in practice is by expressing the VAR model as a VMA – that is, the vector autoregressive model is written as a vector moving average. Provided that the system is stable, the shock should gradually die away.

Variance decompositions offer a slightly different method for examining VAR system dynamics. They give the proportion of the movements in the dependent variables that is due to their 'own' shocks versus shocks to the other variables. A shock to the $i^{th}$ variable will of course directly affect that variable, but it will also be transmitted to all of the other variables in the system through the dynamic structure of the VAR. Variance decompositions determine how much of the $s$-step ahead forecast error variance of a given variable is explained by innovations to each explanatory variable for $s = 1, 2, \ldots$. In practice, it is usually observed that own-series shocks explain most of the (forecast) error variance of the series in a VAR. To some extent, impulse responses and variance decompositions offer very similar information.

For calculating impulse responses and variance decompositions, the ordering of the variables is important. To see why this is the case, recall that the impulse responses refer to a unit shock to the errors of one VAR equation alone. This implies that the error terms of all other equations in the VAR system are held constant. However, this is not realistic since the error terms are likely to be correlated across equations to some extent. Thus, assuming that they are completely independent would lead to a mis-representation of the system dynamics. In practice, the errors will have a common component that cannot be associated with a single variable alone.

The usual approach to this difficulty is to generate orthogonalised impulse responses. In the context of a bivariate VAR, the whole of the common component of the errors is attributed somewhat arbitrarily to the first variable in the VAR. In the general case where there are more than two variables in the VAR, the calculations are more complex but the interpretation is the same. Such a restriction in effect implies an 'ordering' of variables, so that the equation for $y_{1t}$ would be estimated first and then that of $y_{2t}$, a bit like a recursive or triangular system.

It is necessary to assume a particular ordering in order to compute the impulse responses and variance decompositions, although the restriction underlying the ordering used may not be supported by the data. Again, ideally, financial theory should suggest an ordering (in other words, that movements in some variables are likely to follow, rather than precede, others). Failing this, the sensitivity of the results to changes in the ordering can be observed by assuming one ordering and then exactly reversing it and re-computing the impulse responses and variance decompositions. It is also worth noting that the more highly correlated are the residuals from an estimated equation, the more the variable ordering will be important. But when the residuals are almost uncorrelated, the ordering of the variables will make little difference (see Lütkepohl, 1991, Chapter 2 for further details).

Impulse responses and variance decompositions can be constructed in RATS using the IMPULSE and ERRORS commands respectively. Additionally, the latter has an IMPULSES option, so that the ERRORS command can be used to compute both impulse responses and variance decompositions. The instruction to estimate impulse responses for the above model would be

**IMPULSE(MODEL=FXVAR,RESULT=IMPS,STEPS=10)**

Obviously, this line needs to be placed after the VAR model estimation instructions. The output is shown in Box 6.7.

Unfortunately, RATS does not provide standard errors by default (although these can be produced using the MONTEVAR procedure), but even without confidence bands it is easy to see from these values that

| Box 6.7 | | | |

**Responses to Shock in REUR**

| Entry | REUR | RGBP | RJPY |
|---|---|---|---|
| 1 | 0.4677521 | 0.3064024 | 0.2343483 |
| 2 | -0.0117099 | 0.0129357 | 0.0030877 |
| 3 | 0.0101915 | 0.0172257 | 0.0149743 |
| 4 | 0.0010266 | 0.0082176 | 0.0036517 |
| 5 | -0.0227336 | -0.0099657 | 0.0043512 |
| 6 | -0.0001450 | -0.0011704 | -0.0005090 |
| 7 | -0.0017216 | -0.0015016 | -0.0007587 |
| 8 | -0.0001590 | -0.0008278 | 0.0002559 |
| 9 | 0.0003139 | 0.0002396 | -0.0013408 |
| 10 | 0.0000443 | 0.0000547 | 0.0000188 |

**Responses to Shock in RGBP**

| Entry | REUR | RGBP | RJPY |
|---|---|---|---|
| 1 | 0.0000000 | 0.2738899 | 0.0575433 |
| 2 | -0.0211676 | 0.0088131 | -0.0175180 |
| 3 | 0.0070390 | -0.0033410 | -0.0050676 |
| 4 | -0.0018337 | -0.0073634 | -0.0014769 |
| 5 | -0.0100396 | -0.0045326 | -0.0028037 |
| 6 | 0.0004311 | 0.0003116 | 0.0000987 |
| 7 | 0.0000817 | -0.0002665 | 0.0003617 |
| 8 | 0.0002890 | -0.0001298 | -0.0000029 |
| 9 | 0.0003396 | 0.0001845 | -0.0002014 |
| 10 | -0.0000037 | 0.0000317 | 0.0000428 |

**Responses to Shock in RJPY**

| Entry | REUR | RGBP | RJPY |
|---|---|---|---|
| 1 | 0.0000000 | 0.0000000 | 0.3651989 |
| 2 | -0.0074279 | -0.0110346 | 0.0042735 |
| 3 | -0.0039180 | -0.0007069 | 0.0136505 |
| 4 | 0.0075594 | -0.0033444 | 0.0163452 |
| 5 | -0.0146041 | -0.0028765 | -0.0253819 |
| 6 | 0.0005365 | 0.0007489 | 0.0000661 |
| 7 | -0.0000237 | -0.0003937 | -0.0017688 |
| 8 | -0.0011217 | -0.0003565 | -0.0019189 |
| 9 | 0.0012723 | 0.0003563 | 0.0011249 |
| 10 | -0.0000699 | -0.0000383 | -0.0001013 |

the responses to shocks are very small indeed, except for the first-step response of a variable to its own shock. This result confirms that of the Granger causality statistics in showing a lack of any connectivity between the three series.

To estimate the variance decompositions, use the command

**ERRORS(MODEL=FXVAR,RESULT=ERRS,STEPS=10)**

and they appear as in Box 6.8.

**Box 6.8**

```
Decomposition of Variance for Series REUR
Step      Std Error        REUR        RGBP        RJPY
   1     0.46775212     100.000       0.000       0.000
   2     0.46843613      99.771       0.204       0.025
   3     0.46861623      99.741       0.227       0.032
   4     0.46868191      99.714       0.228       0.058
   5     0.46956749      99.572       0.273       0.155
   6     0.46956801      99.572       0.273       0.155
   7     0.46957118      99.572       0.273       0.155
   8     0.46957263      99.572       0.273       0.155
   9     0.46957459      99.571       0.273       0.156
  10     0.46957459      99.571       0.273       0.156

Decomposition of Variance for Series RGBP
Step      Std Error        REUR        RGBP        RJPY
   1     0.41097214      55.585      44.415       0.000
   2     0.41141812      55.564      44.364       0.072
   3     0.41179273      55.638      44.290       0.072
   4     0.41195411      55.634      44.288       0.079
   5     0.41210960      55.650      44.266       0.083
   6     0.41211206      55.650      44.266       0.084
   7     0.41211507      55.651      44.265       0.084
   8     0.41211608      55.651      44.265       0.084
   9     0.41211634      55.651      44.265       0.084
  10     0.41211635      55.651      44.265       0.084

Decomposition of Variance for Series RJPY
Step      Std Error        REUR        RGBP        RJPY
   1     0.43772201      28.663       1.728      69.608
   2     0.43810414      28.618       1.885      69.497
   3     0.43860173      28.670       1.894      69.436
   4     0.43892387      28.635       1.892      69.473
   5     0.43968761      28.545       1.890      69.565
   6     0.43968793      28.545       1.890      69.565
   7     0.43969229      28.545       1.890      69.565
   8     0.43969655      28.545       1.890      69.565
   9     0.43970008      28.545       1.890      69.565
  10     0.43970009      28.545       1.890      69.565
```

The first column of RATS output (after the number of steps ahead) is the standard error of the forecast of the variable in this model. The remaining columns provide the decomposition. By construction, the percentage of the error variance attributable to own shocks for the first variable in the first step is 100%. The behaviour immediately settles down to a steady state. Over 99% of the error variance in the euro series is attributable to own shocks, while the other two series between them explain less than 1% of its variation. It would be tempting to suggest that the results are more interesting for the decompositions of the pound and yen series, since the euro appears able to explain 55% of the variation of the former and 28% of the latter.

But it is important to remember that the ordering of the variables has an impact on the impulse responses and variance decompositions. When, as in this case, financial theory does not suggest an obvious ordering of the series, some sensitivity analysis should be undertaken. The order of the three variables can be reversed by simply re-running the instructions for the VAR but replacing the instruction 'VARIABLES REUR RGBP RJPY' with 'VARIABLES RJPY RGBP REUR'. We then obtain the following decompositions for the reverse order (Box 6.9).

It is evident that changing the ordering has had an overwhelming effect on the proportion of the error variance explained by each series. In

**Box 6.9**

| Step | Std Error | RJPY | RGBP | REUR |
|---|---|---|---|---|
| 1 | 0.43670752 | 100.000 | 0.000 | 0.000 |
| 2 | 0.43708904 | 99.830 | 0.080 | 0.090 |
| 3 | 0.43758479 | 99.786 | 0.081 | 0.133 |
| 4 | 0.43790563 | 99.763 | 0.103 | 0.134 |
| 5 | 0.43866645 | 99.607 | 0.181 | 0.212 |
| 6 | 0.43866676 | 99.607 | 0.181 | 0.212 |
| 7 | 0.43867111 | 99.607 | 0.181 | 0.212 |
| 8 | 0.43867535 | 99.606 | 0.182 | 0.212 |
| 9 | 0.43867887 | 99.605 | 0.183 | 0.213 |
| 10 | 0.43867888 | 99.605 | 0.183 | 0.213 |

Decomposition of Variance for Series RGBP

| Step | Std Error | RJPY | RGBP | REUR |
|---|---|---|---|---|
| 1 | 0.41083902 | 23.851 | 76.149 | 0.000 |
| 2 | 0.41128343 | 23.800 | 76.184 | 0.016 |
| 3 | 0.41165621 | 23.796 | 76.080 | 0.124 |
| 4 | 0.41181671 | 23.778 | 76.021 | 0.201 |
| 5 | 0.41197199 | 23.801 | 75.995 | 0.204 |
| 6 | 0.41197444 | 23.801 | 75.995 | 0.205 |
| 7 | 0.41197744 | 23.801 | 75.994 | 0.205 |
| 8 | 0.41197844 | 23.801 | 75.994 | 0.205 |
| 9 | 0.41197870 | 23.801 | 75.994 | 0.205 |
| 10 | 0.41197871 | 23.801 | 75.994 | 0.205 |

```
Decomposition of Variance for Series REUR
Step    Std Error      RJPY       RGBP       REUR
   1    0.46674727    28.746     30.784     40.470
   2    0.46743267    28.769     30.836     40.395
   3    0.46761277    28.751     30.881     40.367
   4    0.46767815    28.763     30.881     40.356
   5    0.46856361    28.954     30.838     40.208
   6    0.46856413    28.954     30.838     40.208
   7    0.46856729    28.954     30.838     40.208
   8    0.46856874    28.954     30.838     40.208
   9    0.46857068    28.955     30.838     40.207
  10    0.46857069    28.955     30.838     40.207
```

the previous instance, where the euro was ordered first, it explained 69% of the variation in the yen returns, but in the second case where the yen is ordered first, the euro is not even able to explain 1% of the yen's variation. Taken in sum, it would be concluded that there is little evidence of useful lead-lag relationships between the three currency return series investigated. Further RATS code is available for automatically plotting the impulse responses and also for constructing confidence intervals for them using simulated standard errors (see the RATS *User Guide* and sample programs on the Estima web site).

# 7 Modelling long-run relationships

## 7.1 Testing for unit roots

The early and pioneering work on testing for a unit root in time-series was done by Dickey and Fuller (Dickey and Fuller 1979, Fuller 1976). The basic objective of the test is to examine the null hypothesis that $\phi = 1$ in

$$y_t = \phi y_{t-1} + u_t \tag{7.1}$$

against the one-sided alternative that $\phi < 1$. Thus the hypotheses of interest are

$H_0$: series contains a unit root
vs. $H_1$: series is stationary.

In practice, the following regression is employed, rather than (7.1), for ease of computation and interpretation:

$$\Delta y_t = \psi y_{t-1} + u_t \tag{7.2}$$

so that a test of $\phi = 1$ is equivalent to a test of $\psi = 0$ (since $\phi - 1 = \psi$). The test statistic for the Dickey–Fuller (DF) test is defined as

$$\text{test statistic} = \frac{\hat{\psi}}{\widehat{SE(\hat{\psi})}} \tag{7.3}$$

Such test statistics do not follow the usual $t$-distribution under the null hypothesis, since the null is one of non-stationarity, but rather they follow non-standard distribution. Critical values are derived from simulations experiments in, for example, Fuller (1976). A discussion and example of how such critical values are derived using simulations methods are presented in Chapter 12.

Dickey–Fuller-type unit root tests can be accomplished in RATS by calling the DFUNIT sub-routine. The command syntax to call it is

**SOURCE DFUNIT.SRC**

This example uses the same data on UK house prices as employed in Chapters 1 and 5. Assuming that the data have been loaded and the variables are defined as before, the Dickey–Fuller test is run by using the following commands:

**@DFUNIT(TTEST) PRICE**
**@DFUNIT(TTEST) DHP**
**@DFUNIT(TTEST,LAGS=5) PRICE**
**@DFUNIT(TTEST,LAGS=5) DHP**

The first two lines will run a Dickey–Fuller test on the raw house price series and then on the house price percentage changes using the standard *t*-test approach. The last two lines will run an Augmented Dickey–Fuller (ADF) test on the two series with five lags of the dependent variable in each of the test regressions.

By default, RATS includes a constant in the test regression, but not a trend. If it is deemed appropriate to include a trend as well, the option DET=TREND should be used with the command, e.g. '@DFUNIT(TTEST,DET=TREND) PRICE', or the option DET=NONE would be used if the regression were to employ neither a constant nor a trend: '@DFUNIT(TTEST,DET=NONE) PRICE' etc. Running these four unit root tests would give output of the form in Box 7.1 respectively.

We can see that the conclusions are very strong and accord with what we would have expected; the house price levels series is non-stationary (the null hypothesis of a unit root cannot be rejected even at the 10% level), whether a plain Dickey–Fuller or the ADF test is used. And the percentage changes in house prices is clearly a stationary series since the test statistic is more negative than the critical value, even at the 1% level, indicating that the null hypothesis of a unit root can be rejected. The DF and ADF test regressions could also, of course, have been conducted by hand using the 'LINREG' command, although there would be little point in doing so.

The number of lags in the ADF test has been arbitrarily set to 5 here, so as an exercise, try to design a set of instructions that will choose the lag length optimally using an information criterion and determine whether the conclusion from the ADF test with that number of lags remains the same.

There is also a Phillips–Perron unit root test procedure available in RATS, PPUNIT.SRC. It operates in exactly the same way as the

```
         Box 7.1

Dickey-Fuller Unit Root Test, Series PRICE
Regression Run From 1991:02 to 2007:05
Observations 197
With intercept with 0 lags on the differences
T-test statistic    6.21910
Critical values: 1%= -3.465 5%= -2.876 10%= -2.575


Dickey-Fuller Unit Root Test, Series DHP
Regression Run From 1991:03 to 2007:05
Observations 196
With intercept with 0 lags on the differences
T-test statistic   -10.71437
Critical values: 1%= -3.465 5%= -2.876 10%= -2.575


Dickey-Fuller Unit Root Test, Series PRICE
Regression Run From 1991:07 to 2007:05
Observations 192
With intercept with 5 lags on the differences
T-test statistic    2.79236
Critical values: 1%= -3.466 5%= -2.877 10%= -2.575


Dickey-Fuller Unit Root Test, Series DHP
Regression Run From 1991:08 to 2007:05
Observations 191
With intercept with 5 lags on the differences
T-test statistic   -4.21602
Critical values: 1%= -3.466 5%= -2.877 10%= -2.575
```

Dickey–Fuller test and we could apply it to the house price series by using the commands

> SOURCE(NOECHO) PPUNIT.SRC
> @PPUNIT(TTEST) PRICE

The options available are identical to those of the DFUNIT procedure, although the LAGS option will have a different meaning.

## 7.2 Testing for cointegration and modelling cointegrated variables

If we believe that a set of I(1) variables may be cointegrated, we could test this by estimating a regression containing all of the variables and testing the residuals for a unit root. For example, suppose that we have the following model:

$$y_t = \beta_1 + \beta_2 x_{2t} + \beta_3 x_{3t} + \cdots + \beta_n x_{nt} + u_t \tag{7.4}$$

$u_t$ should be I(0) if the variables $y_t, x_{2t}, \ldots x_{kt}$ are cointegrated, but $u_t$ will still be non-stationary if they are not. Thus it is necessary to test the residuals of equation (7.4) to see whether they are non-stationary or stationary. The DF or ADF test can be used on $\hat{u}_t$, using a regression of the form

$$\Delta \hat{u}_t = \psi \hat{u}_{t-1} + v_t \tag{7.5}$$

with $v_t$ an iid error term.

However, since this is a test on residuals of a model, $\hat{u}_t$, then the critical values are changed compared with a DF or an ADF test on a series of raw data. Engle and Granger (1987) have tabulated a new set of critical values for this application and hence the test is known as the Engle–Granger test. The residuals have been constructed from a particular set of coefficient estimates, and the sampling estimation error in those coefficients will change the distribution of the test statistic. Engle and Yoo (1987) tabulate a new set of critical values that is each larger in absolute value (i.e. more negative) than the corresponding DF critical values. The critical values also become more negative as the number of variables in the potentially cointegrating regression increases.

What are the null and alternative hypotheses for any unit root test applied to the residuals of a potentially cointegrating regression?

$H_0: \hat{u}_t \sim I(1)$
$H_1: \hat{u}_t \sim I(0).$

Thus, under the null hypothesis, there is a unit root in the potentially cointegrating regression residuals, while under the alternative, the residuals are stationary. Under the null hypothesis, therefore, a stationary linear combination of the non-stationary variables has not been found. Hence, if this null hypothesis is not rejected, there is no cointegration. The appropriate strategy for econometric modelling in this case would be to employ specifications in first differences only. Such models would have no long-run equilibrium solution, but this would not matter since no cointegration implies that there is no long-run relationship anyway.

However, if the null of a unit root in the potentially cointegrating regression's residuals is rejected, it would be concluded that a stationary linear combination of the non-stationary variables had been found. Therefore, the variables would be classed as cointegrated. The appropriate strategy for econometric modelling in this case would be to form and estimate an error-correction model, using a method described below.

```
┌──────────────────────────────────────────────────────────────────────┐
│ ███ Box 7.2 ████████████████████████████████████████████████████████  │
├──────────────────────────────────────────────────────────────────────┤
│ Linear Regression - Estimation by Least Squares                        │
│ Dependent Variable LSPOT                                               │
│ Monthly Data From 2002:02 To 2007:07                                   │
│ Usable Observations          66      Degrees of Freedom      64        │
│ Centered R**2          0.959158   R Bar **2      0.958519              │
│ Uncentered R**2        0.999980   T x R**2          65.999             │
│ Mean of Dependent Variable       7.0435686902                         │
│ Std Error of Dependent Variable 0.1567267588                          │
│ Standard Error of Estimate       0.0319202000                         │
│ Sum of Squared Residuals         0.0652095469                         │
│ Regression F(1,64)               1502.9980                            │
│ Significance Level of F          0.00000000                           │
│ Log Likelihood                   134.70359                            │
│ Durbin-Watson Statistic          2.012684                             │
│                                                                        │
│      Variable           Coeff        Std Error      T-Stat    Signif   │
│ **************************************************************************│
│ 1.   Constant      0.1144110511  0.1787747375     0.63997  0.52447449 │
│ 2.   LFUTURES      0.9838087892  0.0253764865    38.76852  0.00000000 │
└──────────────────────────────────────────────────────────────────────┘
```

The S&P500 spot and futures series that were discussed in Chapter 2 will now be examined for cointegration. If the two series are cointegrated, this means that the spot and futures prices have a long-term relationship, which prevents them from wandering apart without bound. To test for cointegration using the Engle–Granger approach, the residuals of a regression of the log of the spot price on the log of the futures price are examined.[12] So we need to re-open the SANDPHEDGE.PRG set of instructions that we saved previously. Now, **create two new variables** for the log spot series and the log futures series, and call them LSPOT and LFUTURES respectively. Then **run the regression of LSPOT on a CONSTANT and LFUTURES, saving the residual series as RESIDS**. The regression results are shown in Box 7.2.

The slope parameter in this regression measures the long-run relationship between the two series and this is almost 1:1. It would be tempting to jump in and conduct a test of the hypothesis that the true value of the slope parameter is 1, but remember that it is not valid to examine anything other than the coefficient values in this regression, since

---

[12] Note that it is common to run a regression of the log of the spot price on the log of the futures rather than a regression in levels; the main reason for using logarithms is that the differences of the logs are returns, whereas this is not true for the levels.

the residuals will be non-stationary if the series are not cointegrated. And even if the series are cointegrated, because they are in log-levels form, the residuals from this regression are likely to be highly autocorrelated, making the standard errors and therefore any inferences potentially unreliable.

Now, we should run a Dickey–Fuller test on the RESIDS series, which are the residuals from this regression, and for comparison we also run the test on the log-spot and log-futures prices. All of the commands needed so far in this section are

**LINREG LSPOT / RESIDS**
**# CONSTANT LFUTURES**
**SOURCE DFUNIT.SRC**
**@DFUNIT(TTEST) LSPOT**
**@DFUNIT(TTEST) LFUTURES**
**@DFUNIT(TTEST) RESIDS**

The results are shown in Box 7.3.

The contrast between the raw logged series and the residuals is clear: the former are non-stationary while the latter are stationary. This suggests that we have found a linear combination of the two non-stationary

---

**Box 7.3**

```
Dickey-Fuller Unit Root Test, Series LSPOT
Regression Run From 2002:03 to 2007:07
Observations 66
With intercept with 0 lags on the differences
T-test statistic    -0.26381
Critical values: 1%= -3.531 5%= -2.906 10%= -2.590

Dickey-Fuller Unit Root Test, Series LFUTURES
Regression Run From 2002:03 to 2007:07
Observations 66
With intercept with 0 lags on the differences
T-test statistic     0.18865
Critical values: 1%= -3.531 5%= -2.906 10%= -2.590

Dickey-Fuller Unit Root Test, Series RESIDS
Regression Run From 2002:03 to 2007:07
Observations 66
With intercept with 0 lags on the differences
T-test statistic    -8.05054
Critical values: 1%= -3.531 5%= -2.906 10%= -2.590
```

series that is stationary and therefore that the two series are cointegrated. The next stage in the analysis would be to form an error-correction model. We would do this by running a regression of the spot returns on a constant, the futures returns, and the one-period lagged error-correction term, which will be the lagged residual from the cointegrating regression above:

**LINREG DSPOT**
**# CONSTANT DFUTURES RESIDS{1}**

Running this gives us the results in Box 7.4.

The futures returns and error-correction terms have the correct signs but are of implausible magnitudes. The former suggests that spot returns move in the same direction as futures returns, but to a greater extent. The parameter value of −180 on the error-correction term means that whatever the disequilibrium at any particular time $t$, the spot returns will adjust to correct this by 180% − in other words, it will over-compensate or overshoot by 1.8 times the required amount to restore equilibrium. These slightly odd parameter values may result from the fairly short sample period that has been used in this example.

### Box 7.4

```
Linear Regression - Estimation by Least Squares
Dependent Variable DSPOT
Monthly Data From 2002:03 To 2007:07
Usable Observations            65      Degrees of Freedom      62
Centered R**2          0.240775   R Bar **2       0.216284
Uncentered R**2        0.251519   T x R**2        16.349
Mean of Dependent Variable         0.4212026598
Std Error of Dependent Variable  3.5429920081
Standard Error of Estimate         3.1365312100
Sum of Squared Residuals         609.94533796
Regression F(2,62)                 9.8311
Significance Level of F            0.00019565
Log Likelihood                     -164.99792
Durbin-Watson Statistic            2.015851
```

| | Variable | Coeff | Std Error | T-Stat | Signif |
|---|---|---|---|---|---|
| 1. | Constant | -0.2676014 | 0.4193434 | -0.63814 | 0.52573007 |
| 2. | DFUTURES | 1.7503217 | 0.3955766 | 4.42474 | 0.00003980 |
| 3. | RESIDS{1} | -180.0435641 | 41.7846317 | -4.30885 | 0.00005967 |

## 7.3 Using the systems-based approach to testing for cointegration

In order to use the Johansen's (1988) test, the testing framework involves the estimation of a vector error-correction model (VECM) of the form

$$\Delta y_t = \Pi y_{t-k} + \Gamma_1 \Delta y_{t-1} + \Gamma_2 \Delta y_{t-2} + \cdots + \Gamma_{k-1} \Delta y_{t-(k-1)} + u_t \qquad (7.6)$$

where $\Pi = \left( \sum_{j=1}^{k} \beta_i \right) - I_g$ and $\Gamma_i = \left( \sum_{j=1}^{i} \beta_j \right) - I_g$.

This VAR contains $g$ variables in first-differenced form on the LHS and $k - 1$ lags of the dependent variables (differences) on the RHS, each with a $\Gamma$ coefficient matrix attached to it. In fact, the Johansen test can be affected by the lag length employed in the VECM, so it is useful to attempt to select the lag length optimally, as outlined in the previous chapter. The Johansen test centres around an examination of the $\Pi$ matrix. $\Pi$ can be interpreted as a long-run coefficient matrix, since in equilibrium all the $\Delta y_{t-i}$ will be zero, and setting the error terms, $u_t$, to their expected value of zero will leave $\Pi y_{t-k} = 0$. Notice the parallel between this set of equations and the testing equation for an ADF test, which has a first-differenced term as the dependent variable, together with a lagged-levels term and lagged differences on the right-hand side.

The test for cointegration between the $y$s is calculated by looking at the rank of the $\Pi$ matrix via its eigenvalues.[13] The rank of a matrix is equal to the number of its characteristic roots (eigenvalues) that are different from zero. The eigenvalues, denoted $\lambda_i$, are put in ascending order

$$\lambda_1 \geq \lambda_2 \geq \cdots \geq \lambda_g$$

If the $\lambda$s are roots, in this context they must be less than one in absolute value and positive, and $\lambda_1$ will be the largest (i.e. the closest to one), while $\lambda_g$ will be the smallest (i.e. the closest to zero). If the variables are not cointegrated, the rank of $\Pi$ will not be significantly different from zero, so $\lambda_i \approx 0 \; \forall \; i$. The test statistics actually incorporate $\ln(1 - \lambda_i)$, rather than the $\lambda_i$ themselves, but still, when $\lambda_i = 0$, $\ln(1 - \lambda_i) = 0$.

Suppose now that rank $(\Pi) = 1$, then $\ln(1 - \lambda_1)$ will be negative and $\ln(1 - \lambda_i) = 0 \; \forall \; i > 1$. If the eigenvalue $i$ is non-zero, then $\ln(1 - \lambda_i) < 0 \; \forall \; i > 1$. That is, for $\Pi$ to have a rank of one, the largest eigenvalue must be significantly non-zero, while others will not be significantly different from zero.

---

[13] Strictly, these are not eigenvalues of the $\Pi$ matrix, but this slight inaccuracy vastly simplifies the exposition.

There are two test statistics for cointegration under the Johansen approach, which are formulated as

$$\lambda_{trace}(r) = -T \sum_{i=r+1}^{g} \ln(1 - \hat{\lambda}_i) \qquad (7.7)$$

and

$$\lambda_{max}(r, r + 1) = -T \ln(1 - \hat{\lambda}_{r+1}) \qquad (7.8)$$

where $r$ is the number of cointegrating vectors under the null hypothesis and $\hat{\lambda}_i$ is the estimated value for the $i$th ordered eigenvalue from the $\Pi$ matrix. Intuitively, the larger is $\hat{\lambda}_i$, the more large and negative will be $\ln(1 - \hat{\lambda}_i)$ and hence the larger will be the test statistic. Each eigenvalue will have associated with it a different cointegrating vector. A significantly non-zero eigenvalue indicates a significant cointegrating vector.

$\lambda_{trace}$ is a joint test where the null is that the number of cointegrating vectors is less than or equal to $r$ against an unspecified or general alternative that there are more than $r$. It starts with $p$ eigenvalues and then successively the largest is removed. $\lambda_{trace} = 0$ when all the $\lambda_i = 0$, for $i = 1, \ldots, g$.

$\lambda_{max}$ conducts separate tests on each eigenvalue and has as its null hypothesis that the number of cointegrating vectors is $r$ against an alternative of $r + 1$.

Johansen and Juselius (1990) provide critical values for the two statistics. The distribution of the test statistics is non-standard and the critical values depend on the value of $g - r$, the number of non-stationary components and whether constants are included in each of the equations. Intercepts can be included either in the cointegrating vectors themselves or as additional terms in the VAR. The latter is equivalent to including a trend in the data-generating processes for the levels of the series. Osterwald-Lenum (1992) provides a fairly complete set of critical values for the Johansen test.

If the test statistic is greater than the critical value, reject the null hypothesis that there are $r$ cointegrating vectors in favour of the alternative that there are $r + 1$ (for $\lambda_{trace}$) or more than $r$ (for $\lambda_{max}$). The testing is conducted in a sequence and under the null, $r = 0, 1, \ldots, g - 1$ so that the hypotheses for $\lambda_{trace}$ are

$$
\begin{array}{lll}
H_0: & r = 0 & \text{vs} \quad H_1: 0 < r \le g \\
H_0: & r = 1 & \text{vs} \quad H_1: 1 < r \le g \\
H_0: & r = 2 & \text{vs} \quad H_1: 2 < r \le g \\
& \quad \vdots & \quad \vdots \quad\quad \vdots \\
H_0: & r = p - 1 & \text{vs} \quad H_1: r = g
\end{array}
$$

The first test involves a null hypothesis of no cointegrating vectors (corresponding to $\Pi$ having zero rank). If this null is not rejected, it would be concluded that there are no cointegrating vectors and the testing would be completed. However, if $H_0$: $r = 0$ is rejected, the null that there is one cointegrating vector (i.e. $H_0$: $r = 1$) would be tested and so on. Thus the value of $r$ is continually increased until the null is no longer rejected.

But how does this correspond to a test of the rank of the $\Pi$ matrix? $r$ is the rank of $\Pi$. $\Pi$ cannot be of full rank ($g$) since this would correspond to the original $y_t$ being stationary. If $\Pi$ has zero rank, then by analogy to the univariate case, $\Delta y_t$ depends only on $\Delta y_{t-j}$ and not on $y_{t-1}$, so that there is no long-run relationship between the elements of $y_{t-1}$. Hence there is no cointegration. For $1 < \text{rank } (\Pi) < g$, there are $r$ cointegrating vectors. $\Pi$ is then defined as the product of two matrices, $\alpha$ and $\beta'$, of dimension ($g \times r$) and ($r \times g$) respectively, i.e.

$$\Pi = \alpha\beta' \tag{7.9}$$

The matrix $\beta$ gives the cointegrating vectors, while $\alpha$ gives the amount of each cointegrating vector entering each equation of the VECM, also known as the 'adjustment parameters'.

For example, suppose that $g = 4$, so that the system contains four variables. The elements of the $\Pi$ matrix would be written

$$\Pi = \begin{pmatrix} \pi_{11} & \pi_{12} & \pi_{13} & \pi_{14} \\ \pi_{21} & \pi_{22} & \pi_{23} & \pi_{24} \\ \pi_{31} & \pi_{32} & \pi_{33} & \pi_{34} \\ \pi_{41} & \pi_{42} & \pi_{43} & \pi_{44} \end{pmatrix} \tag{7.10}$$

If $r = 1$, so that there is one cointegrating vector, then $\alpha$ and $\beta$ will be ($4 \times 1$):

$$\Pi = \alpha\beta' = \begin{pmatrix} \alpha_{11} \\ \alpha_{12} \\ \alpha_{13} \\ \alpha_{14} \end{pmatrix} \begin{pmatrix} \beta_{11} & \beta_{12} & \beta_{13} & \beta_{14} \end{pmatrix}. \tag{7.11}$$

If $r = 2$, so that there are two cointegrating vectors, then $\alpha$ and $\beta$ will be ($4 \times 2$):

$$\Pi = \alpha\beta' = \begin{pmatrix} \alpha_{11} & \alpha_{21} \\ \alpha_{12} & \alpha_{22} \\ \alpha_{13} & \alpha_{23} \\ \alpha_{14} & \alpha_{24} \end{pmatrix} \begin{pmatrix} \beta_{11} & \beta_{12} & \beta_{13} & \beta_{14} \\ \beta_{21} & \beta_{22} & \beta_{23} & \beta_{24} \end{pmatrix} \tag{7.12}$$

and so on for $r = 3, \ldots$.

Suppose now that $g = 4$ and $r = 1$, as in equation (7.11) above, so that there are four variables in the system, $y_1$, $y_2$, $y_3$ and $y_4$, that exhibit one cointegrating vector. Then $\Pi y_{t-k}$ will be given by

$$\Pi = \begin{pmatrix} \alpha_{11} \\ \alpha_{12} \\ \alpha_{13} \\ \alpha_{14} \end{pmatrix} \begin{pmatrix} \beta_{11} & \beta_{12} & \beta_{13} & \beta_{14} \end{pmatrix} \begin{pmatrix} y_1 \\ y_2 \\ y_3 \\ y_4 \end{pmatrix}_{t-k} \tag{7.13}$$

Equation (7.13) can also be written

$$\Pi = \begin{pmatrix} \alpha_{11} \\ \alpha_{12} \\ \alpha_{13} \\ \alpha_{14} \end{pmatrix} \begin{pmatrix} \beta_{11} y_1 & \beta_{12} y_2 & \beta_{13} y_3 & \beta_{14} y_4 \end{pmatrix}_{t-k} \tag{7.14}$$

Given (7.14), it is possible to write out the separate equations for each variable $\Delta y_t$. It is also common to 'normalise' on a particular variable, so that the coefficient on that variable in the cointegrating vector is one. For example, normalising on $y_1$ would make the cointegrating term in the equation for $\Delta y_1$ be $\frac{\alpha_{11}}{\beta_{11}}(y_1 + \frac{\beta_{12}}{\beta_{11}} y_2 + \frac{\beta_{13}}{\beta_{11}} y_3 + \beta_{14} y_4)_{t-k}$, etc. Finally, it must be noted that the above description is not exactly how the Johansen procedure works, but is an intuitive approximation to it.

The application we will examine centres on whether the yields on Treasury bills of different maturities are cointegrated. **Re-open the MACRO.PRG instruction file** that was created in Chapter 3. There are six interest rate series corresponding to maturities of three and six months, and one, three, five, and ten years. Each series has a name in the file starting with the letters 'USTB'. The first step in any cointegration analysis is to ensure that the variables are all non-stationary in their levels forms, so **confirm that this is the case** for each of the six series by running a unit root test on each one.

In RATS, the Johansen test is most easily accomplished using the 'CATS in RATS' add-in software developed by Dennis, Hansen, Johansen and Juselius. This is packaged as a '.SRC' file, which can be called in the usual fashion as a sub-routine. If you have CATS2, the easiest way to run it is to use the Wizard, by clicking Statistics and then CATS Cointegration.[14] Screenshot 7.1 will appear.

Enter the following list of variables in the 'Endogenous Variables' box:

**USTB3M USTB6M USTB1Y USTB3Y USTB5Y USTB10Y**

---

[14] Readers who are particularly interested in running cointegrating applications within a VAR framework using CATS version 2 are advised to consult the book by Juselius (2006).

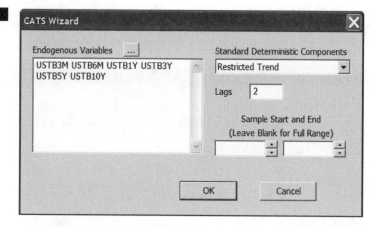

Also choose whether you require any deterministic components in the VAR (these are the options for including either a constant or a trend in the cointegrating vector of the VAR or both), then click **OK**. Note that, for now, the number of lags of each variable to use in the VAR has been set arbitrarily at 2. The code segment that using this Wizard will create is

> **SOURCE 'C:\CATS2\CATS.SRC'**
> **@CATS(LAGS=2,DETTREND=CIMEAN)**
> **# USTB3M USTB6M USTB1Y USTB3Y USTB5Y USTB10Y**

DETTREND=CIMEAN implies that a constant is included in the cointegrating vector, which implies a deterministic trend in the changes of the variables. The LAGS=2 option tells CATS to use two lags in the VAR, while the supplementary cards after the @CATS command give the variables used for the test. The results of such an estimation would be as shown in Box 7.5.

By default, CATS does not present the results of a Johansen test for cointegration. It only produces estimates of the cointegrating combinations of variables (not normalised) in BETA transposed, the amounts of each cointegrating relationship that appear in each equation in the VAR (ALPHA, also known as the adjustment coefficients), and the coefficient matrix on the levels terms of the VAR (i.e. PI or Π).

When you run the code including the @CATS command, you will notice that a whole new set of additional menus is shown at the top of the RATS window, which now appears as in Screenshot 7.2.

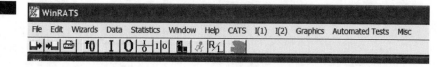

## Box 7.5

```
CATS for RATS version 2 - 12/02/2007 14:26
MODEL SUMMARY
Sample:                    1986:03 to 2006:12 (250 observations)
Effective Sample:          1986:05 to 2006:12 (248 observations)
Obs. - No. of variables:   235
System variables:          USTB3M USTB6M USTB1Y USTB3Y USTB5Y USTB10Y
Constant/Trend:            Restricted Constant
Lags in VAR:               2


I(2) analysis not available for the specified model.


The unrestricted estimates:
```

BETA(transposed)

|         | USTB3M  | USTB6M   | USTB1Y  | USTB3Y   | USTB5Y   | USTB10Y | CONSTANT |
|---------|---------|----------|---------|----------|----------|---------|----------|
| Beta(1) | 10.050  | -11.778  | 1.255   | 1.220    | -1.039   | 0.523   | -0.193   |
| Beta(2) | 3.431   | -11.518  | 12.524  | -15.409  | 18.836   | -7.758  | 0.626    |
| Beta(3) | 5.576   | -9.745   | -0.744  | 15.273   | -13.006  | 2.215   | 2.285    |
| Beta(4) | 2.149   | -9.235   | 11.258  | -1.870   | -7.336   | 5.069   | 0.133    |
| Beta(5) | 0.658   | 1.161    | -2.737  | 4.323    | -3.184   | -0.132  | 0.286    |
| Beta(6) | -0.106  | 0.365    | -0.458  | -0.660   | 2.470    | -2.179  | 3.289    |

ALPHA

|        | Alpha(1)  | Alpha(2)  | Alpha(3) | Alpha(4) | Alpha(5)  | Alpha(6) |
|--------|-----------|-----------|----------|----------|-----------|----------|
| DUSTB3 | -0.082    | -0.021    | 0.022    | 0.025    | -0.007    | 0.006    |
|        | (-6.666)  | (-1.727)  | (1.792)  | (1.993)  | (-0.529)  | (0.472)  |
| DUSTB6 | -0.053    | -0.024    | 0.037    | 0.034    | -0.012    | 0.008    |
|        | (-3.869)  | (-1.745)  | (2.680)  | (2.462)  | (-0.893)  | (0.587)  |
| DUSTB1 | -0.037    | -0.045    | 0.031    | 0.034    | -0.015    | 0.012    |
|        | (-2.313)  | (-2.844)  | (1.962)  | (2.168)  | (-0.924)  | (0.751)  |
| DUSTB3 | -0.008    | -0.048    | 0.012    | 0.057    | -0.009    | 0.017    |
|        | (-0.411)  | (-2.503)  | (0.657)  | (2.992)  | (-0.448)  | (0.895)  |
| DUSTB5 | 0.002     | -0.049    | 0.014    | 0.057    | 0.000     | 0.017    |
|        | (0.115)   | (-2.618)  | (0.760)  | (3.045)  | (0.014)   | (0.890)  |
| DUSTB1 | 0.008     | -0.033    | 0.015    | 0.043    | 0.006     | 0.018    |
|        | (0.471)   | (-1.913)  | (0.893)  | (2.490)  | (0.371)   | (1.059)  |

PI

|        | USTB3M   | USTB6M  | USTB1Y   | USTB3Y  | USTB5Y   | USTB10Y | CONSTANT |
|--------|----------|---------|----------|---------|----------|---------|----------|
| DUSTB3 | -0.727   | 0.764   | -0.094   | 0.487   | -0.747   | 0.283   | 0.073    |
|        | (-4.838) | (2.917) | (-0.447) | (1.777) | (-2.488) | (2.352) | (1.466)  |
| DUSTB6 | -0.346   | 0.219   | 0.016    | 0.742   | -1.059   | 0.393   | 0.106    |
|        | (-2.072) | (0.751) | (0.070)  | (2.438) | (-3.176) | (2.938) | (1.912)  |
| DUSTB1 | -0.286   | 0.317   | -0.212   | 0.987   | -1.388   | 0.548   | 0.089    |
|        | (-1.483) | (0.943) | (-0.782) | (2.806) | (-3.599) | (3.542) | (1.386)  |

| DUSTB3 | -0.057 | -0.011 | 0.041 | 0.760 | -1.399 | 0.645 | 0.061 |
|---|---|---|---|---|---|---|---|
| | (-0.247) | (-0.026) | (0.126) | (1.797) | (-3.016) | (3.466) | (0.793) |
| DUSTB5 | 0.054 | -0.119 | 0.012 | 0.859 | -1.488 | 0.665 | 0.064 |
| | (0.235) | (-0.300) | (0.037) | (2.062) | (-3.259) | (3.631) | (0.838) |
| DUSTB1 | 0.149 | -0.249 | 0.043 | 0.692 | -1.125 | 0.473 | 0.081 |
| | (0.707) | (-0.676) | (0.146) | (1.795) | (-2.663) | (2.792) | (1.148) |

Log-Likelihood = 3733.478

---

**Box 7.6**

```
I(1)-ANALYSIS
p-r   r   Eig.Value    Trace    Trace*    Frac95   P-Value   P-Value*
6     0     0.261     174.202  168.136   103.679    0.000     0.000
5     1     0.130      99.359   94.183    76.813     0.000     0.001
4     2     0.119      64.893   61.692    53.945     0.003     0.008
3     3     0.093      33.603   31.872    35.070     0.072     0.109
2     4     0.030       9.326    8.609    20.164     0.708     0.772
1     5     0.007       1.821    1.682     9.142     0.807     0.831
```

To run the cointegration test, click on the **I(1) menu** and choose **Rank Test Statistics**. The $\lambda_{trace}$ statistics will automatically be calculated and appear as in Box 7.6.

Comparing the trace statistic (174.202) with the corresponding critical value (Frac95 = 103.679), we can see that the null hypothesis of no cointegrating vectors ($r = 0$) is convincingly rejected, as is the null of 1, and of 2 cointegrating vectors, until we reach $r = 3$, where the statistic is slightly lower than the critical value (with $p$-value 0.07) and therefore the null is not rejected and we conclude that there are three linearly independent combinations of these interest rate series that are stationary. Note that the non-rejection at $r = 3$ is a very marginal result and hence it would be possible to argue for a fourth cointegrating vector. CATS also enables the user to test hypotheses about the estimated beta or alpha vectors, to produce a variety of plots and to run a host of diagnostic procedures. Unfortunately, however, there is no on-line help for CATS instructions and so one must resort to the more traditional paper form.

# 8 Modelling volatility and correlation

All of the examples in this chapter will revert to the daily exchange rate data used in Chapter 6. So this material assumes that the file FX.PRG (or the name that you gave the file) has been re-opened and the data re-read into RATS' memory. Recall that there are three exchange rate series – the British pound, the euro and the Japanese yen – all crossed with the US dollar. There are a total of 1,827 observations (although the first of these is 'lost' when we construct the returns), running from 7 July 2002 to 7 July 2007.

## 8.1 Estimating EWMA models

The exponentially weighted moving average (EWMA) model is essentially a simple extension of the historical average volatility measure, which allows more recent observations to have a stronger impact on the forecast of volatility than older data points. Under an EWMA specification, the latest observation carries the largest weight, and weights associated with previous observations decline exponentially over time. The exponentially weighted moving average model can be expressed in several ways, e.g.

$$\sigma_t^2 = (1 - \lambda) \sum_{j=1}^{\infty} \lambda^j (r_{t-j} - \bar{r})^2 \tag{8.1}$$

where $\sigma_t^2$ is the estimate of the variance for period $t$, which also becomes the forecast of future volatility for all periods, $\bar{r}$ is the average return estimated over the observations and $\lambda$ is the 'decay factor', which determines how much weight is given to recent versus older observations. The decay factor could be estimated, but in many studies is set at 0.94 as recommended by RiskMetrics, producers of popular risk-measurement software. Note also that RiskMetrics and many academic papers assume that the average return, $\bar{r}$, is zero. For data that is of daily frequency or higher, this is not an unreasonable assumption and is likely to lead to negligible loss of accuracy since the actual value of $\bar{r}$ will typically be very small.

The following RATS code can be used to compute an exponentially weighted moving average estimate, which then becomes the forecast, for the pound–dollar returns data. There are, unsurprisingly, several methods that could be used to compute the EWMA, but the crucial element in each case is to remember that when the infinite sum in equation (8.1) is replaced with a finite sum of observable data, the weights from the given expression will now sum to less than one.

In the case of small samples, this could make a large difference to the computed EWMA. However, in the present case, there are so many lags that the weights that would have appeared on lags further into the past if the data had been available would have been extremely small. Thus, for large samples, a correction is not necessary. The commands are

```
STATS(NOPRINT) RGBP
SET USQ = (RGBP - %MEAN)**2
ESMOOTH(ALPHA=0.06,SMOOTHED=EWMAS) USQ
PRINT / EWMAS
```

The first stage is to compute the summary statistics of the returns series so that we obtain (without printing) the mean. Then, since a EWMA model for volatility is essentially an exponential smoothing of the squared series, we set up the squared de-meaned returns series and then estimate a EWMA model on that with the desired parameter fixed at 0.06 and with the smoothed series being stored in EWMAS. The final PRINT command will display the entries of the EWMAS series, although only the last entry, which will give the EWMA estimate for all information up to and including observation 1827, is of interest. The estimate obtained is around 0.03, which would also constitute the forecasts for any observations retained as an out-of-sample period. Note that this compares with an unconditional variance for this series of about 0.17, indicating that the series was below its 'typical' level of volatility towards the end of this sample period in July 2007.

## 8.2 Testing for ARCH-effects

A particular non-linear model in widespread usage in finance is known as an 'ARCH' model, which stands for the autoregressive conditionally heteroscedastic formulation due to Engle (1982). An important feature of many series of financial asset returns that provides a motivation for the ARCH class of models is known as 'volatility clustering' or 'volatility pooling'. Volatility clustering describes the tendency of large changes in asset prices (of either sign) to follow large changes and small changes (of either sign) to follow small changes. In other words, the current level of volatility tends to be positively correlated with its level during the immediately preceding periods.

A test for determining whether 'ARCH-effects' are present in the residuals of an estimated model may be conducted using the following steps.

1. Run any postulated linear regression of the form given in the equation above, e.g.

$$y_t = \beta_1 + \beta_2 x_{2t} + \beta_3 x_{3t} + \beta_4 x_{4t} + u_t \tag{8.2}$$

saving the residuals, $\hat{u}_t$.

2. Square the residuals and regress them on $q$ own lags to test for ARCH of order $q$, i.e. run the regression

$$\hat{u}_t^2 = \gamma_0 + \gamma_1 \hat{u}_{t-1}^2 + \gamma_2 \hat{u}_{t-2}^2 + \cdots + \gamma_q \hat{u}_{t-q}^2 + v_t \tag{8.3}$$

where $v_t$ is an error term.

Obtain $R^2$ from this regression.

3. The test statistic is defined as $TR^2$ (the number of observations multiplied by the coefficient of multiple correlation) from the last regression and is distributed as a $\chi^2(q)$.

4. The null and alternative hypotheses are

$H_0 : \gamma_1 = 0$ and $\gamma_2 = 0$ and $\gamma_3 = 0$ and ... and $\gamma_q = 0$
$H_1 : \gamma_1 \neq 0$ or $\gamma_2 \neq 0$ or $\gamma_3 \neq 0$ or ... or $\gamma_q \neq 0$.

Thus, the test is one of a joint null hypothesis that all $q$ lags of the squared residuals have coefficient values that are not significantly different from zero. If the value of the test statistic is greater than the critical value from the $\chi^2$ distribution, then reject the null hypothesis. The test can also be thought of as a test for autocorrelation in the squared residuals. As well as testing the residuals of an estimated model, the ARCH test is frequently applied to raw returns data.

To run the test for ARCH using RATS on the pound–dollar returns, we could use the ARCHTEST procedure, or we could compute the test statistic manually. To do the latter, regress the series on a constant and save the residuals (U)

```
LINREG(NOPRINT) RGBP / U
# CONSTANT
```

Now create a new variable that is the square of the residuals and call it USQ

**Box 8.1**

```
Chi-Squared(5)= 30.412343 with Significance Level 0.00001223
```

**SET USQ = U**2**

Now regress USQ on a constant and five lags

**LINREG(NOPRINT) USQ**
**# CONSTANT USQ{1 TO 5}**

The next step is to compute $TR^2$ and its level of significance. Following regression estimation, RATS will define a number of quantities relating to the results. Recall that these saved quantities start with '%...'. For example, '%NOBS' is the number of observations being used in the estimation procedure and '%RSQUARED' is the $R^2$. The following lines construct the test statistic and calculate the significance level of $TR^2$:

**COMPUTE CHISTAT = %NOBS\*%RSQUARED**
**CDF CHISQ CHISTAT 5**

The result for the Engle test calculated on the RGBP file using these instructions is shown in Box 8.1.

The test statistic is highly significant, suggesting that the pound–dollar returns show evidence of ARCH-effects.

## 8.3  GARCH model estimation

The GARCH model was developed independently by Bollerslev (1986) and Taylor (1986). The GARCH model allows the conditional variance to be dependent upon its own lags, so that the conditional variance equation in the simplest case is now

$$\sigma_t^2 = \alpha_0 + \alpha_1 u_{t-1}^2 + \beta \sigma_{t-1}^2 \tag{8.4}$$

This is a GARCH(1,1) model. $\sigma_t^2$ is known as the conditional variance since it is a one-period ahead estimate for the variance calculated based on any past information thought relevant. Using the GARCH model it is possible to interpret the current fitted variance, $\sigma_t^2$, as a weighted function of a long-term average value (dependent on $\alpha_0$), information about volatility during the previous period ($\alpha_1 u_{t-1}^2$), and the fitted variance from the model during the previous period ($\beta \sigma_{t-1}^2$). This model can be extended to a GARCH($p,q$), where there are $p$ lags of the conditional variance and $q$ lags of the squared error, in the obvious way.

Since the model is no longer of the usual linear form, OLS cannot be used for GARCH model estimation. There is a variety of reasons for this, but the simplest and most fundamental is that OLS minimises the residual sum of squares. The *RSS* depends only on the parameters in the conditional mean equation, not the conditional variance, and hence RSS minimisation is no longer an appropriate objective. In order to estimate models from the GARCH family, another technique known as maximum likelihood is employed. Essentially, the method works by finding the most likely values of the parameters given the actual data. More specifically, a log-likelihood function is formed and the values of the parameters that maximise it are sought. Maximum likelihood estimation can be employed to find parameter values for both linear and non-linear models.

The steps involved in actually estimating an ARCH or GARCH model are as follows.

1. Specify the appropriate equations for the mean and the variance – e.g. an AR(1)-GARCH(1,1) model

$$y_t = \mu + \phi y_{t-1} + u_t, u_t \sim N\left(0, \sigma_t^2\right) \tag{8.5}$$
$$\sigma_t^2 = \alpha_0 + \alpha_1 u_{t-1}^2 + \beta \sigma_{t-1}^2 \tag{8.6}$$

2. Specify the log-likelihood function (*LLF*) to maximise under a normality assumption for the disturbances

$$L = -\frac{T}{2}\log(2\pi) - \frac{1}{2}\sum_{t=1}^{T}\log\left(\sigma_t^2\right) - \frac{1}{2}\sum_{t=1}^{T}(y_t - \mu - \phi y_{t-1})^2/\sigma_t^2 \tag{8.7}$$

3. The computer will maximise the function and generate parameter values that maximise the *LLF* and will construct their standard errors.

There is now a RATS Wizard that can be used to estimate a variety of GARCH-type models. To estimate a 'plain vanilla' GARCH(1,1) model, click **Statistics**, then **ARCH/GARCH**. The window in Screenshot 8.1 will appear.

By default, RATS will estimate a GARCH model with one lag of the squared error ('Lagged u**2 Terms') and one lag of the conditional variance ('Lagged Variance Terms'), but this number can be increased to estimate any model of order $(p,q)$. You specify the dependent variable (**RJPY** say) and then click **OK**. The code that this will create is the compact

    GARCH(P=1,Q=1) / RJPY

and the output will be as in Box 8.2.

**Screenshot 8.1**

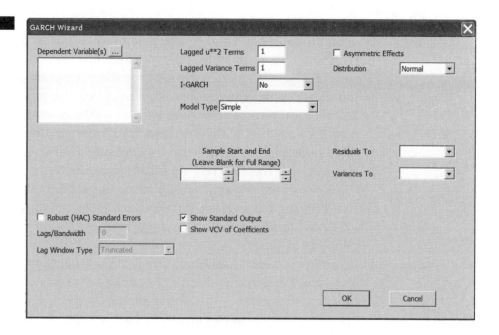

**Box 8.2**

```
GARCH Model - Estimation by BFGS
NO CONVERGENCE IN 18 ITERATIONS
LAST CRITERION WAS 0.0000031
ESTIMATION POSSIBLY HAS STALLED OR MACHINE ROUNDOFF IS MAKING FURTHER PROGRESS
DIFFICULT.
TRY HIGHER SUBITERATIONS LIMIT, TIGHTER CVCRIT, DIFFERENT SETTING FOR EXACTLINE
OR ALPHA ON NLPAR.
RESTARTING ESTIMATION FROM LAST ESTIMATES OR DIFFERENT INITIAL GUESSES MIGHT
ALSO WORK
Daily(7) Data From 2002:07:08 To 2007:07:07
Usable Observations   1826
Log Likelihood                    -1074.91271850


     Variable              Coeff        Std Error      T-Stat        Signif
***********************************************************************************
1.   Mean               0.0016240542  0.0104922725    0.15479     0.87699023
2.   C                  0.0743918245  0.0073774130   10.08373     0.00000000
3.   A                  0.0879770177  0.0239330914    3.67596     0.00023696
4.   B                  0.5337287200  0.0627984118    8.49908     0.00000000
```

In this particular case, the estimation routine has failed to converge upon an optimum[15] and so the parameter estimates and their standard errors may be unreliable. Unfortunately, this is a common occurrence with relatively complex non-linear models such as this one where the estimation requires the use of a non-linear iterative procedure rather than an analytical formula as would be used in the case of, for example, ordinary least squares. If this happens, fixing the problem is more of an art than a science, but would involve choosing a different opimisation routine, running the SIMPLEX algorithm to obtain better starting values for the final estimation approach, choosing initial guesses for the parameters, changing the convergence criterion, etc.

The optimisation methods employed by RATS are based on the determination of the first and second derivatives of the log-likelihood function with respect to the parameter values at each iteration, known as the gradient and Hessian (the matrix of second derivatives of the log-likelihood function with respect to the parameters) respectively. An algorithm for optimisation due to Berndt, Hall, Hall and Hausman (1974), known as BHHH, is available in RATS. BHHH employs only first derivatives (calculated numerically rather than analytically) and approximations to the second derivatives. Not calculating the actual Hessian at each iteration at each time step increases computational speed, but the approximation may be poor when the log-likelihood function (LLF) is a long way from its maximum value, requiring more iterations to reach the optimum. However, another optimisation method is available (and is used by default if the user does not specify otherwise), due to Broyden, Fletcher, Goldfarb, Shanno, known as BFGS (see Broyden 1965, 1967; Fletcher and Powell, 1963). BFGS calculates the gradient in the same way as described above for BHHH, but it differs in its construction of the Hessian matrix of second derivatives. The two methods are asymptotically equivalent, but they may lead to quite different estimates of the standard errors for small samples. All of these optimisation methods are described in detail in Press *et al.* (1992). So arguably the simplest trick to try to get convergent optimisation is to use the METHOD=BHHH option instead of the BFGS default, so the command is

    GARCH(P=1,Q=1, METHOD=BHHH) / RJPY

The output is shown in Box 8.3.

---

[15] However, this problem no longer arises and convergence is achieved in RATS version 7.10.

```
           Box 8.3

GARCH Model - Estimation by BHHH
Convergence in 16 Iterations. Final criterion was 0.0000065 <= 0.0000100
Daily(7) Data From 2002:07:08 To 2007:07:07
Usable Observations   1826
Log Likelihood                     -1039.27742054


     Variable              Coeff      Std Error      T-Stat      Signif
**********************************************************************************
1.  Mean               0.0055649900  0.0092875486     0.59919   0.54904736
2.  C                  0.0012552361  0.0005457840     2.29988   0.02145520
3.  A                  0.0294564864  0.0042235837     6.97429   0.00000000
4.  B                  0.9640150834  0.0058120416   165.86514   0.00000000
```

Note that convergence has now occurred and the results are more plausible than previously. The coefficients on both the lagged squared residual and lagged conditional variance terms in the conditional variance equation are highly statistically significant. Also, as is typical of GARCH model estimates for financial asset returns data, the sum of the coefficients on the lagged squared error and lagged conditional variance is very close to unity (approximately 0.99). This implies that shocks to the conditional variance will be highly persistent, as can be seen by considering the equations for forecasting future values of the conditional variance using a GARCH model given in a subsequent section. A large sum of these coefficients will imply that a large positive or a large negative return will lead future forecasts of the variance to be high for a protracted period. 'Mean' is the estimate of the intercept parameter in the conditional mean equation, which is very small as we would expect for the average daily percentage change. The individual conditional variance coefficients are also as one would expect. The variance intercept term 'C' is very small, and the lagged squared error parameter ('A') is around 0.03, while the coefficient on the lagged conditional variance ('B') is larger at 0.96. All three of the conditional variance parameters are highly statistically significant.

### GARCH model options

It is possible to estimate heteroscedasticity consistent standard errors (by checking the 'Robust (HAC) Standard Errors' box) or heteroscedasticity and autocorrelation consistent (HAC) standard errors and then choosing a non-zero number of lags. Also, by default, RATS will estimate a symmetric model, where positive or negative shocks will have the same impact on the next-period conditional variance. But by checking the 'Asymmetric Effects' box, a GJR-type model can be estimated. It is also possible to choose an alternative distributional assumption – either the Student's $t$ or Generalised Exponential Distribution (GED) rather than the Normal distribution (default). Finally, under 'Model Type', you can choose an exponential GARCH (EGARCH)-type model either with or without the asymmetric terms.

We will examine a number of these other models below, but for now, let us consider the difference when a GARCH model with Student's $t$ distributed errors is employed. In such a case, the model should be better able to capture the fat tails of the distributions that often characterise financial time-series. While GARCH models with Gaussian (normally distributed) innovations can generate series which are unconditionally leptokurtic, these fitted distributions are often not sufficiently fat tailed to describe the actual distributions of asset price returns, which motivates the use of the $t$-distribution that can account for fat tails via the degrees of freedom parameter. The required command simply adds the DISTRIB=T option:

    GARCH(P=1,Q=1, DISTRIB=T) / RJPY

If we estimate this model, one of the resulting parameters is negative, which would therefore represent an inadmissible model. To fix this we could try one of the range of suggestions listed above.

*Specifying and estimating GARCH models – The old-fashioned brute-force way*

Being able to set up and run a GARCH model in just one line of code is a much easier way to do things than specifying the model, the log likelihood, the estimation routine and the sample in detail and writing the code manually. But this is exactly what was required in versions of RATS before 6.0. The range of GARCH models that can be estimated using the GARCH instruction is wide, but there may be situations where additional flexibility is required and where the user will need to be able to work with the detailed code. Since such situations are now likely to be uncommon, interested readers are directed towards Section 12.1.8 in the RATS 7.0 *User Guide* and no annotated code is presented here.

## 8.4  Estimating GJR and EGARCH models

One of the primary restrictions of GARCH models is that they enforce a symmetric response of volatility to positive and negative shocks. This arises since the conditional variance in equations such as (8.4) is a function of the magnitudes of the lagged residuals and not their signs (in other words, by squaring the lagged error in (8.4), the sign is lost). However, it has been argued that a negative shock to financial time-series is likely to cause volatility to rise by more than a positive shock of the same magnitude. In the case of equity returns, such asymmetries are typically attributed to leverage effects, whereby a fall in the value of a firm's stock causes the firm's debt-to-equity ratio to rise. This leads shareholders, who bear the residual risk of the firm, to perceive their future cashflow stream as being relatively more risky.

An alternative view is provided by the 'volatility-feedback' hypothesis. Assuming constant dividends, if expected returns increase when stock price volatility increases, then stock prices should fall when volatility rises. Although asymmetries in returns series other than equities cannot be attributed to changing leverage, there is equally no reason to suppose that such asymmetries exist only in equity returns.

Two popular asymmetric formulations are explained below: the GJR model, named after the authors Glosten, Jagannathan and Runkle (1993), and the exponential GARCH (EGARCH) model proposed by Nelson (1991).

The GJR model is a simple extension of GARCH with an additional term added to account for possible asymmetries. The conditional variance is now given by

$$\sigma_t^2 = \alpha_0 + \alpha_1 u_{t-1}^2 + \beta \sigma_{t-1}^2 + \gamma u_{t-1}^2 I_{t-1} \tag{8.8}$$

where $I_{t-1} = 1$ if $u_{t-1} < 0$

$\quad\quad\quad = 0$ otherwise

For a leverage effect, we would see $\gamma > 0$.

There are various ways to express the conditional variance equation for the EGARCH model, but one possible specification is given by

$$\log\left(\sigma_t^2\right) = \omega + \beta \log\left(\sigma_{t-1}^2\right) + \gamma \frac{u_{t-1}}{\sqrt{\sigma_{t-1}^2}} + \alpha \left[ \frac{|u_{t-1}|}{\sqrt{\sigma_{t-1}^2}} - \sqrt{\frac{2}{\pi}} \right] \tag{8.9}$$

The model has several advantages over the pure GARCH specification. First, since $\log(\sigma_t^2)$ is modelled, then even if the parameters are negative, $\sigma_t^2$ will be positive. There is thus no need to artificially impose non-negativity constraints on the model parameters. Second, asymmetries are allowed for under the EGARCH formulation, since if the relationship between volatility and returns is negative, $\gamma$ will be negative. Note that given the way that Nelson specified the model, this implies that for a leverage effect, the sign on gamma will be the opposite of that in the GJR model.[16]

Note also that in the original formulation, Nelson assumed a Generalised Exponential Distribution structure for the errors. GED is a very broad family of distributions that can be used for many types of series. However, due to its computational ease and intuitive interpretation, almost all applications of EGARCH employ conditionally normal errors as discussed previously rather than using GED.

As stated above, these asymmetric models can be estimated easily in RATS by clicking the appropriate button in the GARCH Wizard or by adding the appropriate option in parentheses to the GARCH instruction. The relevant commands to estimate a GJR and an (asymmetric) EGARCH model would be respectively

> **GARCH(P=1,Q=1, METHOD=BHHH, ASYMMETRIC) / RJPY**
> **GARCH(P=1,Q=1, METHOD=BHHH, EXPONENTIAL, ASYMMETRIC) / RJPY**

Since the BHHH algorithm worked well for this series, let us stick with it for these more general models. Note that for the EGARCH model, the default is to estimate a symmetric model with an exponential formulation, so to allow for asymmetries, the ASYMMETRC option would also need to be used here. The output would be as in Box 8.4.

For both specifications, the asymmetry terms (which RATS has labelled D) are not statistically significant (although it is almost significant in the case of the EGARCH model). Also in both cases, the coefficient estimates are negative, suggesting that positive shocks imply a higher next-period conditional variance than negative shocks of the same sign. This is the opposite to what would have been expected in the case of the application of a GARCH model to a set of stock returns. But arguably neither the *leverage effect* nor the *volatility feedback* explanations for asymmetries in the context of stocks applies here since we are modelling exchange rate returns. For a positive return shock, this implies more yen per dollar and therefore a strengthening dollar and a weakening yen. Thus the results suggest that a strengthening dollar (weakening yen) leads to higher next-period volatility than when the yen strengthens by the same amount.

The negative parameter estimates C and D in the context of an EGARCH model present no problems because of the exponential formulation of

---

[16] RATS does not include the mean correction on the absolute value of the exponential, so this becomes incorporated into the intercept in the conditional variance equation.

```
┌──────────────────────────────────────────────────────────────────────────┐
│   Box 8.4                                                                  │
├──────────────────────────────────────────────────────────────────────────┤

GARCH Model - Estimation by BHHH
Convergence in 15 Iterations. Final criterion was 0.0000081 <= 0.0000100
Daily(7) Data From 2002:07:08 To 2007:07:07
Usable Observations   1826
Log Likelihood              -1039.27594682


        Variable            Coeff       Std Error     T-Stat      Signif
**************************************************************************************

1.  Mean                 0.005634523  0.009574762    0.58848   0.55621247
2.  C                    0.001262758  0.000560605    2.25249   0.02429117
3.  A                    0.029745260  0.005493998    5.41414   0.00000006
4.  B                    0.963941961  0.005913903  162.99590   0.00000000
5.  D                   -0.000493282  0.006202172   -0.07953   0.93660811


E-GARCH Model - Estimation by BHHH
Convergence in 34 Iterations. Final criterion was 0.0000085 <= 0.0000100
Daily(7) Data From 2002:07:08 To 2007:07:07
Usable Observations   1826
Log Likelihood              -1075.47705439


        Variable            Coeff       Std Error     T-Stat      Signif
**************************************************************************************

1.  Mean                 0.003670899  0.010022379    0.36627   0.71416344
2.  C                   -1.356016988  0.205306374   -6.60485   0.00000000
3.  A                    0.217916530  0.035211270    6.18883   0.00000000
4.  B                    0.274286673  0.119419117    2.29684   0.02162787
5.  D                   -0.046279728  0.025172351   -1.83851   0.06598665
└──────────────────────────────────────────────────────────────────────────┘
```

the variance equation, which implies that even when the parameters are negative, the conditional variance is guaranteed to remain positive. However, is the negative value for the parameter D in the GJR model a potential issue? The answer is in fact no. While we would have cause for concern if A, B or C were negative, the non-negativity condition is slightly weaker for D because D is also a parameter on the lagged squared error (as is A). When the lagged error is positive, the parameter on the lagged squared error will be A, while when the lagged error is negative, the parameter on the lagged squared error will be (A + D) combined. The non-negativity condition for D is that $A + D/2 \geq 0$, under the assumption that $E(I_t) = 0.5$, or that the disturbances are negative half of the time. Clearly, for this GJR model, the condition is satisfied and hence the model is admissible.

## 8.5  Tests for sign and size bias

Engle and Ng (1993) have proposed a set of tests for asymmetry in volatility, known as sign and size bias tests. The Engle and Ng tests should thus be used to determine whether an asymmetric model is required for a given series, or whether the symmetric GARCH model can be deemed adequate. In practice, the Engle–Ng tests are usually applied to the residuals of a GARCH fit to the returns data. Define $S_{t-1}^-$ as an indicator dummy that takes the value one if $\hat{u}_{t-1} < 0$ and zero otherwise. The test for sign bias is based on the significance or otherwise of $\phi_1$ in

$$\hat{u}_t^2 = \phi_0 + \phi_1 S_{t-1}^- + v_t \tag{8.10}$$

where $v_t$ is an IID error term. If positive and negative shocks to $\hat{u}_{t-1}$ impact differently upon the conditional variance, then $\phi_1$ will be statistically significant.

It could also be the case that the magnitude or size of the shock will affect whether the response of volatility to shocks is symmetric or not. In this case, a negative size bias test would be conducted, based on a regression where $S_{t-1}^-$ is now used as a slope dummy variable. Negative size bias is argued to be present if $\phi_1$ is statistically significant in the regression

$$\hat{u}_t^2 = \phi_0 + \phi_1 S_{t-1}^- u_{t-1} + v_t \tag{8.11}$$

Finally, defining $S_{t-1}^+ = 1 - S_{t-1}^-$, so that $S_{t-1}^+$ picks out the observations with positive innovations, Engle and Ng propose a joint test for sign and size bias based on the regression

$$\hat{u}_t^2 = \phi_0 + \phi_1 S_{t-1}^- + \phi_2 S_{t-1}^- u_{t-1} + \phi_3 S_{t-1}^+ u_{t-1} + v_t \tag{8.12}$$

Significance of $\phi_1$ indicates the presence of sign bias, where positive and negative shocks have differing impacts upon future volatility, compared with the symmetric response required by the standard GARCH formulation. However, the significance of $\phi_2$ or $\phi_3$ would suggest the presence of size bias, where not only the sign but the magnitude of the shock is important. A joint test statistic is formulated in the standard fashion by calculating $TR^2$ from regression (8.12), which will asymptotically follow a $\chi^2$ distribution with 3 degrees of freedom under the null hypothesis of no asymmetric effects.

The Engle–Ng test for asymmetry in volatility can be computed in RATS using the following commands, which would enter the program immediately after the GARCH instruction, but we need an additional option in that instruction to save the conditional variance series (call it H) and the residuals (call them U):

```
GARCH(P=1,Q=1, METHOD=BHHH, HSERIES=H,RESIDS=U) / RJPY
SET U1 = U(T)/SQRT(H(T))
SET U2 = (U(T)*U(T))/H(T)
SET SMINUS = U1<0.0
SET SPLUS = 1 - SMINUS
SET USMINUS = U1*SMINUS
SET USPLUS = U1*SPLUS
LINREG U2
# CONSTANT SMINUS{1}
LINREG U2
# CONSTANT USMINUS{1}
LINREG U2
# CONSTANT USPLUS{1}
LINREG U2
# CONSTANT SMINUS{1} USMINUS{1} USPLUS{1}
COMPUTE CHISTAT = %NOBS*%RSQUARED
CDF CHISQ CHISTAT 3
```

No annotation is offered for these instructions since they do not involve anything new or complex. The output from these commands would appear as in Box 8.5.

---

**Box 8.5**

```
Linear Regression - Estimation by Least Squares
Dependent Variable U2
Daily(7) Data From 2002:07:09 To 2007:07:07
Usable Observations   1825        Degrees of Freedom   1823
Centered R**2      0.000584       R Bar **2      0.000035
Uncentered R**2    0.187058       T x R**2       341.382
Mean of Dependent Variable        1.0079068585
Std Error of Dependent Variable   2.1050334150
Standard Error of Estimate        2.1049962433
Sum of Squared Residuals          8077.7297432
Regression F(1,1823)                    1.0644
Significance Level of F             0.30234614
Log Likelihood                    -3946.93475
Durbin-Watson Statistic              1.931716


     Variable           Coeff        Std Error       T-Stat     Signif
************************************************************************
1.   Constant        0.9551683919  0.0709997611    13.45312   0.00000000
2.   SMINUS{1}       0.1017417564  0.0986149488     1.03171   0.30234614
```

```
Linear Regression - Estimation by Least Squares
Dependent Variable U2
Daily(7) Data From 2002:07:09 To 2007:07:07
Usable Observations    1825          Degrees of Freedom   1823
Centered R**2       0.003510         R Bar **2      0.0.002963
Uncentered R**2     0.189439         T x R**2             345.726
Mean of Dependent Variable          1.0079068585
Std Error of Dependent Variable     2.1050334150
Standard Error of Estimate          2.1019121130
Sum of Squared Residuals            8054.0769493
Regression F(1,1823)                      6.4212
Significance Level of F                0.01135947
Log Likelihood                      -3944.25889
Durbin-Watson Statistic                1.999066


      Variable              Coeff     Std Error      T-Stat     Signif
************************************************************************
1.    Constant          0.937625960  0.056480707    16.60082   0.00000000
2.    USMINUS{1}       -0.197190500  0.077817385    -2.53402   0.01135947


Linear Regression - Estimation by Least Squares
Dependent Variable U2
Daily(7) Data From 2002:07:09 To 2007:07:07
Usable Observations    1825          Degrees of Freedom   1823
Centered R**2       0.000104         R Bar **2     -0.000445
Uncentered R**2     0.186668         T x R**2             340.669
Mean of Dependent Variable          1.0079068585
Std Error of Dependent Variable     2.1050334150
Standard Error of Estimate          2.1055017118
Sum of Squared Residuals            8081.6095866
Regression F(1,1823)                      0.1887
Significance Level of F                0.66403759
Log Likelihood                      -3947.37293
Durbin-Watson Statistic                1.921184


      Variable              Coeff     Std Error      T-Stat     Signif
************************************************************************
1.    Constant          1.020274354  0.056917601    17.92546   0.00000000
2.    USPLUS{1}        -0.035678330  0.082129359    -0.43442   0.66403759


Linear Regression - Estimation by Least Squares
Dependent Variable U2
Daily(7) Data From 2002:07:09 To 2007:07:07
Usable Observations    1825       Degrees of Freedom   1821
Centered R**2       0.003630      R Bar **2      0.001989
Uncentered R**2     0.189537      T x R**2             345.905
```

```
Mean of Dependent Variable        1.0079068585
Std Error of Dependent Variable   2.1050334150
Standard Error of Estimate        2.1029389130
Sum of Squared Residuals          8053.1031230
Regression F(3,1821)                    2.2117
Significance Level of F              0.08486357
Log Likelihood                     -3944.14855
Durbin-Watson Statistic               2.012001


     Variable                Coeff      Std Error      T-Stat       Signif
*******************************************************************************
1.   Constant            0.938228473   0.102319092    9.16963    0.00000000
2.   SMINUS{1}          -0.031080438   0.138600776   -0.22424    0.82259235
3.   USMINUS{1}         -0.217810551   0.092740763   -2.34860    0.01895077
4.   USPLUS{1}           0.023537486   0.102464051    0.22971    0.81833936

Chi-Squared(3)= 6.625607 with Significance Level 0.08483835
```

The individual regression results show that the residuals of the symmetric GARCH model do not suffer from sign bias and/or positive size bias, but they do exhibit negative size bias. In addition, the $\chi^2(3)$ joint test statistic has a $p$-value of 0.08, demonstrating a very marginal rejection of the null of no asymmetries. The results overall would thus suggest only limited motivation for estimating an asymmetric volatility model for this particular series.

## 8.6 The GARCH(1,1)-M model

Most models used in finance suppose that investors should be rewarded for taking additional risk by obtaining a higher expected return. One way to operationalise this concept is to let the return of a security be partly determined by its risk. Engle, Lilien and Robins (1987) suggested an ARCH-M specification, where the conditional variance of asset returns enters into the conditional mean equation. Since GARCH models are now considerably more popular than ARCH, it is more common to estimate a GARCH-M model. An example of a GARCH-M model is given by the specification

$$y_t = \mu + \delta\sigma_t + u_t, \quad u_t \sim \mathrm{N}(0, \sigma_t^2) \tag{8.13}$$
$$\sigma_t^2 = \alpha_0 + \alpha_1 u_{t-1}^2 + \beta\sigma_{t-1}^2 \tag{8.14}$$

If $\delta$ is positive and statistically significant, then increased risk, given by an increase in the conditional standard deviation, leads to a rise in the mean return. Thus $\delta$ can be interpreted as a risk premium. In some

```
    Box 8.6

GARCH Model - Estimation by BHHH
Convergence in 18 Iterations. Final criterion was 0.0000081 <= 0.0000100
Daily(7) Data From 2002:07:08 To 2007:07:07
Usable Observations   1826
Log Likelihood              -1039.16718372


      Variable              Coeff      Std Error      T-Stat      Signif
************************************************************************
1.   Constant          0.016966744   0.027483824      0.61734   0.53701337
2.   GARCH-V          -0.067488378   0.151385476     -0.44580   0.65573823
3.   C                 0.001285256   0.000549853      2.33745   0.01941573
4.   A                 0.029857891   0.004260469      7.00812   0.00000000
5.   B                 0.963472200   0.005859910    164.41757   0.00000000
```

empirical applications, the conditional variance term, $\sigma_t^2$, appears directly in the conditional mean equation (and this is what will be produced by default using the RATS command below) rather than in square root form, $\sigma_t$. Also, in some applications the term is lagged, $\sigma_{t-1}^2$ rather than contemporaneous.

Estimating a GARCH-in-mean model again requires only a simple modification to the GARCH instruction. First, we need to add the option REGRESSORS to the list in parentheses and this tells RATS to expect one or more variables will be added to the mean. These variables are then added as supplementary cards following the # symbol in the usual way:

**GARCH(P=1,Q=1, METHOD=BHHH, REGRESSORS) / RJPY**
**# CONSTANT %GARCHV**

In this case, the estimated parameter on the mean equation has a negative sign but is not statistically significant (see Box 8.6). If we were estimating a model for stock return volatilities, the variance in mean term could be interpreted as a kind of risk premium; but for currency returns, we would have to rationalise any feedback we found from the conditional variance to the conditional mean in a different way. Here, however, we would conclude that there is no feedback.

Note that we could add any exogenous variable we wished to the conditional mean equation simply by including it on this list, or we could use the lagged conditional variance rather than the current value. We could also specify a model that includes exogenous variables in the conditional variance equation as well as or instead of the mean. So, suppose that we wished to estimate a model that contains only an intercept in the conditional mean but a January dummy variable that we had created in the conditional variance. We would use the XREG option in parentheses:

**GARCH(P=1,Q=1, METHOD=BHHH, XREG) / RJPY**
**# JANUARY**

Note that we do not require the REGRESSORS option because RATS will include an intercept in the conditional mean by default, and of course we do not need to specify any of the GARCH variables or the conditional variance intercept in this list.

## 8.7 Forecasting from GARCH models

GARCH-type models can be used to forecast volatility. GARCH is a model to describe movements in the conditional variance of an error term, $u_t$, which may not appear particularly useful. But it is possible to show that

$$\text{Var}(y_t \mid y_{t-1}, y_{t-2}, \ldots) = \text{Var}(u_t \mid u_{t-1}, u_{t-2}, \ldots) \qquad (8.15)$$

So the conditional variance of $y$, given its previous values, is the same as the conditional variance of $u$, given its previous values. Hence, modelling $\sigma_t^2$ will give models and forecasts for the variance of $y_t$ as well. Thus, if the dependent variable in a regression, $y_t$, is an asset return series, forecasts of $\sigma_t^2$ will be forecasts of the future variance of $y_t$. So one primary usage of GARCH-type models is in forecasting volatility. Producing forecasts from models of the GARCH class is relatively simple and the algebra involved is very similar to that required to obtain forecasts from ARMA models. $s$-step ahead forecasts would be produced by

$$h_{s,T}^f = \alpha_0 \sum_{i=1}^{s-1} (\alpha_1 + \beta)^{i-1} + (\alpha_1 + \beta)^{s-1} h_{1,T}^f \qquad (8.16)$$

for any value of $s \geq 2$.

Forecasts from GARCH models using RATS can be produced in the following way. We first estimate the desired model (which can be any from the ARCH or GARCH family, but not EGARCH). Then, either the GARCHFORE procedure is used, or several additional lines are required after the GARCH instruction. For example, in the context of a standard GARCH(1,1) model, using the procedure would involve writing

**GARCH(P=1,Q=1,METHOD=BHHH,HSERIES=H,RESIDS=U) $**
**2002:07:09 2006:07:07 RJPY**
**SOURCE GARCHFORE.SRC**
**@GARCHFORE(STEPS=365) H U**

To compute the forecasts manually, the required code would be

```
GARCH(P=1,Q=1,METHOD=BHHH,HSERIES=H,RESIDS=U) 2002:07:09 $
   2006:07:07 RJPY
SET UU = U**2
COM VC=%BETA(2), VB=%BETA(4), VA=%BETA(3)
FRML HEQ H = VC + VB*H{1} + VA*UU{1}
FRML UEQ UU = H
GROUP GARCHMOD HEQ>>H UEQ>>UU
FORECAST(MODEL=GARCHMOD, FROM=2006:07:08, TO=2007:07:07)
PRINT 2006:07:08 2007:07:07 H
```

While these commands are essentially redundant given the availability of the pre-written GARCHFORE procedure, the general principles may be applied when forecasting from any system of equations and hence the code is now discussed. The first line estimates the GARCH(1,1) model over the period 9 July 2002 to 7 July 2006, which allows a year of hold-out data for out-of-sample forecasting. The second line constructs a series of squared residuals from the residuals to use in the recursive formulae for calculating the forecasts. The third line copies the parameters out of the %BETA vector so that they can be used easily in the formula. Line 4 sets up a formula for the conditional variance equation and calls it HEQ, while line 5 sets up a formula for computing the out-of-sample squared innovations. Given these two equations (and the order is important for some models), RATS can recursively compute the forecasts. The GROUP line will construct a group of equations, called GARCHMOD, which are linked together. The results of the HEQ formula are placed in the H series by the HEQ>>H part, and so on. Finally, the FORECAST command actually computes the multi-step ahead forecasts for the GARCHMOD group of equations for the last year in the sample as specified, and the PRINT command will print them out. The conditional variance predictions are as in Box 8.7 (for the first and last few entries only rather than all 365 of them!).

We can see that very quickly these multi-step ahead forecasts converge upon the long-term unconditional volatility of the currency returns.

Suppose now that we were interested in estimating a set of rolling one-step ahead forecasts rather than a set of multi-step ahead forecasts. We would do that by nesting the entire set of instructions inside a loop that indexed over the observations, adding one each time to the in-sample estimation period and then producing a single out-of-sample, one-step ahead forecast each time:

```
DO J=1,365
   GARCH(P=1,Q=1, METHOD=BHHH, HSERIES=H2,RESIDS=U2,NOPRINT) $
   2002:07:09 2006:07:06+J RJPY
```

---

**Box 8.7**

```
ENTRY              H
2006:07:08   0.208104700806
2006:07:09   0.215838129955
2006:07:10   0.218270285339
2006:07:11   0.219035195665
2006:07:12   0.219275759163
      :            :
2007:07:04   0.219386126564
2007:07:05   0.219386126564
2007:07:06   0.219386126564
2007:07:07   0.219386126564
```

---

**Box 8.8**

```
ENTRY              H2
2006:07:08   0.171312414094
2006:07:09   0.177977617752
2006:07:10   0.182789880392
2006:07:11   0.177451088918
2006:07:12   0.173030928349
      :            :
2007:07:04   0.079287120841
2007:07:05   0.080470665642
2007:07:06   0.078949626681
2007:07:07   0.078293320547
```

```
     SET UU2 = U2**2
     COM VC=%BETA(2), VB=%BETA(4), VA=%BETA(3)
     FRML HEQ H2 = VC + VB*H2{1} + VA*UU2{1}
     FRML UEQ UU2 = H2
     GROUP GARCHMOD2 HEQ>>H2 UEQ>>UU2
     FORECAST(MODEL=GARCHMOD2, FROM=2006:07:07+J, TO=2006:07:07+J)
     END DO J
PRINT 2006:07:08 2007:07:07 H2
```

The resulting series of forecasts, H2, is then printed at the end (Box 8.8).

These forecasts obviously do not converge upon a long-term mean since they are only produced for one-step ahead each time. It is worth noting as well that in this instance, the parameters will have been estimated every time that a forecast is made using information up to and including that observation. An alternative strategy, which would have been computationally quicker, would have been to estimate the model only once (for the first in-sample period) and then to assume that the parameter values were constant. As the one-step ahead forecasts are rolled through the sample, this would have become increasingly inappropriate. For the last forecast, the parameters would have been based on information up to observation 7 July 2006, but observations through to 6 July 2007 are now available. So it is clearly preferable to re-estimate the parameters at every time-step as we did. The importance of this will depend on how stable the parameter estimates are over time and on the length of the out-of-sample period.

## 8.8  Multivariate GARCH models

Multivariate GARCH models are in spirit very similar to their univariate counterparts, except that the former also specify equations for how the covariances move over time. Several different multivariate GARCH formulations have been proposed in the literature, including the *VECH*, the diagonal *VECH* and the *BEKK* models. Each of these is discussed in turn below; for a more detailed discussion, see Kroner and Ng (1998). In each case, it is assumed for simplicity here that there are two assets whose return variances and covariances are to be modelled.

A common specification of the *VECH* model, initially due to Bollerslev, Engle and Wooldridge (1988), is

$$VECH(H_t) = C + A\,VECH(\Xi_{t-1}\Xi'_{t-1}) + B\,VECH(H_{t-1}) \tag{8.17}$$
$$\Xi_t \,|\psi_{t-1} \sim N(0, H_t),$$

where $H_t$ is a $2 \times 2$ conditional variance-covariance matrix, $\Xi_t$ is a $2 \times 1$ innovation (disturbance) vector, $\psi_{t-1}$ represents the information set at time $t-1$, $C$ is a $3 \times 1$ parameter vector, $A$ and $B$ are $3 \times 3$ parameter matrices and $VECH(\cdot)$ denotes the column-stacking operator applied to the upper portion of the symmetric matrix. The model requires the estimation of 21 parameters ($C$ has three elements, $A$ and $B$ each have nine elements). In order to gain a better understanding of how the *VECH* model works, the elements are written out below. Define

$$H_t = \begin{bmatrix} h_{11t} & h_{12t} \\ h_{21t} & h_{22t} \end{bmatrix}, \quad C = \begin{bmatrix} c_{11} \\ c_{21} \\ c_{31} \end{bmatrix}, \quad A = \begin{bmatrix} a_{11} & a_{12} & a_{13} \\ a_{21} & a_{22} & a_{23} \\ a_{31} & a_{32} & a_{33} \end{bmatrix},$$

$$B = \begin{bmatrix} b_{11} & b_{12} & b_{13} \\ b_{21} & b_{22} & b_{23} \\ b_{31} & b_{32} & b_{33} \end{bmatrix}, \quad \Xi_t = \begin{bmatrix} u_{1t} \\ u_{2t} \end{bmatrix}.$$

The *VECH* operator takes the 'upper triangular' portion of a matrix and stacks each element into a vector with a single column. For example, in the case of $VECH(H_t)$, this becomes

$$VECH(H_t) = \begin{bmatrix} h_{11t} \\ h_{12t} \\ h_{22t} \end{bmatrix}$$

where $h_{iit}$ represent the conditional variances at time $t$ of the two asset return series ($i = 1, 2$) used in the model and $h_{ijt}(i \neq j)$ represent the conditional covariances between the asset returns. In the case of $VECH(\Xi_t \Xi'_t)$, this can be expressed as

$$VECH(\Xi_t \Xi'_t) = VECH\left(\begin{bmatrix} u_{1t} \\ u_{2t} \end{bmatrix} \begin{bmatrix} u_{1t} & u_{2t} \end{bmatrix}\right)$$

$$= VECH\begin{pmatrix} u^2_{11t} & u_{1t}u_{2t} \\ u_{2t}u_{1t} & u^2_{22t} \end{pmatrix} = \begin{bmatrix} u^2_{1t} \\ u^2_{2t} \\ u_{1t}u_{2t} \end{bmatrix}$$

The *VECH* model in full is given by

$$h_{11t} = c_{11} + a_{11}u^2_{1t-1} + a_{12}u^2_{2t-1} + a_{13}u_{1t}u_{2t-1} + b_{11}h_{11t-1}$$
$$+ b_{12}h_{22t-1} + b_{13}h_{12t-1} \tag{8.18}$$
$$h_{12t} = c_{31} + a_{31}u^2_{1t-1} + a_{32}u^2_{2t-1} + a_{33}u_{1t}u_{2t-1} + b_{31}h_{11t-1}$$
$$+ b_{32}h_{22t-1} + b_{33}h_{12t-1} \tag{8.19}$$
$$h_{22t} = c_{21} + a_{21}u^2_{1t-1} + a_{22}u^2_{2t-1} + a_{23}u_{1t}u_{2t-1} + b_{21}h_{11t-1}$$
$$+ b_{22}h_{22t-1} + b_{23}h_{12t-1} \tag{8.20}$$

Thus, it is clear that the conditional variances and conditional covariances depend on the lagged values of all of the conditional variances of and conditional covariances between, all of the asset returns in the series, as well as the lagged squared errors and the error cross-products. Estimation of such a model would be quite a formidable task, even in the two-asset case considered here. As the number of assets employed in the model increases, the estimation of the *VECH* model can quickly become infeasible. Hence the *VECH* model's conditional variance-covariance matrix has been restricted to the form developed by Bollerslev, Engle and Wooldridge (1988), in which $A$ and $B$ are assumed to be diagonal. This reduces the number of parameters to be estimated and the model, known as a diagonal *VECH*, is now characterised by

$$h_{ij,t} = \omega_{ij} + \alpha_{ij}u_{i,t-1}u_{j,t-1} + \beta_{ij}h_{ij,t-1} \quad \text{for } i, j = 1, 2, \tag{8.21}$$

where $\omega_{ij}$, $\alpha_{ij}$ and $\beta_{ij}$ are parameters.

A disadvantage of the *VECH* model (in either form) is that there is no guarantee of a positive semi-definite covariance matrix. The *BEKK* model (Engle and Kroner, 1995) addresses the difficulty with *VECH* of ensuring that the *H* matrix is always positive definite. It is represented by

$$H_t = W'W + A'H_{t-1}A + B'\Xi_{t-1}\Xi'_{t-1}B \tag{8.22}$$

where *A* and *B* are $3 \times 3$ matrices of parameters and *W* is an upper triangular $3 \times 3$ matrix. The positive definiteness of the covariance matrix is ensured due to the quadratic nature of the terms on the equation's right-hand side.

Estimating a multivariate GARCH model using RATS requires no new instructions and is made very simple by the GARCH instruction. Unrestricted VECH, diagonal VECH, BEKK, constant conditional correlation (CCC) and dynamic conditional correlation (DCC) forms of the model can all be estimated. The diagonal VECH is the default specification. Suppose that we wished to estimate such a model for the three exchange rate return series. The command would be

**GARCH(P=1,Q=1, METHOD=BHHH) / RJPY REUR RGBP**

The high degree of connectivity and large number of parameters make multivariate GARCH models inherently more difficult to estimate than their univariate counterparts and this particular example also entails some problems. As well as switching to an alternative optimisation method, it is often useful to employ the SIMPLEX method for a number of iterations before switching to the standard BFGS or BHHH approach. SIMPLEX is a derivative-free method which cannot be used to calculate standard errors but is often useful for improving the starting values prior to employing BFGS/BHHH to finish the job. Running SIMPLEX with 100 iterations first (using the PMETHOD=SIMPLEX option in parentheses) leads to convergence with plausible parameter estimates in this case

**GARCH(P=1,Q=1,METHOD=BHHH,PMETHOD=SIMPLEX,PITERS=100) $
/ RJPY REUR RGBP**

The results are shown in Box 8.9.

All of the options for estimation in the context of univariate models, such as the possibility of incorporating asymmetries or the use of Student's *t* or GED innovations, still apply here. To estimate a different type of MGARCH model (e.g. the BEKK), use the option MV=... in parentheses, where ... can be BEKK or DIAGONAL or CC or DCC or VECH or EWMA. The latter option will estimate a multivariate EWMA model à la JP Morgan, for both the variances and the covariance, and these can be thought of as

---

### Box 8.9

```
GARCH Model - Estimation by BHHH
Convergence in 31 Iterations. Final criterion was 0.0000001 <= 0.0000100
Daily(7) Data From 2002:07:08 To 2007:07:07
Usable Observations   1826
Log Likelihood               -1929.50433115
```

| | Variable | Coeff | Std Error | T-Stat | Signif |
|---|---|---|---|---|---|
| 1. | Mean(1) | 0.008043040 | 0.009414849 | 0.85429 | 0.39294264 |
| 2. | Mean(2) | -0.020385546 | 0.009100559 | -2.24003 | 0.02508882 |
| 3. | Mean(3) | -0.012353027 | 0.008904641 | -1.38726 | 0.16536340 |
| 4. | C(1,1) | 0.006251986 | 0.001291464 | 4.84101 | 0.00000129 |
| 5. | C(2,1) | 0.005078605 | 0.001184160 | 4.28878 | 0.00001797 |
| 6. | C(2,2) | 0.005144203 | 0.000547684 | 9.39264 | 0.00000000 |
| 7. | C(3,1) | 0.026851023 | 0.003999730 | 6.71321 | 0.00000000 |
| 8. | C(3,2) | 0.033231148 | 0.005776307 | 5.75301 | 0.00000001 |
| 9. | C(3,3) | 0.132136813 | 0.008391927 | 15.74571 | 0.00000000 |
| 10. | A(1,1) | 0.035190090 | 0.005126514 | 6.86433 | 0.00000000 |
| 11. | A(2,1) | 0.025326958 | 0.004491086 | 5.63938 | 0.00000002 |
| 12. | A(2,2) | 0.025802417 | 0.002593075 | 9.95051 | 0.00000000 |
| 13. | A(3,1) | 0.056384958 | 0.007623281 | 7.39642 | 0.00000000 |
| 14. | A(3,2) | 0.032771428 | 0.004552096 | 7.19919 | 0.00000000 |
| 15. | A(3,3) | 0.103151644 | 0.012676588 | 8.13718 | 0.00000000 |
| 16. | B(1,1) | 0.932056982 | 0.010445827 | 89.22769 | 0.00000000 |
| 17. | B(2,1) | 0.928423408 | 0.014106740 | 65.81417 | 0.00000000 |
| 18. | B(2,2) | 0.949499311 | 0.004268247 | 222.45652 | 0.00000000 |
| 19. | B(3,1) | 0.625169217 | 0.049577467 | 12.60995 | 0.00000000 |
| 20. | B(3,2) | 0.727377196 | 0.043750614 | 16.62553 | 0.00000000 |
| 21. | B(3,3) | 0.117883153 | 0.042539981 | 2.77111 | 0.00558648 |

---

### Box 8.10

```
GARCH Model - Estimation by BHHH
Convergence in 19 Iterations. Final criterion was 0.0000089 <= 0.0000100
Daily(7) Data From 2002:07:08 To 2007:07:07
Usable Observations   1826
Log Likelihood               -1872.53363133
```

| | Variable | Coeff | Std Error | T-Stat | Signif |
|---|---|---|---|---|---|
| 1. | Mean(1) | 0.004018805 | 0.008570630 | 0.46890 | 0.63913809 |
| 2. | Mean(2) | -0.019058468 | 0.008838356 | -2.15634 | 0.03105742 |
| 3. | Mean(3) | -0.016507158 | 0.008262648 | -1.99780 | 0.04573783 |
| 4. | Alpha | 0.014888006 | 0.000800539 | 18.59748 | 0.00000000 |

a restricted form of IGARCH model. Such a model will estimate a single decay parameter that is assumed to apply to all variance and covariance series. The code and results for the multivariate EWMA model are

**GARCH(P=1,Q=1, METHOD=BHHH, MV=EWMA) / RJPY REUR RGBP**

See Box 8.10.

The estimated alpha parameter is very small, indicating a very high degree of persistence in the variance and covariance series, with little variation from one period to the next in the fitted values.

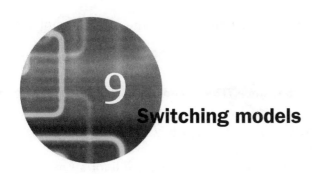

# 9

# Switching models

## 9.1 Dummy variables for seasonality

In the context of financial markets, and especially in the case of equities, a number of 'seasonal effects' have been noted. Such effects are usually known as 'calendar anomalies' or 'calendar effects' and result in systematically different behaviour in one or more seasons compared with the others. Examples include open- and close-of-market effects, the 'January effect', weekend effects and bank holiday effects.

One very simple method for coping with this and examining the degree to which seasonality is present is the inclusion of dummy variables in regression equations. The number of dummy variables that could sensibly be constructed to model the seasonality would depend on the frequency of the data. For example, four dummy variables would be created for quarterly data, twelve for monthly data, five for daily data and so on. In the case of quarterly data, the four dummy variables would be defined as follows:

$D1_t = 1$ in quarter 1 and zero otherwise
$D2_t = 1$ in quarter 2 and zero otherwise
$D3_t = 1$ in quarter 3 and zero otherwise
$D4_t = 1$ in quarter 4 and zero otherwise

It is important to remember that if an intercept term is used in the regression, the number of dummies that could also be included would be one less than the 'seasonality' of the data. So for quarterly data, we could either use four dummy variables and no intercept or three dummies and an intercept to avoid falling into the 'dummy variable trap'.

The dummies operate by changing the intercept, so that the average value of the dependent variable, given all of the explanatory variables, is permitted to change across the seasons. Consider the following regression:

$$y_t = \beta_1 + \gamma_1 D1_t + \gamma_2 D2_t + \gamma_3 D3_t + \beta_2 x_{2t} + \cdots + u_t \qquad (9.1)$$

During each period, the intercept will be changed. The intercept will be

- $\hat{\beta}_1 + \hat{\gamma}_1$ in the first quarter, since $D1 = 1$ and $D2 = D3 = D4 = 0$ for all quarter 1 observations.
- $\hat{\beta}_1 + \hat{\gamma}_2$ in the second quarter, since $D2 = 1$ and $D1 = D3 = D4 = 0$ for all quarter 2 observations.
- $\hat{\beta}_1 + \hat{\gamma}_3$ in the third quarter, since $D3 = 1$ and $D1 = D2 = D4 = 0$ for all quarter 3 observations.
- $\hat{\beta}_1$ in the fourth quarter, since $D1 = D2 = D3 = D4 = 0$ for all quarter 4 observations.

As well as, or instead of, intercept dummies, slope dummy variables can be used. These operate by changing the slope of the regression line, leaving the intercept unchanged. For example, if the data were quarterly, the following set-up could be used, with $D1_t \ldots D3_t$ representing quarters 1 to 3.

$$y_t = \alpha + \beta x_t + \gamma_1 D1_t x_t + \gamma_2 D2_t x_t + \gamma_3 D3_t x_t + u_t \tag{9.2}$$

In this case, since there is also a term in $x_t$ with no dummy attached, the interpretation of the coefficients on the dummies ($\gamma_1$, etc.) is that they represent the deviation of the slope for that quarter from the average slope over all quarters. Meanwhile, if the four-slope dummy variables were included (and not $\beta x_t$), the coefficients on the dummies would be interpreted as the average relationship between $y$ and $x$ during each quarter.

There are several ways to generate seasonal dummies in RATS. The first, for monthly or quarterly data, is to use the SEASONAL command. Let us return to the monthly data that we examined previously for Microsoft stock and the S&P500 index (MACRO.PRG). For example, if we run the following command at any point after the data has been read into RATS' memory

    SEASONAL SEASONS

this will create one 0–1 dummy variable for the last month in the year (December). Instead of creating further dummy variables for the other months of the year, a regression containing all of the dummy variables could be conducted using the 'leads' of SEASONS, e.g.

    LINREG RSANDP
    # SEASONS{-11 TO 0}

The output would be that shown in Box 9.1.

```
Box 9.1
```

```
Linear Regression - Estimation by Least Squares
Dependent Variable RSANDP
Monthly Data From 1986:04 To 2007:04
Usable Observations     253          Degrees of Freedom     241
Centered R**2     0.041723          R Bar **2   -0.002015
Uncentered R**2   0.067418          T X R**2       17.057
Mean of Dependent Variable         0.7214831553
Std Error of Dependent Variable    4.3552197934
Standard Error of Estimate         4.3596061048
Sum of Squared Residuals           4580.4858587
Regression F(11,241)                  0.9539
Significance Level of F            0.48942157
Log Likelihood                     -725.35706
Durbin-Watson Statistic              2.048506
```

| | Variable | Coeff | Std Error | T-Stat | Signif |
|---|---|---|---|---|---|
| 1. | SEASONS{-11} | 0.675778817 | 0.951344046 | 0.71034 | 0.47817941 |
| 2. | SEASONS{-10} | 1.078319085 | 0.929471145 | 1.16014 | 0.24713874 |
| 3. | SEASONS{-9} | 1.708633656 | 0.951344046 | 1.79602 | 0.07374370 |
| 4. | SEASONS{-8} | 0.490168459 | 0.951344046 | 0.51524 | 0.60685910 |
| 5. | SEASONS{-7} | 0.458490410 | 0.951344046 | 0.48194 | 0.63028619 |
| 6. | SEASONS{-6} | -0.625629471 | 0.951344046 | -0.65763 | 0.51140549 |
| 7. | SEASONS{-5} | -1.115743183 | 0.951344046 | -1.17281 | 0.24203103 |
| 8. | SEASONS{-4} | 0.738013851 | 0.951344046 | 0.77576 | 0.43865179 |
| 9. | SEASONS{-3} | 1.383781933 | 0.951344046 | 1.45455 | 0.14709374 |
| 10. | SEASONS{-2} | 1.927077049 | 0.951344046 | 2.02564 | 0.04390417 |
| 11. | SEASONS{-1} | 1.691402130 | 0.951344046 | 1.77791 | 0.07667986 |
| 12. | SEASONS | 0.230512941 | 0.951344046 | 0.24230 | 0.80875193 |

So SEASONS{-11} would be the January dummy, SEASONS{-10} would be the February dummy, ..., and SEASONS would be the December dummy. The results we find here for the S&P are not particularly exciting, but show marginally significant and positive March, October and November effects.

An alternative method for generating a January dummy variable would be to use the command

    SET JANDUMMY = %MONTH(T) == 1

For daily data, the corresponding command to create a Friday dummy variable would be

    SET FRIDUMMY = %DAY(T) == 5

```
Box 9.2

Linear Regression - Estimation by Least Squares
Dependent Variable RMSOFT
Monthly Data From 1986:04 To 2007:04
Usable Observations    253          Degrees of Freedom    250
Centered R**2      0.188772        R Bar **2    0.182283
Uncentered R**2   0.188776         T X R**2       47.760
Mean of Dependent Variable         0.033600543
Std Error of Dependent Variable    15.420559877
Standard Error of Estimate         13.944462700
Sum of Squared Residuals           48612.010000
Regression F(2,250)                   29.0874
Significance Level of F             0.00000000
Log Likelihood                    -1024.15835
Durbin-Watson Statistic               2.145128


      Variable          Coeff        Std Error       T-Stat        Signif
**************************************************************************
1.    Constant        -1.149368837   0.890398184    -1.29085     0.19794877
2.    RSANDP           1.355290000   0.210425919     6.44070     0.00000000
3.    SLOPEJAN         1.461257923   0.702569552     2.07988     0.03855588
```

(where Monday is numbered 1 in the %DAY instruction, Tuesday is numbered 2, etc., and '==' denotes that two equals signs are used one after the other).

Suppose that we wanted to use this form of command to determine whether the CAPM beta for Microsoft stock is different in January compared with other months of the year. We would want to use a slope dummy variable that allowed for this, so we could use the code segment

```
SET JANDUMMY = %MONTH(T) == 1
SET SLOPEJAN = JANDUMMY*RSANDP
LINREG RMSOFT
# CONSTANT RSANDP SLOPEJAN
```

The results would be as shown in Box 9.2.

The coefficient on RSANDP will represent the beta for all months except January, whereas the beta in January will be the sum of the coefficients on SLOPEJAN and RSANDP. Another way to think about this would be to say that SLOPEJAN represents the difference in beta between January and the rest of the year, or alternatively, the slope estimate is significantly higher in January than in other months. This parameter needs to be interpreted with some caution, however, since even in a sample of 20 years' length, there will be only 20 January data points and so the January slope dummy is effectively estimated using a small sample and could be influenced by one or two extreme outliers.

Creating (deterministic) time trends can also be achieved easily using the SET instruction. So

    SET TREND = T
    SET TRENDSQ = T**2

would construct two new series, TREND and TRENDSQ, that would contain linear and quadratic trends respectively.

Finally, we can also create dummy variables to draw out particular observations. For example

    SET RLARGE = RMSOFT > 3
    SET RSMALL = RMSOFT < −3

will create two new dummy variables, RLARGE and RSMALL. RLARGE will contain the value 1 for all observations where the Microsoft return is greater than 3 and zero elsewhere; RSMALL will contain 1 for all RMSOFT observations less than −3 and zero elsewhere.

## 9.2  Markov switching models

The Markov regime switching model as it is used in economics and finance is primarily associated with Hamilton (1989, 1990). Under the Markov switching approach, the universe of possible occurrences is split into $m$ states of the world, corresponding to $m$ regimes. In other words, it is assumed that $y_t$ switches regime according to some unobserved variable, $s_t$, that takes on integer values. In the remainder of this chapter, it will be assumed that $m = 2$. Movements of the state variable between regimes are governed by a Markov process. This Markov property can be expressed as

$$P[a < y_t \leq b | y_1, y_2, \ldots, y_{t-1}] = P[a < y_t \leq b | y_{t-1}] \tag{9.3}$$

This equation states that the probability distribution of the state at any time $t$ depends only on the state at time $t − 1$ and not on the states that were passed through at times $t − 2, t − 3, \ldots$. The model's strength lies in its flexibility, being capable of capturing changes in the variance between state processes as well as changes in the mean.

The most basic form of Hamilton's model, also known as 'Hamilton's filter' (see Hamilton, 1989), comprises an unobserved state variable, denoted $z_t$, which is postulated to evaluate according to a first-order Markov process:

$$\text{Prob}[z_t = 1 \mid z_{t-1} = 1] = p_{11} \qquad (9.4)$$

$$\text{Prob}[z_t = 2 \mid z_{t-1} = 1] = 1 - p_{11} \qquad (9.5)$$

$$\text{Prob}[z_t = 2 \mid z_{t-1} = 2] = p_{22} \qquad (9.6)$$

$$\text{Prob}[z_t = 1 \mid z_{t-1} = 2] = 1 - p_{22} \qquad (9.7)$$

where $p_{11}$ and $p_{22}$ denote the probability of being in regime one, given that the system was in regime one during the previous period, and the probability of being in regime two, given that the system was in regime two during the previous period respectively. Thus $1 - p_{11}$ defines the probability that $y_t$ will change from state 1 in period $t - 1$ to state 2 in period $t$, and $1 - p_{22}$ defines the probability of a shift from state 2 to state 1 between times $t - 1$ and $t$. It can be shown that under this specification, $z_t$ evolves as an AR(1) process:

$$z_t = (1 - p_{11}) + \rho z_{t-1} + \eta_t \qquad (9.8)$$

where $\rho = p_{11} + p_{22} - 1$. Loosely speaking, $z_t$ can be viewed as a generalisation of a dummy variables approach for one-off shifts in a series. Under the Markov switching approach, there can be multiple shifts from one set of behaviour to another.

In this framework, the observed returns series evolves as given by (9.9):

$$y_t = \mu_1 + \mu_2 z_t + \left(\sigma_1^2 + \phi z_t\right)^{1/2} u_t \qquad (9.9)$$

where $u_t \sim N(0, 1)$. The expected values and variances of the series are $\mu_1$ and $\sigma_1^2$ respectively in state 1 and $(\mu_1 + \mu_2)$ and $\sigma_1^2 + \phi$ in state 2 respectively. The variance in state 2 is also defined as $\sigma_2^2 = \sigma_1^2 + \phi$. The unknown parameters of the model $(\mu_1, \mu_2, \sigma_1^2, \sigma_2^2, p_{11}, p_{22})$ are estimated using maximum likelihood. Details are beyond the scope of this book, but are most comprehensively given in Engel and Hamilton (1990).

If a variable follows a Markov process, all that is required to forecast the probability that it will be in a given regime during the next period is the current period's probability and a set of transition probabilities, given for the case of two regimes by equations (9.4)–(9.7). In the general case where there are $m$ states, the transition probabilities are best expressed in a matrix as

$$P = \begin{bmatrix} P_{11} & P_{12} & \cdots & P_{1m} \\ P_{21} & P_{22} & \cdots & P_{2m} \\ \cdots & \cdots & \cdots & \cdots \\ P_{m1} & P_{m2} & \cdots & P_{mm} \end{bmatrix} \qquad (9.10)$$

where $P_{ij}$ is the probability of moving from regime $i$ to regime $j$. Since, at any given time, the variable must be in one of the $m$ states, it must be true that

$$\sum_{j=1}^{m} P_{ij} = 1 \,\forall\, i \qquad (9.11)$$

A vector of current state probabilities is then defined as

$$\pi_t = [\pi_1 \quad \pi_2 \quad \cdots \quad \pi_m] \qquad (9.12)$$

where $\pi_i$ is the probability that the variable $y$ is currently in state $i$. Given $\pi_t$ and $P$, the probability that the variable $y$ will be in a given regime next period can be forecast using

$$\pi_{t+1} = \pi_t P \qquad (9.13)$$

The probabilities for $S$ steps into the future will be given by

$$\pi_{t+s} = \pi_t P^s \qquad (9.14)$$

The RATS newsletter ('RATSletter') of December 1998 presented sample code for estimating various specifications of the Markov switching model. The code required to compute the statistics for a two-regime model with unknown regime and separate means and variances for each model is shown on the following page.

It is assumed that the series to be examined is called Y, and A01 and A02 denote the means for states 1 and 2 respectively, with all other notation explained below. The number of lines of code required to estimate this model is fairly large, and many of them will not be familiar, but the approach used here is the way that all GARCH models had to be estimated before the GARCH instruction came along!

The example considered here focuses on modelling the time-series behaviour of the gilt-equity yield ratio (GEYR), defined as the ratio of the income yield on long-term government bonds (termed 'gilts' in the UK) to the dividend yield on equities. It has been suggested that the current value of the GEYR might be a useful tool for investment managers or market analysts in determining whether to invest in equities or whether to invest in gilts. The GEYR is assumed to have a long-run equilibrium level, deviations from which are taken to signal that equity prices are at an unsustainable level. If the GEYR becomes high relative to its long-run level, equities are viewed as being expensive relative to bonds. The expectation, then, is that for given levels of bond yields, equity yields must rise which will occur via a fall in equity prices, and *vice versa*.

The paper by Brooks and Persand (2001) discusses the usefulness of the Markov switching approach in this context and considers whether

profitable trading rules can be developed on the basis of forecasts derived
from the model. Brooks and Persand employ monthly stock index dividend
yields and income yields on government bonds covering the period January 1975 to August 1997 (272 observations) for three countries – the UK,
the US and Germany, although only the UK series is employed here. The
series used are the dividend yield and index values of the FTSE 100, while
the bond indices and redemption yields are based on the clean prices of
UK government consols (irredeemable bonds).

```
OPEN DATA 'C:\CHRIS\BOOK\RATS HANDBOOK\GEYRR.XLS'
CALENDAR(M) 1975
ALL 1997:08
DATA(FORMAT=XLS,ORG=COLUMNS) 1975:01 1997:08 GEYR
SET Y = GEYR
NONLIN P12 P21 A01 A02 SIGMA1 SIGMA2
FRML REG1 = Y-A01
FRML REG2 = Y-A02
*
COMPUTE P12=0.7
COMPUTE P21=0.3
LINREG(NOPRINT) Y
# CONSTANT
COMPUTE A01=%BETA(1)+0.5
COMPUTE A02=%BETA(1)
COMPUTE SIGMA1=SQRT(%SEESQ)
COMPUTE SIGMA2=SQRT(%SEESQ)
*
SET PSTAR 1 272 = 0.5
FRML MARKOV = $
  F1=%DENSITY(REG1{0}/SIGMA1)/SIGMA1 , $
  F2=%DENSITY(REG2{0}/SIGMA2)/SIGMA2 , $
  RP1=F1*(P21*(1-PSTAR{1})+(1-P12)*PSTAR{1}) , $
  RP2=F2*((1-P21)*(1-PSTAR{1})+P12*PSTAR{1}) , $
  PSTAR=RP1/(RP1+RP2) , $
  LOG(RP1+RP2)
MAXIMIZE(ROBUST) MARKOV 2 272
PRINT 1 272 PSTAR
```

Given that most of these instructions are new, some annotation will now
follow. The first four lines obviously just read in the data from an Excel
file, and the following one defines the dependent variable used in the
program (Y). The next line tells RATS that a non-linear estimation will
be conducted and the parameters to be estimated are listed: P12 P21 etc.
FRML then defines the formulae for the residuals for each regime, then
some initial starting value guesses are offered for the probabilities. The
linear regression and the four COMPUTE instructions that follow it also
generate initial guesses, but for the means and variances in each regime.

```
┌─────────────────────────────────────────────────────────────────────────┐
│    Box 9.3                                                                 │
├─────────────────────────────────────────────────────────────────────────┤
│ MAXIMIZE - Estimation by BFGS                                             │
│ Convergence in 15 Iterations. Final criterion was 0.0000088 <= 0.0000100  │
│ With Heteroscedasticity/Misspecification Adjusted Standard Errors         │
│ Monthly Data From 1975:02 To 1997:08                                      │
│ Usable Observations   271                                                 │
│ Function Value                    52.59207092                             │
│                                                                           │
│      Variable          Coeff       Std Error      T-Stat      Signif      │
│ ***********************************************************************     │
│ 1.  P12            0.0604684471  0.0371214652    1.62893   0.10332682     │
│ 2.  P21            0.0124004131  0.0074475580    1.66503   0.09590662     │
│ 3.  A01            2.6694842266  0.0625870338   42.65235   0.00000000     │
│ 4.  A02            2.1223427585  0.0152292509  139.35963   0.00000000     │
│ 5.  SIGMA1         0.2292422194  0.0296724035    7.72577   0.00000000     │
│ 6.  SIGMA2         0.1736851588  0.0100295265   17.31738   0.00000000     │
└─────────────────────────────────────────────────────────────────────────┘
```

The vector PSTAR will contain the probabilities of being in state 1 at each point in time for the sample and this must be initialised. The next FRML constructs a formula, called MARKOV, that defines the log-likelihood as a function of the parameters, and finally the MAXIMIZE command does the estimation.

A crucial point in the analysis above is that different starting values are used for some of the parameters in each state. Without that, the model is not globally identified in the sense that the two states could be flipped without affecting the results. The log-likelihood function, called MARKOV, is maximised using the BFGS procedure. Note that in this application, the maximisation must start at observation 2. The results obtained using the above code for the UK GEYR series are shown in Box 9.3.

Comparing the results to those from the Brooks and Persand (2001) paper, which used code written by James Hamilton, the probabilities of a switch from one regime to another are comparable (the corresponding figures from the paper are 0.045 and 0.028), while the means for each state and the variances are slightly different. The model can be easily extended to allow the variable to follow an autoregressive process within each regime (see Hamilton, 1994, or the RATSletter discussed above).

## 9.3 Threshold autoregressive models

Threshold autoregressive (TAR) models are one class of non-linear autoregressive models. Such models are a relatively simple relaxation of standard linear autoregressive models that allow for a locally linear approximation over a number of states. According to Tong (1990, p. 99), the threshold principle 'allows the analysis of a complex stochastic system by decomposing it into a set of smaller sub-systems'. The key difference between TAR and Markov switching models is that under the former, the state variable is assumed known and observable, while it is latent under the latter. A very simple example of a threshold autoregressive model is given by equation (9.15). The model contains a first-order autoregressive process in each of two regimes, and there is only one threshold. Of course, the number of thresholds will always be the number of regimes minus one. Thus, the dependent variable $y_t$ is purported to follow an autoregressive process with intercept coefficient $\mu_1$ and autoregressive coefficient $\phi_1$ if the value of the state-determining variable lagged $k$ periods, denoted $s_{t-k}$, is lower than some threshold value $r$. If the value of the state-determining variable lagged $k$ periods, is equal to or greater than that threshold value $r$, $y_t$ is specified to follow a different autoregressive process, with intercept coefficient $\mu_2$ and autoregressive coefficient $\phi_2$. The model would be written

$$y_t = \begin{cases} \mu_1 + \phi_1 y_{t-1} + u_{1t} & \text{if } s_{t-k} < r \\ \mu_2 + \phi_2 y_{t-1} + u_{2t} & \text{if } s_{t-k} \geq r \end{cases} \tag{9.15}$$

But what is $s_{t-k}$, the state-determining variable? It can be any variable that is thought to make $y_t$ shift from one set of behaviour to another. Obviously, financial or economic theory should have an important role to play in making this decision. If $k = 0$, it is the current value of the state-determining variable that influences the regime that $y$ is in at time $t$, but in many applications $k$ is set to 1, so that the immediately preceding value of $s$ is the one that determines the current value of $y$.

The simplest case arises when the state-determining variable is the variable under study, i.e. $s_{t-k} = y_{t-k}$. This situation is known as a self-exciting TAR, or a SETAR, since it is the lag of the variable $y$ itself that determines the regime that $y$ is currently in. The model would now be written

$$y_t = \begin{cases} \mu_1 + \phi_1 y_{t-1} + u_{1t} & \text{if } y_{t-k} < r \\ \mu_2 + \phi_2 y_{t-1} + u_{2t} & \text{if } y_{t-k} \geq r \end{cases} \tag{9.16}$$

The models of (9.15) or (9.16) can of course be extended in several directions. The number of lags of the dependent variable used in each regime may be higher than one, and the number of lags need not be the same for both regimes. The number of states can also be increased to more than two. A general threshold autoregressive model that notationally permits the existence of more than two regimes and more than one lag may be written

$$y_t = \sum_{j=1}^{J} I_t^{(j)} \left( \phi_0^{(j)} + \sum_{i=1}^{p_j} \phi_i^{(j)} y_{t-i} + u_t^{(j)} \right), \quad r_{j-1} \leq z_{t-d} \leq r_j \qquad (9.17)$$

where $I_t^{(j)}$ is an indicator function for the $j^{\text{th}}$ regime taking the value one if the underlying variable is in state $j$ and zero otherwise. $z_{t-d}$ is an observed variable determining the switching point and $u_t^{(j)}$ is a zero-mean independently and identically distributed error process. Again, if the regime changes are driven by own lags of the underlying variable, $y_t$ (i.e. $z_{t-d} = y_{t-d}$), then the model is a SETAR.

As alluded to previously, the estimation of threshold models is considerably more complex than is the case for other models described in this book. Part of the reason for this is that determination of the lag length for each regime, the regime switching variable, the value of the threshold, and the coefficients all need to be estimated, and the estimates of each will depend on the estimates of the others. To fully address these issues requires algebra and techniques that are well beyond the scope of this text, but instead a simple and imperfect example to illustrate the technique will be employed.

In the early 1990s, the requirement that currencies in the European Monetary Union zone (prior to the formation of the euro) remain within a certain band around their central parity forced central banks to intervene in the markets to bring about either an appreciation or a depreciation in their currency. A study by Chappell *et al.* (1996) considered the effect that such interventions might have on the dynamics and time-series properties of the French franc–German mark (hereafter FRF–DEM) exchange rate. 'Core currency pairs' such as the FRF–DEM were allowed to move up to $\pm 2.25\%$ either side of their central parity within the exchange rate mechanism (ERM). The study used daily data from 1 May 1990 until 30 March 1992. The first 450 observations were used for model estimation, with the remaining 50 being retained for out-of-sample forecasting.

A SETAR model was employed to allow for different types of behaviour according to whether the exchange rate was close to the ERM boundary. The argument was that, close to the boundary, the respective central banks would be required to intervene in the opposite direction in order to drive the exchange rate back towards its central parity. Such intervention might be expected to affect the usual market dynamics that ensured fast reaction to news and the absence of arbitrage opportunities.

Let $E_t$ denote the log of the FRF–DEM exchange rate at time $t$. Chappell *et al.* estimated two models: one with two thresholds and one with one threshold. The former was anticipated to be most appropriate for the data at hand since exchange rate behaviour was likely to be affected by intervention if the exchange rate came close to either the ceiling or the floor of the band. However, over the sample period employed, the mark was never a weak currency and therefore the FRF–DEM exchange rate was either at the top of the band or in the centre, never close to the bottom. Therefore, a model with one threshold was more appropriate since any second estimated threshold was deemed likely to be spurious. The Chappell *et al.* (1996) coefficient estimates for a SETAR with one threshold whose value had been estimated was

$$\hat{E}_t = 0.0222 + 0.9962 E_{t-1} \qquad \text{For} \qquad (9.18)$$
$$\quad (0.0458) \quad (0.0079) \qquad E_{t-1} < 5.8306$$

$$\hat{E}_t = 0.3486 + 0.4394 E_{t-1} + 0.3057 E_{t-2} + 0.1951 E_{t-3} \quad \text{For} \qquad (9.19)$$
$$\quad (0.2391) \quad (0.0889) \qquad (0.1098) \qquad (0.0866) \quad E_{t-1} \geq 5.8306$$

It is possible to replicate their results, given the number of regimes, the value of the threshold and the number of lags in each state, using the following RATS code:

```
OPEN DATA 'C:\CHRIS\BOOK\RATS HANDBOOK\FFDMR.XLS'
CALENDAR(D) 1990:5:1
ALL 1992:03:30
DATA(FORMAT=XLS,ORG=COLUMNS) 1990:05:01 1992:03:30 FFDM
SET Y = FFDM
COMPUTE R=5.8306
NONLIN A0 A1 B0 B1 B2 B3
FRML SETAR Y = %IF(Y{1}<R, A0+A1*Y{1}, $
B0+B1*Y{1}+B2*Y{2}+B3*Y{3})
LINREG(NOPRINT) Y
# CONSTANT Y{1}
COMPUTE A0=%BETA(1)
COMPUTE A1=%BETA(2)
LINREG(NOPRINT) Y
# CONSTANT Y{1} Y{2} Y{3}
COMPUTE B0=%BETA(1)
COMPUTE B1=%BETA(2)
COMPUTE B2=%BETA(3)
COMPUTE B3=%BETA(4)
NLLS(FRML=SETAR,ITERATIONS=100,ROBUSTERRORS) Y 1990:5:4 $
    1992:03:30
```

The first four lines of code read in the data from the Excel file and then define Y as the variable to be modelled. The threshold value is specified as 5.8306, followed by the NONLIN instruction that, as for GARCH-type models, specifies the parameters to be estimated. The FRML instruction defines the SETAR model. It states that if the one-period lagged value of Y is less than R, then set the term in brackets (Y{1}<R,1,0) to 1, else set the term to zero. The %IF statement will pick out any observations for lagged Y where it is greater than or equal to the specified value of the threshold. Thus, if the lagged value of Y is less than the threshold, the current value of Y will be modelled as (A0+A1*Y(T−1)), while if the lagged value of Y is greater than or equal to the threshold, the current value of Y will be modelled as (B0+B1*Y(T−1)+B2*Y(T−2)+B3*Y(T−3)). The two sets of LINREG instructions together with their corresponding COMPUTE statements set up starting values for the parameters for the AR(1) and AR(3) regimes as the estimates obtained from a linear regression of that form. Finally, the NLLS instruction estimates the SETAR model using Non-linear Least Squares, with heteroscedasticity-robust standard errors for observations from 4 May 1990 to 30 March 1992 (observation numbers 4 to 500). The results that would be obtained are shown in Box 9.4.

### Box 9.4

```
Nonlinear Least Squares - Estimation by Gauss-Newton
Convergence in 2 Iterations. Final criterion was 0.0000004 <= 0.0000100
With Heteroscedasticity-Consistent (Eicker-White) Standard Errors
Dependent Variable Y
Daily(5) Data From 1990:05:04 To 1992:03:30
Usable Observations    497      Degrees of Freedom      491
Centered R**2      0.986799     R Bar **2      0.986664
Uncentered R**2    1.000000     T X R**2       497.000
Mean of Dependent Variable        5.8248665836
Std Error of Dependent Variable   0.0065341741
Standard Error of Estimate        0.0007545681
Sum of Squared Residuals          0.0002795621
Log Likelihood                    2870.92022
Durbin-Watson Statistic              1.914210
```

| Variable | Coeff | Std Error | T-Stat | Signif |
|---|---|---|---|---|
| 1. A0 | 0.0358256962 | 0.0337796593 | 1.06057 | 0.28888532 |
| 2. A1 | 0.9938559273 | 0.0058017751 | 171.30204 | 0.00000000 |
| 3. B0 | 0.0891014437 | 0.2144240445 | 0.41554 | 0.67774774 |
| 4. B1 | 0.5095427582 | 0.1164738018 | 4.37474 | 0.00001216 |
| 5. B2 | 0.2388951159 | 0.1251466123 | 1.90892 | 0.05627216 |
| 6. B3 | 0.2362801742 | 0.1088076544 | 2.17154 | 0.02989038 |

As can be seen, these parameter estimates are fairly close to those obtained by Chappell *et al.*, although they use only the first 450 data points for estimation rather than the full 500 used here, and the sources of data may also be different. The standard error estimates in both cases should be interpreted with extreme caution, however, since the residuals of the model are likely to be highly autocorrelated even if we accept the Chappell *et al.* argument that the exchange rate was stationary over this period.

It would be possible and relatively easy to generalise this procedure to incorporate more than one threshold, or to allow for different numbers of lags in each regime. It would also be valid, given the threshold value, to use an information criterion to guide the choice of how many lags to include. However, estimation of the threshold value itself would be considerably more difficult. One approach, for a given number of lags in each state, would be to estimate the model over a whole range of values of R and to choose the model that minimised the residual sum of squares. This would be known as a grid-search procedure and could be accomplished in RATS using the DOFOR instruction. For example, in the context of the FRF–DEM example, all of the sample data lies in the range (5.812,5.835). It is undesirable to allow the threshold to occur right at one end of the range or another, since this would imply that the parameters of one regime were to be estimated using a very small number of observations. Instead, suppose that it were determined to constrain the value of the threshold to lie within the central 80% of the distribution of the data points (i.e. the threshold is not permitted to lie within the lowest 10% or the highest 10% of the data). The relevant range would then be (5.814,5.833). Then the threshold value could be chosen using the following grid-search approach:

```
DOFOR R = 5.814 5.815 5.816 5.817 5.818 5.819 5.820 5.821 5.822 $
5.823 5.824 5.825 5.826 5.827 5.828 5.829 5.830 5.831 5.832 5.833
NONLIN A0 A1 B0 B1 B2 B3
FRML SETAR Y = (%IF(Y{1}<R,1,0))*(A0+A1*Y(T-1)) + $
%IF(Y{1}>=R,1,0)*(B0+B1*Y(T-1)+B2*Y(T-2)+B3*Y(T-3))
LINREG(NOPRINT) Y
# CONSTANT Y{1}
COMPUTE A0=%BETA(1)
COMPUTE A1=%BETA(2)
LINREG(NOPRINT) Y
# CONSTANT Y{1} Y{2} Y{3}
COMPUTE B0=%BETA(1)
COMPUTE B1=%BETA(2)
COMPUTE B2=%BETA(3)
COMPUTE B3=%BETA(4)
```

```
NLLS(FRML=SETAR,ITERATIONS=100,ROBUSTERRORS,NOPRINT) $
   Y 1990:5:4 1992:03:30
DIS R %RSS
END DOFOR R
```

This will print the value of the residual sum of squares for each value of R. Clearly, it does not use a very fine grid with only 20 points, and therefore the optimal threshold value is not likely to be calculated with much accuracy. But the procedure could be generalised to measure R to more decimal places (assuming that sufficient accuracy is available in the original data) and to search over a finer grid.

The DOFOR instruction above could have been simplified to

```
DOFOR R = %SEQA(5.814,0.001,20)
```

It is an extremely useful instruction since it can be used to loop over series as well as numbers. For example, suppose that we wanted to estimate an AR(1) model for three series: X, Y and Z. We could use the commands

```
DOFOR A = X Y Z
LINREG A
# CONSTANT A{1}
END DOFOR
```

Although it would have been easy to just run these three regressions separately, imagine if we had wanted to apply a long and complex set of instructions to 30 or 300 series. In situations like this, DOFOR can be invaluable.

# 10 Panel data

The situation often arises in financial modelling where we have data comprising both time-series and cross-sectional elements, and such a dataset would be known as a panel of data or longitudinal data. A panel of data will embody information across both time and space. Importantly, a panel keeps the same individuals or objects (henceforth we will call these 'entities') and measures some quantity about them over time. This chapter will present and discuss the important features of panel analysis and will describe the techniques used to model such data.

Econometrically, the set-up we may have is as described in the following equation:

$$y_{it} = \alpha + \beta x_{it} + u_{it} \tag{10.1}$$

where $y_{it}$ is the dependent variable, $\alpha$ is the intercept term, $\beta$ is a $k \times 1$ vector of parameters to be estimated on the explanatory variables, and $x_{it}$ is a $1 \times k$ vector of observations on the explanatory variables, $t = 1, \ldots, T$; $i = 1, \ldots, N$.[17]

## 10.1 Setting up the panel

The estimation of panel models with either fixed or random effects is very easy with RATS; the harder part is organising the data so that the software can recognise that you have a panel of data and can apply the techniques accordingly. RATS requires the data file to have a particular structure. Each variable must have a single list of values for each individual (so that both the time-series and cross-sectional observations on a given variable are stacked up in a single column). The data can be grouped *by individual*

---

[17] Note that $k$ is defined slightly differently in this chapter compared with others in the book. Here, $k$ represents the number of slope parameters to be estimated (rather than the total number of parameters as it is elsewhere), which is equal to the number of explanatory variables in the regression model.

**Table 10.1** Data grouped by individual and by time

| Grouped by individual | Grouped by time |
|---|---|
| Individual 1, 1997 | Individual 1, 1997 |
| Individual 1, 1998 | Individual 2, 1997 |
| Individual 1, 1999 | Individual 1, 1998 |
| Individual 2, 1997 | Individual 2, 1998 |
| Individual 2, 1998 | Individual 1, 1999 |
| Individual 2, 1999 | Individual 2, 1999 |

or grouped *by time*. Examples of each (taken from the RATS 7 *User Guide*, p. 542) are shown in Table 10.1.

Use of the technique is probably best explained with the aid of an example. The application to be considered here is that of a variant on an early test of the capital asset pricing model due to Fama and MacBeth (1973). Their test involves a two-step estimation procedure: first, the betas are estimated in separate time-series regressions for each firm, and second, for each separate point in time, a cross-sectional regression of the excess returns on the betas is conducted

$$R_{it} - R_{ft} = \lambda_0 + \lambda_m \beta_{Pi} + u_i \qquad (10.2)$$

where the dependent variable, $R_{it} - R_{ft}$, is the excess return of the stock $i$ at time $t$ and the independent variable is the estimated beta for the portfolio ($P$) that the stock has been allocated to. The betas of the firms themselves are not used on the RHS, but rather, the betas of portfolios formed on the basis of firm size. If the CAPM holds, then $\lambda_0$ should not be significantly different from zero and $\lambda_m$ should approximate the (time average) equity market risk premium, $R_m - R_f$. Fama and MacBeth proposed estimating this second-stage (cross-sectional) regression separately for each time period and then taking the average of the parameter estimates to conduct hypothesis tests. However, one could also achieve a similar objective using a panel approach. We will use an example in the spirit of Fama–MacBeth comprising the annual returns and 'second pass betas' for 11 years on 2,500 UK firms.[18]

The data are contained in four columns in the Excel file PANELEXR.XLS. The first column is a firm identifier (simply a number associated with each firm, although this column is not strictly necessary with RATS and will

---

[18] *Source*: computation by Keith Anderson and the author. There would be some severe limitations of this analysis if it purported to be a piece of original research, but the range of freely available panel datasets is severely limited and so hopefully it will suffice as an example of how to estimate panel models with RATS. No doubt readers with access to a wider range of data will be able to think of much better applications!

not be used). The second and third columns contain the actual data to be used in the estimation: the excess returns on each stock and the betas of each stock. The final column contains the years that each observation corresponds to. The first and fourth columns are superfluous, but are useful for readers to be able to see how the data is organised inside the spreadsheet; it should be evident that the structure corresponds exactly to the second ('grouped by time') type of data listed above.

Having this organisational structure makes life much easier because RATS can work directly with it, and there is a function on the data-import Wizard for dealing with panel data. We will look at how to use this next, but for now, suppose that the data had been organised in some way other than that described above. For example, suppose that the data on each individual were not in the same order over the years, but rather the individuals were identified by some variable in another column. Or alternatively, suppose that each variable and year of data are listed in separate columns rather than all the years being stacked up in a single column. How would we proceed? The answer is that the data must be re-organised to conform to one of the two types listed above. This could be done either in a spreadsheet or within RATS by using the PFORM instruction (see the RATS *User Guide* for details).

Returning to the case we have here, to read in the data, click **Data** and then choose the **Data (Other Formats)** option from the menu. Then change 'Files of type' to **Excel** and choose the file **PANELEXR.XLS** and click **Open**. RATS will then examine the file and will conclude that it has 27501 Rows and 4 Columns. Click **OK**, then we need to explain how the data are organised. The data are **Annual**, with **1 Period per Year**, and the Structure is a **Panel** with **11 observations per individual. Complete the boxes** in the New Series Date window accordingly and it should appear as in screenshot 10.1.

**Screenshot 10.1**

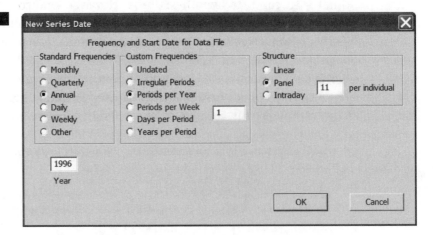

Then click OK and the Wizard will create the following lines of code:

```
OPEN DATA "C:\Chris\book\RATS handbook\panelexr.xls"
CALENDAR(PANELOBS=11,A) 1996
ALL 2500//2006:01
DATA(FORMAT=XLS,ORG=COLUMNS) 1//1996:01 2500//2006:01 $
    firm_ident return beta year
```

## 10.2 Estimating fixed or random effects panel models

To see how the fixed effects model works, we can take equation (10.1) above and decompose the disturbance term, $u_{it}$, into an individual specific effect, $\mu_i$, and the 'remainder disturbance', $v_{it}$, that varies over time and entities (capturing everything that is left unexplained about $y_{it}$)

$$u_{it} = \mu_i + v_{it} \tag{10.3}$$

So we could rewrite equation (10.1) by substituting in for $u_{it}$ from (10.3) to obtain

$$y_{it} = \alpha + \beta x_{it} + \mu_i + v_{it} \tag{10.4}$$

We can think of $\mu_i$ as encapsulating all of the variables that affect $y_{it}$ cross-sectionally but do not vary over time – for example, the sector that a firm operates in, a person's gender, or the country where a bank has its headquarters, etc. This model could be estimated using dummy variables, which would be termed the least squares dummy variable (LSDV) approach.

We can also test for whether the panel approach is really necessary at all. This test would be a slightly modified version of the Chow test described in Chapter 4 and would involve incorporating the restriction that all of the intercept dummy variables have the same parameter (i.e. $H_0: \mu_1 = \mu_2 = \ldots = \mu_N$). If this null hypothesis is not rejected, the data can simply be pooled together and OLS employed. If this null is rejected, however, then it is not valid to impose the restriction that the intercepts are the same over the cross-sectional units and a panel approach must be employed.

It is also possible to have a time-fixed effects model rather than an entity-fixed effects model. We would use such a model where we thought that the average value of $y_{it}$ changes over time but not cross-sectionally. Hence with time-fixed effects, the intercepts would be allowed to vary over time but would be assumed to be the same across entities at each given point in time. We could write a time-fixed effects model as

$$y_{it} = \alpha + \beta x_{it} + \lambda_t + v_{it} \tag{10.5}$$

where $\lambda_t$ is a time-varying intercept that captures all of the variables that affect $y_{it}$ and that vary over time but are constant cross-sectionally. An example would be where the regulatory environment or tax rate changes part-way through a sample period. In such circumstances, this change of environment may well influence $y$, but in the same way for all firms, which could be assumed to all be affected equally by the change.

An alternative to the fixed effects model described above is the random effects model, which is sometimes also known as the error components model. As with fixed effects, the random effects approach proposes different intercept terms for each entity and again these intercepts are constant over time, with the relationships between the explanatory and explained variables assumed to be the same both cross-sectionally and temporally.

However, the difference is that under the random effects model, the intercepts for each cross-sectional unit are assumed to arise from a common intercept $\alpha$ (which is the same for all cross-sectional units and over time), plus a random variable $\varepsilon_i$ that varies cross-sectionally but is constant over time. $\varepsilon_i$ measures the random deviation of each entity's intercept term from the 'global' intercept term $\alpha$. We can write the random effects panel model as

$$y_{it} = \alpha + \beta x_{it} + \omega_{it}, \quad \omega_{it} = \varepsilon_i + v_{it} \tag{10.6}$$

where $x_{it}$ is still a $1 \times k$ vector of explanatory variables, but unlike the fixed effects model, there are no dummy variables to capture the heterogeneity (variation) in the cross-sectional dimension. Instead, this occurs via the $\varepsilon_i$ terms. Note that this framework requires the assumptions that the new cross-sectional error term, $\varepsilon_i$, has zero mean, is independent of the individual observation error term ($v_{it}$), has constant variance $\sigma_\varepsilon^2$ and is independent of the explanatory variables ($x_{it}$).

Returning to RATS, when the data have been imported we are ready to run the panel regressions. The main command for doing this is PREGRESS, with options METHOD=FIXED and METHOD=RANDOM for fixed and random effects models respectively. So the instructions would be

```
PREGRESS(METHOD=FIXED) RETURN
# CONSTANT BETA
PREGRESS(METHOD=RANDOM) RETURN
# CONSTANT BETA
```

And the two sets of results are shown in Box 10.1. and Box 10.2.

```
      Box 10.1

Panel Regression - Estimation by Fixed Effects
Dependent Variable RETURN
Panel(11) of Annual Data From   1//1996:01 To 2500//2006:01
Usable Observations   8856         Degrees of Freedom   6647
Total Observations    27500        Skipped/Missing   18644
Centered R**2      0.313653      R Bar **2       0.085662
Uncentered R**2    0.315031      T x R**2        2789.915
Mean of Dependent Variable       0.0023449901
Std Error of Dependent Variable  0.0522821933
Standard Error of Estimate       0.0499927616
Sum of Squared Residuals         16.612688993
Regression F(2208,6647)                 1.3757
Significance Level of F            0.00000000
Log Likelihood                    15235.89166


     Variable         Coeff         Std Error     T-Stat      Signif
***********************************************************************
1.   Constant     0.0000000000  0.0000000000  0.00000   0.00000000
2.   BETA         0.0015258234  0.0030609629  0.49848   0.61816350
```

```
      Box 10.2

Panel Regression - Estimation by Random Effects
Dependent Variable RETURN
Panel(11) of Annual Data From   1//1996:01 To 2500//2006:01
Usable Observations   8856         Degrees of Freedom   8854
Total Observations    27500        Skipped/Missing   18644
Mean of Dependent Variable       0.0023449901
Std Error of Dependent Variable  0.0522821933
Standard Error of Estimate       0.0485226977
Sum of Squared Residuals         20.846319740
Log Likelihood                   13608.59359
Hausman Test(1)                  0.484883
Significance Level               0.48621903

     Variable         Coeff         Std Error     T-Stat      Signif
***********************************************************************
1.   Constant     0.0021206693  0.0030680609  0.69121   0.48943462
2.   BETA         0.0005410075  0.0027143846  0.19931   0.84201925
```

Although the slope coefficients are not significant for either specification, the estimates are quite different, suggesting that the fixed and random effects models represent rather different characterisations of the data. RATS ignores the intercept in the fixed effects model because it has used dummy variables for each of the individual units. The fixed effects model is exactly equivalent to the LSDV approach and so can be estimated by OLS, but the random effects model must be estimated using GLS. When the random effects model is used, RATS automatically conducts a Hausman test for the validity of random effects approach. In this case, the $p$-value of 0.486 is indicative that it would be permissible and arguably more efficient to use a random effects specification.

The returns in this regression are in proportion terms rather than percentages, so the slope estimate of 0.0015 corresponds to a risk premium of 0.15% per month, or around 1.8% per year, which seems plausible although lower than the actual difference between the average returns on stocks and Treasuries over the sample period. By contrast, if we were to simply run an OLS regression on these variables (with no fixed or random effects), we would observe a slope estimate of 0.000454, corresponding to a risk premium of 0.0454% per month, or around 0.5% per year.

By default, METHOD=FIXED results in the estimation of a model with entity-specific fixed effects. But we could instead estimate a model with time-fixed effects or both individual and time-fixed effects. The command for a time-fixed effects model would be

**PREGRESS(METHOD=FIXED,EFFECTS=TIME) RETURN**
**# CONSTANT BETA**

Notice that while the individual fixed effects model will use some 2,500 dummy variables, the time-fixed effect model will use only 11 (one for each year). Consequently, the slope parameter estimate for the time-fixed effects specification is only slightly different from that of the pooled regression model. It is also possible to estimate models based on the within transformation (METHOD=FD), the between estimator (METHOD=BETWEEN) or using a seemingly unrelated regression (SUR).

Finally, we can run a test for redundant fixed effects, where these could be time-fixed effects, cross-sectional fixed effects, or both; here we opt for the cross-sectional version only since we saw above that only this type of heterogeneity is important. We would achieve this using the PSTATS command after the regression estimation

**LINREG(NOPRINT) RETURN / RESIDS**
**# CONSTANT BETA**
**PSTATS(TESTS,EFFECT=INDIVIDUAL) RESIDS**

The output is shown in Box 10.3.

**Box 10.3**

```
Analysis of Variance for Series RESIDS
Source    Sum of Squares  Degrees   Mean Square      F-Statistic  Signif Level
INDIV      7.591431891518    2207   0.003439706340       1.3765    0.0000000
ERROR     16.612995210168    6648   0.002498946331
TOTAL     24.204427101686    8855
```

The *F*-test statistic is significant even at the 1% level, suggesting that it is important to allow for the individual fixed effects and that simply running a pooled regression ignoring them would not be valid.

# 11

# Limited dependent variable models

There are many situations in financial research where it is the explained variable rather than one or more of the explanatory variables that is qualitative. The qualitative information would then be coded as a dummy variable and the situation would be referred to as a *limited dependent variable* and needs to be treated differently. The term refers to any problem where the values that the dependent variables may take are limited to certain integers (e.g. 0, 1, 2, 3, 4) or even where it is a binary number (only 0 or 1).

The linear probability model (LPM) is by far the simplest way of dealing with binary dependent variables, and it is based on an assumption that the probability of an event occurring is linearly related to a set of explanatory variables. The actual probabilities cannot be observed, so we would estimate a model where the outcomes, $y_i$ (the series of zeros and ones), would be the dependent variable. This is then a linear regression model and would be estimated by OLS. The set of explanatory variables could include either quantitative variables or dummies or both. The fitted values from this regression are the estimated probabilities that $y_i = 1$ for each observation $i$.

The linear probability model has many important flaws and consequently the logit and probit approaches are used instead. Both models are able to overcome the limitation of the LPM that it can produce estimated probabilities that are negative or greater than one. They do this by using a function that effectively transforms the regression model so that the fitted values are bounded within the (0,1) interval. Visually, the fitted regression model will appear as an S-shape rather than a straight line. The logit model is so called because the function $F$ is in fact the cumulative logistic distribution. With the logistic model, 0 and 1 are asymptotes to the function and thus the probabilities will never actually fall to exactly zero or rise to one, although they may come infinitesimally close. Clearly, this model is not linear (and cannot be made linear by a transformation) and thus is not estimable using OLS. Thus maximum likelihood is usually used.

Instead of using the cumulative logistic function to transform the model, the cumulative normal distribution is sometimes employed. This gives rise to the probit model. This function is the cumulative distribution function for a standard normal random variable. As for the logistic approach, this function provides a transformation to ensure that the fitted probabilities will lie between zero and one.

## 11.1 Reading in the data

The example that will be considered here concerns whether it is possible to determine the factors that affect the likelihood that a student will fail his/her MSc. The data comprise an anonymised sample from the student record files for five years of MSc students in finance at the ICMA Centre, University of Reading, contained in the spreadsheet 'MSC_RECORDR.XLS'. Only a sample of 100 students are included for each of five years who completed (or not as the case may be!) their degrees in the years 2003 to 2007 inclusive. Therefore, the data cannot be used to infer actual failure rates on these programmes. The idea for this example is taken from a study by Heslop and Varotto (2007), which seeks to propose an approach to preventing systematic biases in admissions decisions.[19]

The objective here is to analyse the factors that affect the probability of failure of the MSc. The dependent variable ('fail') is binary and takes the value 1 if that particular candidate failed at first attempt in terms of his/her overall grade, and zero elsewhere. Therefore, a model that is suitable for limited dependent variables is required, such as a logit or probit.

The other information in the spreadsheet that will be used includes the age of the student, a dummy variable taking the value 1 if the student is female, a dummy variable taking the value 1 if the student has work experience, a dummy variable taking the value 1 if the student's first language is English, a country code variable that takes values from

---

[19] Note that since this book uses only a sub-set of their sample and variables in the analysis, the results presented below may differ from theirs. When constructing the sample, I systematically endeavoured to retain all of the ones (i.e. the fails) since the proportion of these is quite small. Hence the unconditional probability of failure here will be biased upwards relative to the true value.

1 to 10,[20] a dummy variable that takes the value 1 if the student already has a postgraduate degree, a dummy variable that takes the value 1 if the student achieved an A-grade at the undergraduate level (i.e. a first-class honours degree or equivalent) and a dummy variable that takes the value 1 if the undergraduate grade was less than a B-grade (i.e. the student received the equivalent of a lower second-class degree). The B-grade (or upper second-class degree) is the omitted dummy variable and this will then become the reference point against which the other grades are compared. The reason why these variables ought to be useful predictors of the probability of failure should be fairly obvious and is therefore not discussed. To allow for differences in examination rules and in average student quality across the five-year period, year dummies for 2004, 2005, 2006 and 2007 are created and thus the year 2003 dummy will be omitted from the regression model.

First, use the **data entry Wizard** to read in the 500 undated observations organised into 13 columns. Note that with cross-sectional (undated) data, it is not necessary to use the CALENDAR instruction, only ALLOCATE. Next, estimate a linear probability model as a basis for comparison with the more appropriate methods that will be discussed shortly. Recall that the LPM is simply a linear regression estimated using OLS with a 0–1 binary dependent variable:

> **LINREG FAIL**
> **# CONSTANT AGE ENGLISH FEMALE WORKEXP AGRADE $**
> **BELOWBGRADE PGDEGREE YEAR2004 YEAR2005 $**
> **YEAR2006 YEAR2007**

The results are shown in Box 11.1 and are discussed below in parallel with those from the other models.

## 11.2  The logit and probit models

Next, estimate a *logit* model and a *probit* model using the same dependent and independent variables as above. This is achieved using the DDV (discrete dependent variable) instruction with the option DISTRIBUTION =

---

[20] The exact identities of the countries involved are not revealed in order to avoid any embarrassment for students from countries with high relative failure rates, except that Country 8 is the UK!

```
                                              Box 11.1

Linear Regression - Estimation by Least Squares
Dependent Variable FAIL
Usable Observations    500          Degrees of Freedom    488
Centered R**2    0.066252           R Bar **2   0.045204
Uncentered R**2  0.191374           T x R**2       95.687
Mean of Dependent Variable          0.1340000000
Std Error of Dependent Variable     0.3409934796
Standard Error of Estimate          0.3331972039
Sum of Squared Residuals            54.177943821
Regression F(11,488)                   3.1477
Significance Level of F             0.00039621
Log Likelihood                       -153.88571
Durbin-Watson Statistic               2.032368


        Variable          Coeff        Std Error       T-Stat     Signif
******************************************************************************
1.   Constant          0.103880547  0.120527948      0.86188   0.38917724
2.   AGE               0.001321917  0.004335995      0.30487   0.76059484
3.   ENGLISH          -0.020073137  0.031527607     -0.63668   0.52462894
4.   FEMALE           -0.029380428  0.035053334     -0.83816   0.40234918
5.   WORKEXP          -0.062028081  0.031436064     -1.97315   0.04904228
6.   AGRADE           -0.080700412  0.037720079     -2.13945   0.03289429
7.   BELOWBGRADE       0.092616301  0.050226362      1.84398   0.06579237
8.   PGDEGREE          0.028661454  0.047410145      0.60454   0.54576390
9.   YEAR2004          0.056909819  0.047751378      1.19179   0.23392118
10.  YEAR2005         -0.011101256  0.048367449     -0.22952   0.81856159
11.  YEAR2006          0.141580585  0.048033538      2.94754   0.00335659
12.  YEAR2007          0.085150326  0.049727466      1.71234   0.08746931
```

LOGIT or DISTRIBUTION = PROBIT respectively; the latter is the default if no distribution is specified.

> **DDV(DISTRIBUTION = LOGIT) FAIL**
> **# CONSTANT AGE ENGLISH FEMALE WORKEXP AGRADE $**
> **BELOWBGRADE PGDEGREE YEAR2004 YEAR2005 $**
>    **YEAR2006 YEAR2007**
> **DDV(DISTRIBUTION = PROBIT) FAIL**
> **# CONSTANT AGE ENGLISH FEMALE WORKEXP AGRADE $**
> **BELOWBGRADE PGDEGREE YEAR2004 YEAR2005 $**
> **YEAR2006 YEAR2007**

The logit output is shown in Box 11.2 and the probit output in Box 11.3.

```
       Box 11.2
```

```
Binary Logit - Estimation by Newton-Raphson
Convergence in 6 Iterations. Final criterion was 0.0000044 <= 0.0000100
Dependent Variable FAIL
Usable Observations     500          Degrees of Freedom   488
Log Likelihood        -179.716670
Average Likelihood       0.6980718
Pseudo-R**2              0.0696385
Log Likelihood(Base)  -196.960207
LR Test of Coefficients(11)     34.4871
Significance Level of LR    0.0003010


        Variable          Coeff       Std Error      T-Stat      Signif
*******************************************************************************
1.    Constant          -2.256368303  1.073015229    -2.10283   0.03548066
2.    AGE                0.011011487  0.038131109     0.28878   0.77275004
3.    ENGLISH           -0.165117711  0.282959024    -0.58354   0.55953031
4.    FEMALE            -0.333894010  0.349236210    -0.95607   0.33903724
5.    WORKEXP           -0.568768665  0.288479948    -1.97161   0.04865465
6.    AGRADE            -1.085030590  0.491177262    -2.20904   0.02717181
7.    BELOWBGRADE        0.562350929  0.373507660     1.50559   0.13217140
8.    PGDEGREE           0.212084195  0.419910116     0.50507   0.61350935
9.    YEAR2004           0.653206481  0.500927157     1.30399   0.19223531
10.   YEAR2005          -0.183824429  0.587960384    -0.31265   0.75454838
11.   YEAR2006           1.246576153  0.473666318     2.63176   0.00849438
12.   YEAR2007           0.850421962  0.497067207     1.71088   0.08710341
```

As can be seen, the pseudo-$R^2$ values are quite small at around 7% for both specifications, although this is often the case for limited dependent variable models. Only the work experience and A-grade variables and two of the year dummies have parameters that are statistically significant, and the Below B-grade dummy is almost significant at the 10% level in the probit specification (although slightly less so in the logit).

It is important to note that we cannot interpret the parameter estimates from a logit or probit model in the usual way. In order to be able to do this, we need to calculate the marginal effects, which is fortunately very easy in RATS. This can be achieved using the PRJ command immediately after the estimation of a logit or probit model. In the former case, the syntax is

**PRJ(ATMEAN,DIST=LOGIT)**
**DISPLAY %PRJDENSITY*%BETA**

```
┌──────────────────────────────────────────────────────────────────────────┐
│     Box 11.3                                                                │
├──────────────────────────────────────────────────────────────────────────┤
```

Binary Probit - Estimation by Newton-Raphson
Convergence in 6 Iterations. Final criterion was 0.0000000 <= 0.0000100
Dependent Variable FAIL
Usable Observations     500          Degrees of Freedom   488
Log Likelihood          -179.456344
Average Likelihood        0.6984353
Pseudo-R**2               0.0707004
Log Likelihood(Base)    -196.960207
LR Test of Coefficients(11) 35.0077
Significance Level of   LR 0.0002471

| | Variable | Coeff | Std Error | T-Stat | Signif |
|---|---|---|---|---|---|
| 1. | Constant | -1.287209587 | 0.569222596 | -2.26135 | 0.02373780 |
| 2. | AGE | 0.005677023 | 0.020149189 | 0.28175 | 0.77813564 |
| 3. | ENGLISH | -0.093792251 | 0.153659330 | -0.61039 | 0.54160292 |
| 4. | FEMALE | -0.194107266 | 0.184433861 | -1.05245 | 0.29259351 |
| 5. | WORKEXP | -0.318246532 | 0.156663226 | -2.03141 | 0.04221388 |
| 6. | AGRADE | -0.538814071 | 0.235294017 | -2.28996 | 0.02202359 |
| 7. | BELOWBGRADE | 0.341802603 | 0.214268424 | 1.59521 | 0.11066584 |
| 8. | PGDEGREE | 0.132957086 | 0.230258998 | 0.57742 | 0.56365302 |
| 9. | YEAR2004 | 0.349663153 | 0.257969253 | 1.35545 | 0.17527580 |
| 10. | YEAR2005 | -0.108329878 | 0.292863348 | -0.36990 | 0.71145770 |
| 11. | YEAR2006 | 0.673611722 | 0.246326928 | 2.73462 | 0.00624514 |
| 12. | YEAR2007 | 0.433785277 | 0.259286644 | 1.67300 | 0.09432827 |

While the marginal effects will be printed in a single row, for ease of comparison, Table 11.1 shows the coefficient estimates for the linear probability model (which can be interpreted as marginal effects since there is no transformation under the LPM) and the marginal effects evaluated at the mean of the variables for the logit and probit models together.

This table presents us with values that can be intuitively interpreted in terms of how the variables affect the probability of failure. For example, an age parameter value of 0.0012 would imply that an increase in the age of the student by one year would increase the probability of failure by 0.12%, holding everything else equal, while a female student is around 3–3.7% (depending on the model) less likely than a male student with otherwise identical characteristics to fail. Having an A-grade (first-class) in the bachelors degree makes a candidate either 10.4% or 10.2% (depending on the model) less likely to fail than an otherwise identical student with a B-grade (upper second-class degree). Since the year 2003 dummy has been omitted from the equations, this becomes the reference point. So students

**Table 11.1**  Marginal effects

| Variable | LPM | Logit | Probit |
|---|---|---|---|
| Constant | 0.10388 | −0.21704 | −0.24372 |
| AGE | 0.00132 | 0.00106 | 0.00107 |
| ENGLISH | −0.02007 | −0.01588 | −0.01776 |
| FEMALE | −0.02938 | −0.03212 | −0.03675 |
| WORKEXP | −0.06203 | −0.05471 | −0.06026 |
| AGRADE | −0.08070 | −0.10437 | −0.10202 |
| BELOWBGRADE | 0.09262 | 0.05409 | 0.06472 |
| PGDEGREE | 0.02866 | 0.02040 | 0.02517 |
| YEAR2004 | 0.05691 | 0.06283 | 0.06621 |
| YEAR2005 | −0.01110 | −0.01768 | −0.02051 |
| YEAR2006 | 0.14158 | 0.11991 | 0.12754 |
| YEAR2007 | 0.08515 | 0.08180 | 0.08213 |

were more likely in 2004, 2006 and 2007, but less likely in 2005, to fail the MSc than in 2003. A final interesting note is that despite its severe limitations in theory, the LPM yields marginal effects that are mostly very similar indeed to those from the logit or probit approaches.

RATS can estimate many other types of limited dependent variable models by using the TYPE=... instruction, where ... can be BINARY (the default), ORDERED (for estimating ordered probit or logit models), MULTINOMIAL (for multinomial logit) or COUNT. The Newton–Raphson algorithm is used with maximum likelihood for parameter estimation. Finally, RATS can also estimate censored and truncated dependent variable models. Instead of DDV, the instruction is LDV (limited dependent variable) with the option TRUNCATE or CENSORED – see the RATS *User Guide* for further details.

# 12
## Simulation methods

Simulation studies are often used in econometrics when the properties of a particular estimation method are not known. For example, it may be known from asymptotic theory how a particular test behaves with an infinite sample size, but how will the test behave if only 50 observations are available? Will the test still have the desirable properties of being correctly sized and having high power? In other words, if the null hypothesis is correct, will the test lead to rejection of the null 5% of the time if a 5% rejection region is used? And if the null is incorrect, will it be rejected a high proportion of the time?

The way that such a study would be conducted (with additional steps and modifications where necessary) is as follows.

1. Generate the data according to the desired data-generating process (DGP), with the errors being drawn from some given distribution.
2. Run the regression and calculate the test statistic.
3. Save the test statistic or whatever parameter is of interest.
4. Go back to stage 1 and repeat $N$ times.

A brief explanation of each of these steps is in order. The first stage involves specifying the model that will be used to generate the data. This may be a pure time-series or a structural model. Pure time-series models are usually simpler to implement, as a full structural model would require the researcher to specify a data-generating process for the explanatory variables as well. Assuming that a time-series model is deemed appropriate, the next choice to be made is of the probability distribution specified for the errors. Usually, standard normal draws are used, although any other empirically plausible distribution (such as a Student's $t$) could also be used.

The second stage involves estimation of the parameter of interest in the study. The parameter of interest might be, for example, the value of a coefficient in a regression, or the value of an option at its expiry date. It could instead be the value of a portfolio under a particular set of scenarios governing the way that the prices of the component assets move over time.

The quantity $N$ is known as the number of replications and this should be as large as is feasible. The central idea behind Monte Carlo is that of random sampling from a given distribution. Therefore, if the number of replications is set too small, the results will be sensitive to 'odd' combinations of random number draws. It is also worth noting that asymptotic arguments apply in Monte Carlo studies as well as in other areas of econometrics. That is, the results of a simulation study will be equal to their analytical counterparts (assuming that the latter exist) asymptotically.

## 12.1 Simulating Dickey–Fuller critical values

Recall that the equation for a Dickey–Fuller test applied to a series $y_t$ is the regression

$$y_t = \phi y_{t-1} + u_t \tag{12.1}$$

so that the test is one of $H_0$: $\phi = 1$ against $H_1 : \phi < 1$. The relevant test statistic is given by

$$\tau = \frac{\hat{\phi} - 1}{SE(\hat{\phi})} \tag{12.2}$$

Under the null hypothesis of a unit root, the test statistic does not follow a standard distribution and therefore a simulation would be required to obtain the relevant critical values. Obviously, these critical values are well documented, but it is of interest to see how one could generate them. A very similar approach could then potentially be adopted for situations where there has been less research and where the results are relatively less well known.

The simulation would be conducted in the following steps.

1. Construct the data-generating process under the null hypothesis – that is, obtain a series for $y$ that follows a unit root process. This would be done as follows:
   a. Draw a series of length $T$, the required number of observations, from a normal distribution. This will be the error series, so that $u_t \sim N(0, 1)$.
   b. Assume a first value for $y$, i.e. a value for $y$ at time $t = 1$.
   c. Construct the series for $y$ recursively, starting with $y_2$, $y_3$, and so on

$$y_2 = y_1 + u_2$$
$$y_3 = y_2 + u_3 \tag{12.3}$$
$$\ldots$$
$$y_T = y_{T-1} + u_T$$

2. Calculate the test statistic, $\tau$.
3. Repeat steps 1 and 2 $N$ times to obtain $N$ replications of the experiment. A distribution of values for $\tau$ will be obtained across the replications.
4. Order the set of $N$ values of $\tau$ from the lowest to the highest. The relevant 5% critical value will be the 5th percentile of this distribution.

Some RATS code for conducting such a simulation is given below. The objective is to develop a set of critical values for Dickey–Fuller test regressions. The simulation framework considers sample sizes of 1,000, 500 and 100 observations. For each of these sample sizes, regressions with no constant or trend, a constant but no trend, and a constant and trend are conducted. In each case 50,000 replications are used and the critical values for a one-sided test at the 1%, 5% and 10% levels are determined.

```
ALL 50000
SEED 12345
COM NREPS=50000
COM NOBS =1000
COM NBURN=200
SET TREND = T
CLEAR T1 T2 T3
DOFOR NOBS = 1000 500 100
  DO REPC = 1,NREPS
    CLEAR Y1 U
    SET U 1 NOBS+NBURN = %RAN(1.0)
    SET(FIRST=U) Y1 1 NOBS+NBURN = Y1{1}+U
    SET DY1 = Y1 - Y1{1}
    SMPL NBURN+1 NBURN+NOBS
    LINREG(NOPRINT) DY1
    # Y1{1}
    COM T1(REPC) = %TSTATS(1)
    LINREG(NOPRINT) DY1
    # CONSTANT Y1{1}
    COM T2(REPC) = %TSTATS(2)
    LINREG(NOPRINT) DY1
    # CONSTANT TREND Y1{1}
    COM T3(REPC) = %TSTATS(3)
  END DO REPC
  DISP "DICKEY-FULLER STATISTICS FOR" NOBS "OBSERVATIONS"
  SMPL 1 50000
  ORDER T1
  DIS T1(500) T1(2500) T1(5000)
  ORDER T2
  DIS T2(500) T2(2500) T2(5000)
  ORDER T3
  DIS T3(500) T3(2500) T3(5000)
END DOFOR NOBS
```

Some detailed notation is in order concerning the commands in the above program since this is a fairly extensive simulation. The SEED instruction sets the seed for the artificial random number generation at some arbitrary value. This is always useful to include in simulations programs since it means that the results can be exactly replicated later on if so desired. If this instruction is not used, the seed will be set according to the computer's clock time, which will of course be different if the simulation is re-run at a different time, resulting in different random number draws and possibly different results.

NREPS and NOBS define the number of replications to be used for each experiment and the number of observations generated for each replication for the first experiment. Notice that an additional 200 observations (NBURN) are constructed in each experiment, and the subsequent 'SMPL NBURN+1 NBURN+NOBS' line ensures that these start-up observations are discarded.

The DOFOR loop repeats all the instructions for sample sizes of 1,000, 500 and 100 observations. The 'DO REPC...' line begins the main body of the program.

'SET U 1 NOBS+NBURN = %RAN(1.0)' will draw a set of normally distributed random variates with mean zero and unit standard deviation, and will place them in the column vector U. Note that, by default, the length of U would have been the length of the arrays specified in the 'ALL(OCATE)' statement. The next SET command, with the FIRST=U option, constructs the data under the null hypothesis – which is a unit root process. The subsequent steps involve computing the vector of first differences to be used as the dependent variable (DY1) and then running the test regressions.

'COM T1(REPC)...', 'COM T2(REPC)...', 'COM T3(REPC)...' will place the $t$-ratio on the lagged value of Y from the test regression into the T1, T2 or T3 vector, at row REPC. In RATS, %TSTATS(1) will contain the $t$-ratio for the first ordered parameter and so on. The 'ORDER T1' command will arrange the observations on the series T1 in ascending order, so that the relevant percentile from the distribution of statistics across the replications can be obtained.

The results will be given separately for 1,000, 500 and 100 observations respectively, and the results together and placed in a table are shown in Table 12.1. (The entries within a column refer to a no constant or trend, then a constant, and then a constant and trend.)

If we compare these critical values with those from Fuller's (1976) book, they are only slightly different. This is to be expected, for the use of 50,000 replications should ensure that an approximation to the asymptotic behaviour is obtained. For example, the 5% critical value for a test regression

**Table 12.1** Observations results

| 1% | 5% | 10% |
|---|---|---|
| | Panel A: 1,000 observations | |
| −2.56141 | −1.93146 | −1.61252 |
| −3.46071 | −2.86760 | −2.57511 |
| −3.97570 | −3.41631 | −3.12826 |
| | Panel B: 500 observations | |
| −2.55553 | −1.95352 | −1.62420 |
| −3.42019 | −2.85956 | −2.55720 |
| −3.96312 | −3.41207 | −3.12844 |
| | Panel C: 100 observations | |
| −2.62491 | −1.94439 | −1.60828 |
| −3.49000 | −2.89178 | −2.58480 |
| −4.04632 | −3.45635 | −3.14910 |

with no constant or trend and 500 observations is −1.954 in this simulation and −1.95 in Fuller.

Monte Carlo simulations are, by their very nature, often much slower than other types of analysis due to the requirement to use many replications. So when running them, it is useful to know how far the simulation has got – in other words, how many replications are completed and how many are left. This can be achieved using the INFOBOX instruction. Enders (2003, p. 146) presents a nice example. Suppose that we were conducting a Monte Carlo experiment with 10,000 replications. Just before the DO REPC=1,NREPS instruction, add the command

```
INFOBOX(ACTION=DEFINE,PROGRESS,LOWER=1,UPPER=10000) $
'REPS COMPLETED'
```

Then, right after the DO instruction, add

```
INFOBOX(CURRENT=REPC)
```

Finally, right after the END DO REPC command, add

```
INFOBOX(ACTION=REMOVE)
```

## 12.2 Pricing Asian options

A simple example of how to use a Monte Carlo study for obtaining a price for a financial option is shown below. Although the option used for illustration in the following steps is just a plain vanilla European call option which could be valued analytically using the standard

Black–Scholes (1973) formula, again the method is sufficiently general that only relatively minor modifications would be required to value more complex options. Boyle (1977) gives an excellent and highly readable introduction to the pricing of financial options using Monte Carlo.

The steps involved are as follows.

1. Specify a data-generating process for the underlying asset. A random walk with drift model is usually assumed. Specify also the size of the drift component and the size of the volatility parameter. Specify also a strike price $K$ and a time to maturity, $T$.
2. Draw a series of length $T$, the required number of observations for the life of the option, from a normal distribution. This will be the error series, so that $\varepsilon_t \sim N(0,1)$.
3. Form a series of observations of length $T$ on the underlying asset.
4. Observe the price of the underlying asset at maturity observation $T$. For a call option, if the value of the underlying asset on maturity date $P_T \leq K$, the option expires worthless for this replication. If the value of the underlying asset on maturity date $P_T > K$, the option expires in the money and has value on that date equal to $P_T - K$, which should be discounted back to the present day using the risk-free rate. Use of the risk-free rate relies upon risk-neutrality arguments.
5. Repeat steps 1 to 4 a total of $N$ times and take the average value of the option over the $N$ replications. This average will be the price of the option.

An Asian option is one whose payoff depends upon the average value of the underlying asset over the averaging horizon specified in the contract. Most Asian options contracts specify that arithmetic rather than geometric averaging should be employed. Unfortunately, the arithmetic average of a unit root process with a drift is not well defined. Additionally, even if the asset prices are assumed to be log-normally distributed, the arithmetic average of them will not be. Consequently, a closed-form analytical expression for the value of an Asian option has yet to be developed. Thus, the pricing of Asian options represents a natural application for simulations methods. Determining the value of an Asian option is achieved in almost exactly the same way as for a vanilla call or put. The simulation is conducted identically and the only difference occurs in the very last step where the value of the payoff at the date of expiry is determined.

A sample of RATS code for determining the value of an Asian option is given below. The example is in the context of an arithmetic Asian option on the FTSE 100, and two simulations will be undertaken with different strike prices (one that is out of the money forward and one that is in the money forward). In each case, the life of the option is six months, with daily averaging commencing immediately, and the option value is given for both calls and puts in terms of index points. The parameters are given as follows, with the dividend yield and risk-free rate expressed as percentages:

Simulation 1: strike = 6500, risk-free = 6.24, dividend yield = 2.42, 'today's' FTSE = 6289.70, forward price = 6405.35, implied volatility = 26.52.
Simulation 2: strike = 5500, risk-free = 6.24, dividend yield = 2.42, 'today's' FTSE = 6289.70, forward price = 6405.35, implied volatility = 34.33.

Since no actual estimation is performed, differences between packages are likely to be negligible. All experiments are based on 25,000 replications and their antithetic variates (total: 50,000 sets of draws) to reduce Monte Carlo sampling error. Sample code for the Gaussian draw case is given below.

```
ALL 0 50000
*** SET PARAMETERS: SEED ENSURES THAT THE SAME SET
*** OF RANDOM DRAWS IS USED FOR EACH PARAMETER COMBINATION
*** N = NUMBER OF DAYS; TTM = TIME TO MATURITY IN YEARS
*** NREPS = NUMBER OF REPLICATIONS, IV = VOLATILITY USED TO
*** GENERATE THE PRICE SERIES, EXPRESSED AS A
*** DECIMAL; RF AND DY ARE RISK-FREE AND DIVIDEND YIELD RATES,
*** RESPECTIVELY, K IS THE STRIKE AND S0 IS THE INITIAL FTSE VALUE.
SEED 54321
COM N=125
COM TTM=0.5
COM NREPS=50000
COM IV=0.3433
COM RF=0.0624
COM DY=0.0242
COM DT=TTM/N
COM DRIFT=(RF-DY-(IV**2/2.0))*DT
COM VSQRDT =IV*(DT**0.5)
COM K=5500
COM S0=6289.7
CLEAR APVAL ACVAL SPOT

DO REPC=1,NREPS,2
* MAKES GAUSSIAN DRAWS WITH STD DEV 1.
SET U = %RAN(1)
* GENERATES THE DATA
COM SPOT(1)=S0*EXP(DRIFT+VSQRDT*U(1))
```

```
DO I=2,N
COM SPOT(I)=SPOT(I-1)*EXP(DRIFT+VSQRDT*U(I))
END DO I
SMPL 1 N
STATS(NOPRINT) SPOT

* COMPUTES THE DAILY AVERAGE
COM AV=%MEAN
COM ACPAY=%IF(AV-K.GT.0,AV-K,0)
COM APPAY=%IF(AV-K.LT.0,-AV+K,0)
COM ACVAL(REPC)=ACPAY*EXP(-RF*TTM)
COM APVAL(REPC)=APPAY*EXP(-RF*TTM)

* REPEATS ALL OF THE ABOVE FOR THE ANTITHETIC VARIATES
SET U = -U
COM SPOT(1)=S0*EXP(DRIFT+VSQRDT*U(1))
DO I=2,N
COM SPOT(I)=SPOT(I-1)*EXP(DRIFT+VSQRDT*U(I))
END DO I
STATS(NOPRINT) SPOT
COM AV=%MEAN
COM ACPAY=%IF(AV-K.GT.0,AV-K,0)
COM APPAY=%IF(AV-K.LT.0,-AV+K,0)
COM ACVAL(REPC+1)=ACPAY*EXP(-RF*TTM)
COM APVAL(REPC+1)=APPAY*EXP(-RF*TTM)

END DO REPC

SMPL 1 NREPS
* THE FOLLOWING AVERAGES WILL BE THE CALL AND PUT PRICES
STATS(NOPRINT) ACVAL
DIS %MEAN
STATS(NOPRINT) APVAL
DIS %MEAN
```

Considering the code listed above, 'COM DT=TTM/N' splits the time to maturity (0.5 years) into N discrete time periods. Since daily averaging is required, it is easiest to set N = 125 (the approximate number of trading days in half a year), so that each time period DT represents one day. The model assumes that the log of the underlying asset price follows a geometric Brownian motion, which could be given by

$$S + dS = S \exp\left[\left(rf - dy - \frac{1}{2}\sigma^2\right)dt + \sigma dz\right] \tag{12.4}$$

where $dz$ is a standard Wiener process. Further details of this continuous time representation of the movement of the underlying asset overtime are beyond the scope of this book. A treatment of this and many other useful option-pricing formulae and computer code are given in Haug (1998). The discrete time approximation to this can be written

$$S_t = S_{t-1} \exp\left[\left(rf - dy - \frac{1}{2}\sigma^2\right)dt + \sigma\sqrt{dt}u_t\right]$$

(12.5)

The CLEAR instruction sets up the arrays for the underlying spot price (called SPOT) and for the discounted values of the put (APVAL) and call (ACVAL). The command also sets all entries in these arrays to %NA to be overwritten later. Note that by default, arrays of the length given by the allocate statement (50,000) will be created.

The command 'DO REPC=1,NREPS,2' starts the main do loop for the simulation, looping up to the number of replications, in steps of two. The loop ends at 'END DO REPC'. Steps of two are used because antithetic variates are also employed for each replication, which will create another simulated path for the underlying asset prices and option value.

The random N(0,1) draws are made, which are then constructed into a series of future prices of the underlying asset for the next 125 days. 'STATS(NOPRINT) SPOT' will compute but not display the summary statistics for the underlying asset prices. From this, %MEAN will calculate the average price of the underlying over the lifetime of the option (125 days). The following two COM statements construct the terminal payoffs for the call and the put options respectively. For the call, ACPAY is set to the average underlying price less the strike price if the average is greater than the strike (i.e. if the option expires in the money) and zero otherwise. Vice versa for the put. The payoff at expiry is discounted back to the present using the risk-free rate and placed in the REPC row of the ACVAL or APVAL array for the calls and puts respectively.

The process then repeats using the antithetic variates, constructed using 'SET U = −U'. The call and put present values for these paths are put in the even rows of ACVAL and APVAL.

This completes one cycle of the REPC loop, which starts again with REPC = 3, then 5, 7, 9, . . . , 49999. The result will be two arrays, ACVAL and APVAL, which will contain 50,000 rows comprising the present value of the call and put option for each simulated path. The option prices would then simply be given by the averages over the 50,000 replications.

## 12.3 Simulating the price of an option using a fat-tailed process

A fairly limiting and unrealistic assumption in the above methodology for pricing options is that the underlying asset returns are normally distributed, whereas in practice it is well known that asset returns are fat-tailed. There are several ways to remove this assumption. First, one could employ draws from a fat-tailed distribution, such as a Student's $t$, in step 2 above. Another method, which would generate a distribution of returns with fat tails, would be to assume that the errors and therefore the returns follow a GARCH process. To generate draws from a GARCH process, do the following.

1. Draw a series of length $T$, the required number of observations for the life of the option, from a normal distribution. This will be the error series, so that $\varepsilon_t \sim N(0,1)$.
2. Recall that one way of expressing a GARCH model is:

$$r_t = \mu + u_t \qquad u_t = \varepsilon_t \sigma_t \qquad \varepsilon_t \sim N(0,1) \tag{12.6}$$
$$\sigma_t^2 = \alpha_0 + \alpha_1 u_{t-1}^2 + \beta \sigma_{t-1}^2, \tag{12.7}$$

A series of $\varepsilon_t$, has been constructed and it is necessary to specify initialising values $y_1$ and $\sigma_1^2$ and plausible parameter values for $\alpha_0$, $\alpha_1$, $\beta$. Assume that $y_1$ and $\sigma_1^2$ are set to 0 and 1 respectively. The equations above can then be used to generate the model for $r_t$ as described above.

For the GARCH model case, $u_t$ is no longer iid(0,1), but is now $(0, \sigma_t^2)$. The GARCH data are constructed using the model of (12.6) and (12.7). Investigation revealed that the price of the option was very sensitive to the choice of parameter values. For the purpose of this study, the parameter values were determined by estimating a GARCH model using approximately the last four years of actual FTSE data. The parameter values employed were (0.008, 0.046, 0.95) for $(\alpha_0, \alpha_1, \beta_1)$. RATS code is presented below for the GARCH Monte Carlo. Apart from the innovation process, denoted U in the program, that now follows a GARCH structure, all of the instructions are identical to those above for the Gaussian U case and so are not annotated.

```
ALL 50000
*** SET PARAMETERS
SEED 54321
COM N=125
COM TTM=0.5
COM NREPS=50000
COM IV=0.2652
COM RF=0.0624
COM DY=0.0242
COM DT=TTM/N
COM DRIFT=(RF-DY-(IV**2/2.0))*DT
COM VSQRDT =IV*(DT**0.5)
```

```
COM K=6500
COM S0=6289.7
CLEAR APVAL ACVAL SPOT H Y
DO REPC=1,NREPS,2

SET U = %RAN(1)
* THE FOLLOWING SETS UP A SERIES, Y, THAT FOLLOWS A
* GACRH PROCESS. THEN THE OPTION PRICES ARE CONSTRUCTED
* AS ABOVE.
COM H(1)=1
COM Y(1)=0
DO I=2,N
COM H(I)=0.008+0.046*(Y(I-1)**2)+0.95*H(I-1)
COM Y(I)=U(I)*(H(I)**0.5)
END DO I
SET U = Y
COM SPOT(1)=S0*EXP(DRIFT+VSQRDT*U(1))
DO I=2,N
COM SPOT(I)=SPOT(I-1)*EXP(DRIFT+VSQRDT*U(I))
END DO I
SMPL 1 N
STATS(NOPRINT) SPOT
COM AV=%MEAN
COM ACPAY=%IF(AV-K.GT.0,AV-K,0)
COM APPAY=%IF(AV-K.LT.0,-AV+K,0)
COM ACVAL(REPC)=ACPAY*EXP(-RF*TTM)
COM APVAL(REPC)=APPAY*EXP(-RF*TTM)
SET U = -U

COM SPOT(1)=S0*EXP(DRIFT+VSQRDT*U(1))
DO I=2,N
COM SPOT(I)=SPOT(I-1)*EXP(DRIFT+VSQRDT*U(I))
END DO I
STATS(NOPRINT) SPOT
COM AV=%MEAN
COM ACPAY=%IF(AV-K.GT.0,AV-K,0)
COM APPAY=%IF(AV-K.LT.0,-AV+K,0)
COM ACVAL(REPC+1)=ACPAY*EXP(-RF*TTM)
COM APVAL(REPC+1)=APPAY*EXP(-RF*TTM)

END DO REPC
SMPL 1 NREPS
STATS(NOPRINT) ACVAL
DIS %MEAN
STATS(NOPRINT) APVAL
DIS %MEAN
```

**Table 12.2** Simulated Asian option price values

| Strike = 6500, IV = 26.52 | | Strike = 5500, IV = 34.33 | |
| --- | --- | --- | --- |
| *CALL* | Price | *CALL* | Price |
| Analytical approximation | 203.45 | Analytical approximation | 888.55 |
| Monte Carlo normal | 205.23 | Monte Carlo normal | 886.72 |
| Monte Carlo GARCH | 210.19 | Monte Carlo GARCH | 896.91 |
| *PUT* | Price | *PUT* | Price |
| Analytical approximation | 348.70 | Analytical approximation | 64.52 |
| Monte Carlo normal | 350.09 | Monte Carlo normal | 62.34 |
| Monte Carlo GARCH | 350.20 | Monte Carlo GARCH | 64.07 |

Note that both the call and put values can be calculated easily from a given simulation, since the most computationally expensive step is in deriving the path of simulated prices for the underlying asset. The results are given in Table 12.2, along with the values derived from an analytical approximation to the option price, derived by Levy and estimated using VBA code in Haug (1998, pp. 97–100).

In all cases and as expected, the GARCH simulated prices are higher than those from the simulation using the Normal draws, especially for the second example (right-hand panel of the above table) where the implied volatility is higher. This phenomenon results from the GARCH leading to a fatter-tailed distribution of returns, meaning larger price movements and therefore options for some replications that will be deeper in the money. In both cases, the simulated options prices are quite close to the analytical approximations, although the Monte Carlo seems to overvalue the out-of-the-money call and to undervalue the out-of-the-money put. Some of the errors in the simulated prices relative to the analytical approximation may result from the use of a discrete-time averaging process using only 125 points.

## 12.4 VAR estimation using bootstrapping

Bootstrapping is related to simulation, but with one crucial difference. With simulation, the data are constructed completely artificially. Bootstrapping, meanwhile, is used to obtain a description of the properties of empirical estimators by using the sample data points themselves, and it involves sampling repeatedly with replacement from the actual data – see Davison and Hinkley (1997) for details.

Suppose a sample of data, $y = y_1, y_2, \ldots, y_T$ is available and it is desired to estimate some parameter $\theta$. An approximation to the statistical properties of $\hat{\theta}_T$ can be obtained by studying a sample of bootstrap estimators. This is done by taking $N$ samples of size $m$ with replacement from $y$ and re-calculating $\hat{\theta}$ with each new sample. Effectively, this involves sampling from the sample, i.e. treating the sample as a population from which samples can be drawn. Call the test statistics calculated from the new samples $\hat{\theta}^*$. The samples are likely to be quite different from each other and from the original $\hat{\theta}$ value, since some observations may be sampled several times and others not at all. Thus a distribution of values of $\hat{\theta}^*$ is obtained, from which standard errors or some other statistics of interest can be calculated.

The advantage of bootstrapping over the use of analytical results is that it allows the researcher to make inferences without making strong distributional assumptions, since the distribution employed will be that of the actual data. Instead of imposing a shape on the sampling distribution of the $\hat{\theta}$ value, bootstrapping involves empirically estimating the sampling distribution by looking at the variation of the statistic within sample.

We now employ the Hsieh (1993) and Brooks, Clare and Persand (2000) approaches to calculating minimum capital risk requirements (MCRRs) by way of illustration of how to use a bootstrap in RATS. The first issue is which model to use in order to capture the time-series properties of the data. Hsieh concludes that both the EGARCH and autoregressive volatility (ARV) models present reasonable descriptions of the futures returns series, which are then employed in conjunction with the bootstrap to estimate the value-at-risk estimates. This is achieved by simulating the future values of the futures price series, using the parameter estimates from the two models, and using disturbances obtained by sampling with replacement from the standardised residuals for the EGARCH ($\hat{\eta}_t / \hat{h}_t^{1/2}$) and the ARV models. In this way, 10,000 possible future paths of the series are simulated (i.e. 10,000 replications are used), and in each case the maximum drawdown (loss) can be calculated over a given holding period by

$$Q = (P_0 - P_1) \times \textit{number of contracts} \tag{12.8}$$

where $P_0$ is the initial value of the position and $P_1$ is the lowest simulated price (for a long position) or highest simulated price (for a short position) over the holding period. The maximum loss is calculated assuming holding periods of 1, 5, 10, 15, 20, 25, 30, 60, 90 and 180 days. It is assumed that the futures position is opened on the final day of the sample used to estimate the models, 9 March 1990.

The 90th percentile of these 10,000 maximum losses can be taken to obtain a figure for the amount of capital required to cover losses on 90% of days. It is important for firms to consider the maximum daily losses arising from their futures positions, since firms will be required to post additional funds to their margin accounts to cover such losses. If funds are not made available to the margin account, the firm is likely to have to liquidate its futures position, thus destroying any hedging effects that the firm required from the futures contracts in the first place.

However, Hsieh uses a slightly different approach to the final stage, which is as follows. Assume (without loss of generality) that the number of contracts held is one and that prices are lognormally distributed, i.e. that the logs of the ratios of the prices, $\ln(P_1/P_0)$, are normally distributed. This being the case, an alternative estimate of the 5th percentile of the distribution of returns can be obtained by taking the relevant critical value from the normal statistical tables, multiplying it by the standard deviation and adding it to the mean of the distribution.

The following RATS code can be used to calculate the MCRR for a ten-day holding period using daily S&P500 data. Assume that the data have been read into the program and that the S&P500 index values and corresponding log-returns are defined as P and RT respectively. The code is presented, followed by a further copy of the code, annotated one line at a time, with comments added.

```
ALL 10000
OPEN DATA "C:\CHRIS\BOOK\RATS HANDBOOK\SP500.TXT"
DATA(FORMAT=FREE,ORG=OBS) 1 2610 P
CLEAR RT
SET RT = LOG(P/P{1})
DECLARE SERIES U ;* RESIDUALS
DECLARE SERIES H ;* VARIANCES
CLEAR MIN
CLEAR MAX
SET P 2611 2620 = %NA
SET RT 2611 2620 = %NA
NONLIN B1 VA VB VC
FRML RESID U = RT - B1
FRML HF H = VB + VA*U{1}**2 + VC*H{1}
FRML LOGL = (H(T)=HF(T)),(U(T)=RESID(T)),%LOGDENSITY(H,U)
LINREG(NOPRINT) RT / U
# CONSTANT
COMPUTE B1 = %BETA(1)
COMPUTE VB=%SEESQ,VA=0.2,VC=0.7
```

```
SET H = %SEESQ
NLPAR(CRITERION=VALUE,CVCRIT=0.00001,SUBITERS=50)
MAXIMIZE(PMETHOD=SIMPLEX,PITERS=5,METHOD=BHHH, ITERS=100,ROBUST) $
LOGL 10 2610
SET SRES = (RT-B1)/H**0.5
FRML YEQ RT = B1
GROUP GARCH HF>>H RESID>>U YEQ>>RT
FORECAST(MODEL=GARCH,FROM=2611,TO=2620)
SMPL 2611 2620
DO Z=1,10000
  BOOT ENTRIES / 10 2610
  SET PATH1 = SRES(ENTRIES(T))
  DO J=2611,2620
    COM RT(J) = B1 + ((H(J))**0.5)*PATH1(J)
    COM P(J) = P(J-1) * EXP(RT(J))
  END DO J
  STATS(FRACTILE,NOPRINT) P
  COM MIN(Z) = %MINIMUM
  COM MAX(Z) = %MAXIMUM
END DO Z
SMPL 1 10000
SET L1 = LOG(MIN/1138.73)
STATS(NOPRINT) L1
COM MCRR = 1 - (EXP((-1.645*(%VARIANCE**0.5)) + %MEAN))
DISPLAY 'MCRR=' MCRR

SET S1 = LOG(MAX/1138.73)
STATS(NOPRINT) S1
COM MCRR = (EXP((1.645*(%VARIANCE**0.5)) + %MEAN)) - 1
DISPLAY 'MCRR=' MCRR
```

Now for the code segments again with annotations. Lines 2 and 3 read in the data, which are stored in a single column, raw text file, and the following two lines generate a series of continuously compounded proportion returns.

```
DECLARE SERIES U ;* RESIDUALS
DECLARE SERIES H ;* VARIANCES
CLEAR MIN
CLEAR MAX
```

The first two lines above declare the series for the residuals and the conditional variances for the GARCH estimation. The CLEAR command not only sets up the space for the arrays but also fills those arrays with missing values (%NA in the RATS notation). These arrays will be used to store the minimum and maximum prices observed in the out-of-sample holding period for each replication.

```
SET P 2611 2620 = %NA
SET RT 2611 2620 = %NA
```

The two lines above are used to extend the lengths of the arrays for P and RT to allow them to hold the simulated values for the returns and prices in the out-of-sample holding period. The following lines are used to estimate a standard GARCH(1,1) model on the S&P500 returns data.

```
NONLIN B1 VA VB VC
FRML RESID = RT - B1
FRML HF = VB + VA*U{1}**2 + VC*H{1}
FRML LOGL = (H(T)=HF(T)),(U(T)=RESID(T)),%LOGDENSITY(H,U)
LINREG(NOPRINT) RT / U
# CONSTANT
COMPUTE B1 = %BETA(1)
COMPUTE VB=%SEESQ,VA=0.2,VC=0.7
SET H = %SEESQ
NLPAR(CRITERION=VALUE,CVCRIT=0.00001,SUBITERS=50)
MAXIMIZE(PMETHOD=SIMPLEX,PITERS=5,METHOD=BHHH,ITERS=100,ROBUST) $
LOGL 10 2610
```

The next line below generates a series of standardised residuals from the model: that is, the residuals at each point in time divided by the square root of the corresponding conditional variance estimate.

```
SET SRES = (RT- B1)/H**0.5
```

The following five lines produce the forecasts of the conditional variance for the ten days immediately following the in-sample estimation period (see Chapter 8).

```
FRML HEQ H = VB + VA*U{1}**2 + VC*H{1}
FRML REQ U = RT - B1
FRML YEQ RT = B1
GROUP GARCH HEQ>>H REQ>>U YEQ>>RT
FORECAST(MODEL=GARCH,FROM=2611,TO=2620)
```

Z gives the main loop, and there are 10,000 bootstrap replications used in the simulations study.

```
SMPL 1 2611 2620
DO Z=1,10000
```

The following command is the main bootstrapping engine, and the command will draw observation numbers (integers) randomly with replacement from numbers 10 to 2610, placing the resultant observation numbers in the array ENTRIES. The 'SET PATH1 . . .' command creates a new series of standardised residuals that is constructed from the original series using the observation number series generated by the boot command.

```
BOOT ENTRIES / 10 2610
SET PATH1 = SRES(ENTRIES(T))
```

The following J loop is the inner loop that will construct a series of returns for the ten-day holding sample that starts the day after the in-sample estimation period. The 'COM RT . . .' line constructs the return for observation J, while the next line constructs the price observation given the log-return and the previous price.

```
DO J=2611,2620
COM RT(J) = B1 + ((H(J))**0.5)*PATH1(J)
COM P(J) = P(J-1) * EXP(RT(J))
END DO J
```

The next four lines collectively calculate the minimum and maximum price over the ten-day hold-out sample that will subsequently be used to compute the maximum draw down (i.e. the maximum loss) for a long and short position respectively. These will form the basis of the capital risk requirement. The SMPL instruction is necessary so that RATS picks only the maximum and minimum from the ten-day hold-out sample and not from the whole sample of price observations. The FRACTILES option on the STATS command generates the fractiles for the distribution of P (i.e. the maximum, the 95th percentile, the 90th percentile, . . . , the 1st percentile and the minimum). The minimum and the maximum following the STATS command will be stored in %MINIMUM and %MAXIMUM respectively. These quantities are calculated for each replication Z, so they are placed in arrays called MIN and MAX and they are collected together after the replications loop is completed.

```
STATS(FRACTILE,NOPRINT) P
COM MIN(Z) = %MINIMUM
COM MAX(Z) = %MAXIMUM
```

The next line ends the replication loop

```
END DO Z
```

The following SMPL instruction is necessary to reset the sample period used to cover all observation numbers from 1 to 10,000 (i.e. to incorporate all of the 10,000 bootstrap replications). By default, if this statement were not included, RATS would have continued to use the most recent sample statement, conducting analysis using only observations 2611 to 2620.

    SMPL 1 10000

The following block of four commands generates the MCRR for the long position. The first stage is to construct the log returns for the maximum loss over the ten-day holding period. Notice that the SET command will automatically do this calculation for every element of the MIN array – i.e. for all 10,000 replications. The STATS command is then used to construct summary statistics for the distribution of maximum losses across the replications. The 5th percentile from this distribution could be taken as the MCRR, which would be stored as %FRACT05. However, in order to use information from all of the replications, and under the assumption that the L1 statistic is normally distributed across the replications, the MCRR can also be calculated using the command given. This works as follows. Assuming that $\ln(P_1/P_0)$ is normally distributed with some mean $m$ and standard deviation $sd$, a standard normal variable can be constructed by subtracting the mean and dividing by the standard deviation: $[(\ln(P_1/P_0) - m)/ sd] \sim N(0,1)$. The 5% lower-tail critical value for a standard normal is $-1.645$, so to find the 5th percentile

$$\frac{Ln\left(\frac{P_1}{P_0}\right) - m}{sd} = -1.645 \tag{12.9}$$

Rearranging (12.9),

$$\frac{P_1}{P_0} = \exp[-1.645sd + m] \tag{12.10}$$

From equation (12.8), equation (12.10) can also be written

$$\frac{Q}{P_0} = 1 - \exp[-1.645sd + m] \tag{12.11}$$

which will give the maximum loss or draw down on a long position over the simulated ten days. The maximum draw down for a short position will be given by

$$\frac{Q}{P_0} = \exp[-1.645sd + m] - 1 \tag{12.12}$$

Finally, the MCRRs calculated in this way are displayed using the DISPLAY command.

```
SET L1 = LOG(MIN/1138.73)
STATS(NOPRINT) L1
COM MCRR = 1 - (EXP((-1.645*(%VARIANCE**0.5)) + %MEAN))
DISPLAY 'MCRR=' MCRR
```

The following four lines repeat the above procedure, but replacing the MIN array with MAX to calculate the MCRR for a short position.

```
SET S1 = LOG(MAX/1138.73)
STATS(NOPRINT) S1
COM MCRR = (EXP((1.645*(%VARIANCE**0.5)) + %MEAN)) – 1
DISPLAY 'MCRR=' MCRR
```

The results generated by running the above program are

```
MCRR= 0.04019
MCRR= 0.04891
```

Since no seed has been set for this simulation, unlike the previous ones, the results will differ slightly from one run to another. We could set a seed to ensure that the results always remained the same, or we could increase the number of replications from 10,000 to 100,000 (so that every occurrence of the number 10,000 in the code above would have to be replaced) and this would reduce the Monte Carlo sampling variability and so reduce the variation from one run to another.

These figures represent the minimum capital risk requirement for a long position and a short position respectively as a percentage of the initial value of the position for 95% coverage over a ten-day horizon. This means that, for example, approximately 4% of the value of a long position held as liquid capital will be sufficient to cover losses on 95% of days if the position is held for ten days. The required capital to cover 95% of losses over a ten-day holding period for a short position in the S&P500 Index would be around 4.8%. This is as one would expect since the Index had a positive drift over the sample period. Therefore the index returns are not symmetric about zero as positive returns are slightly more likely than negative returns. Higher capital requirements are thus necessary for a short position since a loss is more likely than for a long position of the same magnitude.

# Appendix: sources of data in this book

I am grateful to the following organisations, which all kindly agreed to allow their data to be used as examples in this book and for it to be copied onto the book's web site: Bureau of Labor Statistics, Federal Reserve Board, Federal Reserve Bank of St Louis, Nationwide, Oanda, and Yahoo! Finance. The following table gives details of the data used and of the provider's web site.

| Provider | Data | Web site |
|---|---|---|
| Bureau of Labor Statistics | CPI | www.bls.gov |
| Federal Reserve Board | US T-bill yields, money supply, industrial production, consumer credit | www.federalreserve.gov |
| Federal Reserve Bank of St Louis | average AAA and BAA corporate bond yields | research.stlouisfed.org/fred2 |
| Nationwide | UK average house prices | www.nationwide.co.uk |
| Oanda | euro–dollar, pound–dollar and yen–dollar exchange rates | www.oanda.com/convert/fxhistory |
| Yahoo! Finance | S&P500 and various US stock and futures prices | finance.yahoo.com |

# References

Bera, A. K. and Jarque, C. M. (1981) An Efficient Large-Sample Test for Normality of Observations and Regression Residuals, *Australian National University Working Papers in Econometrics* 40, Canberra

Berndt, E. K., Hall, B. H., Hall, R. E. and Hausman, J. A. (1974) Estimation and Inference in Nonlinear Structural Models, *Annals of Economic and Social Measurement* 4, 653–65

Black, F. and Scholes, M. (1973) The Pricing of Options and Corporate Liabilities, *Journal of Political Economy* 81(3), 637–54

Bollerslev, T. (1986) Generalised Autoregressive Conditional Heteroskedasticity, *Journal of Econometrics* 31, 307–27

Bollerslev, T., Engle, R. F. and Wooldridge, J. M. (1988) A Capital-Asset Pricing Model with Time-varying Covariances, *Journal of Political Economy* 96(1), 116–31

Box, G. E. P. and Jenkins, G. M. (1976) *Time-series Analysis: Forecasting and Control* 2nd edn., Holden-Day, San Francisco

Boyle, P. P. (1977) Options: A Monte Carlo Approach, *Journal of Financial Economics* 4(3), 323–38

Brooks, C. (2008) *Introductory Econometrics for Finance*, 2nd edn., Cambridge University Press, Cambridge, UK

Brooks, C., Burke, S. P. and Persand, G. (2001) Benchmarks and the Accuracy of GARCH Model Estimation, *International Journal of Forecasting* 17, 45–56

Brooks, C., Burke, S. P. and Persand, G. (2003) Multivariate GARCH Models: Software Choice and Estimation Issues, *Journal of Applied Econometrics* 18, 725–34

Brooks, C., Clare, A. D. and Persand, G. (2000) A Word of Caution on Calculating Market-Based Minimum Capital Risk Requirements, *Journal of Banking and Finance* 14(10), 1557–74

Brooks, C. and Persand, G. (2001) The Trading Profitability of Forecasts of the Gilt-Equity Yield Ratio, *International Journal of Forecasting* 17, 11–29

Broyden, C. G. (1965) A Class of Methods for Solving Nonlinear Simultaneous Equations, *Mathematics of Computation* 19, 577–93

Broyden, C. G. (1967) Quasi-Newton Methods and their Application to Function Minimisation, *Mathematics of Commutation* 21, 368–81

Chappell, D., Padmore, J., Mistry, P. and Ellis, C. (1996) A Threshold Model for the French Franc/Deutschmark Exchange Rate, *Journal of Forecasting* 15, 155–64

Davison, A. C. and Hinkley, D. V. (1997) *Bootstrap Methods and their Application*, Cambridge University Press, Cambridge, UK

Dickey, D. A. and Fuller, W. A. (1979) Distribution of Estimators for Time-series Regressions with a Unit Root, *Journal of the American Statistical Association* 74, 427–31

Doan, T. (2007) *RATS Version 7 Reference Manual*, Estima, Evanston, Illinois

Doan, T. (2007) *RATS Version 7 User Guide*, Estima, Evanston, Illinois

Durbin, J. and Watson, G. S. (1951) Testing for Serial Correlation in Least Squares Regression, *Biometrika* 38, 159–71

Enders, W. (2003) *RATS Programming Manual*, E-book distributed by Estima

Engel, C. and Hamilton, J. D. (1990) Long Swings in the Dollar: Are they in the Data and Do Markets Know It?, *American Economic Review* 80(4), 689–713

Engle, R. F. (1982) Autoregressive Conditional Heteroskedasticity with Estimates of the Variance of United Kingdom Inflation, *Econometrica* 50(4), 987–1007

Engle, R. F. and Granger, C. W. J. (1987) Co-integration, and Error Correction: Representation, Estimation and Testing, *Econometrica* 55, 251–76

Engle, R. F. and Kroner, K. F. (1995) Multivariate Simultaneous Generalised GARCH, *Econometric Theory* 11, 122–50

Engle, R. F., Lilien, D. M. and Robins, R. P. (1987) Estimating Time Varying Risk Premia in the Term Structure: The ARCH-M Model, *Econometrica* 55(2), 391–407

Engle, R. F. and Ng, V. K. (1993) Measuring and Testing the Impact of News on Volatility, *Journal of Finance* 48, 1749–78

Engle, R. F. and Yoo, B. S. (1987) Forecasting and Testing in Cointegrated Systems, *Journal of Econometrics* 35, 143–59

Fama, E. F. and MacBeth, J. D. (1973) Risk, Return and Equilibrium: Empirical Tests, *Journal of Political Economy* 81(3), 607–36

Fletcher, R. and Powell, M. J. D. (1963) A Rapidly Convergent Descent Method for Minimisation, *Computer Journal* 6, 163–8

Fuller, W. A. (1976) *Introduction to Statistical Time-series*, Wiley, New York

Glosten, L. R., Jagannathan, R. and Runkle, D. E. (1993) On the Relation Between the Expected Value and the Volatility of the Nominal Excess Return on Stocks, *Journal of Finance* 48(5), 1779–801

Goldfeld, S. M. and Quandt, R. E. (1965) Some Tests for Homoskedasticity, *Journal of the American Statistical Association* 60, 539–47

Hamilton, J. D. (1989) A New Approach to the Economic Analysis of Nonstationary Time-series and the Business Cycle, *Econometrica* 57(2), 357–84

Hamilton, J. D. (1990) Analysis of Time-series Subject to Changes in Regime, *Journal of Econometrics* 45, 39–70

Hamilton, J. (1994) *Time Series Analysis*, Princeton University Press, Princeton, New Jersey

Haug, E. G. (1998) *The Complete Guide to Options Pricing Formulas*, McGraw-Hill, New York

Heslop, S. and Varotto, S. (2007) Admissions of International Graduate Students: Art or Science? A Business School Experience, *ICMA Centre Discussion Papers in Finance* 2007–8

Hsieh, D. A. (1993) Implications of Nonlinear Dynamics for Financial Risk Management, *Journal of Financial and Quantitative Analysis* 28(1), 41–64

Johansen, S. (1988) Statistical Analysis of Cointegrating Vectors, *Journal of Economic Dynamics and Control* 12, 231–54

Johansen, S. and Juselius, K. (1990) Maximum Likelihood Estimation and Inference on Cointegration with Applications to the Demand for Money, *Oxford Bulletin of Economics and Statistics* 52, 169–210

Juselius, K. (2006) *The Cointegrated VAR Model: Methodology and Applications*, Oxford University Press, Oxford

Kroner, K. F. and Ng, V. K. (1998) Modelling Asymmetric Co-movements of Asset Returns, *Review of Financial Studies* 11, 817–44

Lütkepohl, H. (1991) *Introduction to Multiple Time-series Analysis*, Springer-Verlag, Berlin

Nelson, D. B. (1991) Conditional Heteroskedasticity in Asset Returns: A New Approach, *Econometrica* 59(2), 347–70

Newey, W. K. and West, K. D. (1987) A Simple Positive-Definite Heteroskedasticity and Autocorrelation-Consistent Covariance Matrix, *Econometrica* 55, 703–8

Osterwald-Lenum, M. (1992) A Note with Quantiles of the Asymptotic Distribution of the ML Cointegration Rank Test Statistics, *Oxford Bulletin of Economics and Statistics* 54, 461–72

Press, W. H., Teukolsy, S. A., Vetterling, W. T. and Flannery, B. P. (1992) *Numerical Recipes in Fortran*, Cambridge University Press, Cambridge, UK

Ramanathan, R. (1995) *Introductory Econometrics with Applications* 3rd edn., Dryden Press, Fort Worth, Texas

Ramsey, J. B. (1969) Tests for Specification Errors in Classical Linear Least-Squares Regression Analysis, *Journal of the Royal Statistical Society B* 31(2), 350–71

Sims, C. (1980) Macroeconomics and Reality, *Econometrica* 48, 1–48

Taylor, S. J. (1986) Forecasting the Volatility of Currency Exchange Rates, *International Journal of Forecasting* 3, 159–70

Tong, H. (1990) *Nonlinear Time-series: A Dynamical Systems Approach*, Oxford University Press, Oxford

White, H. (1980) A Heteroskedasticity-consistent Covariance Matrix Estimator and a Direct Test for Heteroskedasticity, *Econometrica* 48, 817–38

# Index